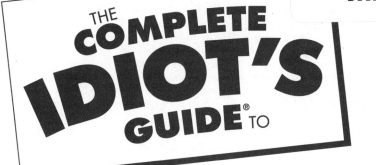

THE COMPLETE IDIOT'S GUIDE® TO

The Popes and the Papacy

by Brandon Toropov

ALPHA

A Pearson Education Company

Publisher: *Marie Butler-Knight*
Product Manager: *Phil Kitchel*
Managing Editor: *Jennifer Chisholm*
Acquisitions Editor: *Gary Goldstein*
Development Editor: *Amy Gordon*
Production Editor: *Billy Fields*
Copy Editor: *Amy Borrelli*
Illustrator: *Chris Eliopolous*
Cover Designer/Book Designer: *Trina Wurst*
Indexer: *Ginny Bess*
Layout/Proofreading: *John Etchison, Gloria Schurick*

Contents at a Glance

Appendixes

Contents

Foreword

Bishop of Rome, Vicar of Christ, Successor to the Prince of the Apostles, Supreme Pontiff of the Universal Church, Patriarch of the West, Primate of Italy, Archbishop and Metropolitan of the Roman Province, Sovereign of the Vatican City State, and Servant of the Servants of God. In addition to the familiar and affectionate *Il Papa*, and the proper protocol of "Holy Father," these are the official titles of the pope.

Welcome to a historical and religious roller-coaster ride that may, indeed, take your breath away with its fantastic highs and lows, twists and turns, and teeth-jarring reversals. The pageant of the papacy of the Roman Catholic Church has been played out against a backdrop of spirituality and splendor, violence and scandal, sin and soaring aspirations for two millenia—ever since Simon bar Jonah, a fisherman from the Roman-occupied Galilee, was commissioned by his Lord, Jesus of Nazareth, to assume leadership of the community of disciples who became known as Christians. Peter witnessed, and others believed through his testimony, the risen Christ and the Gospel message. Peter was the chief of the apostles, those original twelve who answered Jesus' call, and was acknowledged as such by his fellows in the group that became known as the church. He was the "co-founder," with St. Paul, of the Christian community in the capital of the empire, Rome, in the mid-first century.

For the devout Catholic of the twentieth century, it may be discouraging to look too closely at some of the horrendous abuses of power among the men who were heirs to St. Peter. But Pope John Paul II has challenged the Church—that is, the so-called "body of Christ," about 1 billion Catholics worldwide—to be not afraid to face these sometimes disturbing facts of history. It is deeply troubling for any fair-minded person of any faith, or none at all, to read of moral corruption, sexual hypocrisy, anti-Semitism, massacres of civilian populations, racial and cultural biases, blatant nepotism, arrogance, and imperious political manipulations—all carried out in the name of Jesus Christ, the Jewish teacher who was, himself, executed as a criminal by the Roman state authorities in Jerusalem in about 36 C.E.

Yet, this is what we must do—take a good, hard, close look into the historical record—if we are to discover the lessons that lie therein. In my own reflections on the papacy, with the help of the book you now hold in your hands, I try to fit everything within the simple model of the "Petrine Ministry," that is, the true religious foundation of the office itself—which perdures *despite* some of the worst incumbents and *because* of some of the greatest ones. In that regard, it may be helpful to ask three key questions (please, pardon the pun) and attempt to answer them.

First, what is the Petrine Ministry (which is another way of asking, who is the pope)? In its purest Scriptural formulation, from the Gospel of Matthew (16:17–18), the ministry was conferred by the messiah upon a single man:

"Thou art Peter, and upon this rock I will build my church; and the gates of hell shall not prevail against it. And I will give unto thee the keys of the kingdom of heaven: and whatsoever thou shalt bind on earth shall be bound in heaven: and whatsoever thou shalt loose on earth shall be loosed in heaven."

Interpretations of the exact nature and scope of Peter's charge have varied widely over time. The single issue of primacy over all other churches and hierarchs, spiritual and juridical, has made the papacy a lightning rod for critics from the Eastern churches, for reformers such as Martin Luther, and for contemporary skeptics.

Second, who are these 262 men whom we call "the popes" (including St. Peter but discounting the numerous "anti-popes," or false claimants to the office)? These men are as varied as humanly possible, in terms of their talents and temperaments, their family backgrounds and education, and their moral suitability for the office, their holiness if you will. One early Bishop of Rome was a slave, others have been lawyers, monks, peasants, diplomats, and authors. To date, there has been only one Englishman, and one Pole. The most notorious, perhaps, was a Borgia, the most revered a Roman nobleman.

Third, what is the historic context of the papacy, from its now-obscure foundations in the ancient Roman world to our own high-technology, hyper-self-aware age—a span of two thousand years? The fortunes of the papal office have waxed and waned dramatically through long years of decline and frequent periods of reformation. It has not been a static picture, nor a clearly visible march toward holiness.

One of the greatest figures in all of Church history is Pope John XXIII (1958–1963), whom many Catholics remember for his surprising call for an ecumenical council in the 1960s, not to condemn heresies but to open a defensive Church to the modern world. His Second Vatican Council was nothing short of a revolution.

Others have been notable for many reasons: Gregory I (590–604), called the Great, was perhaps the greatest theorist and practitioner of the art of being pope. The scion of a wealthy Roman family, he had turned his properties over to the Church and become a monk, then a papal ambassador to the imperial court at Constantinople, and finally elected pope. Gregory coined the term *Servum Servorum Dei*, Servant of the Servants of God, to describe his conception of the Petrine Ministry—though he was no shrinking violet when it came to asserting papal prerogatives.

With the pontificate of Innocent III (1198–1216), a brilliant young lawyer elected unanimously on the very day of his elderly predecessor's death, the prestige and power of the papacy achieved its apogee—but he pressed for more, bringing kings and emperors to heel, if not quite literally to kiss his feet as Gregory VII (1073–1085) had done. Pius IX (1846–1878) was the longest-reigning Roman pontiff, during whose time the First Vatican Council defined the pope's infallibility when his is speaking *ex cathedra* (from the chair) on faith and morals; he remains a controversial figure, and he "lost" the papal states that had buffered the papacy from temporal threats for more than a thousand years.

And, yes, there were bad popes, terrible popes, loathsome popes—perhaps none more so than John XII (955–964), who almost singlehandedly brought the papacy to its nadir; he was barely eighteen when elected, skilled in the arts of debauchery, and allegedly died of a stroke when he was in bed with a married woman. There was scandal, simony, and sin enough through the centuries to fill volumes of history and fire the souls of reformers and critics.

John Paul II (1978–) will be remembered hundreds of years hence for his tireless travels, his doctrinal orthodoxy, and his personal sanctity. Yes, he has legions of critics within the Church, especially in the U.S., but no one can deny his restless energy and intellectual gifts, his unparalleled ability to present his message on a world stage.

So, I hope this guidebook will answer—and raise—many questions about these successors of the Big Fisherman. As one of my graduate theology professors put it to his students: "Surely the Church is a divine institution if it has survived the worst of these men." And the great mystery remains: Will the Church survive in the coming millennium, even with the best of these men?

Gregory Tobin

Gregory Tobin is the author of *The Wisdom of St. Patrick* (Ballantine Books, 1999), a meditation on the life and moral teachings of the Apostle of Ireland. He was the editor of the acclaimed *Saints and Sinners* (Doubleday, 2000), an anthology of American Catholic writing since World War II. He is the former editor-in-chief of the Book-of-the-Month Club, Inc., and recently served as senior vice president and editor-in-chief of Ballantine Books. He chaired the parish leadership committee for the stewardship initiative of the Archdiocese of Newark, New Jersey.

Introduction

You're about to learn about one of history's most fascinating and enduring institutions.

The Complete Idiot's Guide to the Popes and the Papacy is offered as an opening look at the institution of the papacy. In writing this book, I've renewed my conviction that the subject of the popes is indisputably, incomprehensibly huge. (This is a conviction, of course, that many other writers who have taken on the history of the papacy have also reached.)

I share this fact with you not to earn your sympathy, but because I want to emphasize that what follows is, like any single-volume attempt to tame this topic, only a beginning. My aim has been to make the extraordinary story of the popes accessible to someone approaching it for the very first time, and to highlight, wherever possible, the personalities of the fascinating men who have held this office. In the process, I've had to condense and abridge a jaw-dropping amount of history, theology, controversy, and doctrine. This has to be a humbling experience for any writer; it certainly was for me.

I can only hope that the work I've done will encourage readers to explore the subject further on their own. (Resources for doing just that appear in Appendix C, "Further Reading.")

Five Sections

In this book, you'll find five sections, each devoted to some element of the ongoing, impossible-to-ignore drama that is the papacy. Here's a quick breakdown.

Part 1, "When in Rome ...." This is an overview of the Church and the history and prophecies associated with the papacy.

Part 2, "The Ascent of Christianity." This is a review of the history of the Church and the papacy from the time of St. Peter to the conversion of the Emperor Constantine, and from the time of Constantine to the bitter and corrupt struggles of tenth-century Rome.

Part 3, "Consolidation and Challenge." This part of the book takes you from the time of the Crusades to the turmoil of the Protestant Reformation, and explores the Church's momentous response to the challenge of internal reform, the Council of Trent.

Part 4, "After Trent." Here, you'll learn how the papacy responded to the task of implementing the edicts of the Council of Trent—and to growing political challenges in Europe.

Part 5, "From Potentate to Pastor." In this part of the book, you'll learn how the popes have responded to the tests of the modern world.

The appendixes at the end of the book offer a list of the popes in sequence, as well as a list of the antipopes (men who claimed the papacy but whose claims are regarded as lacking authority). As mentioned above, you'll also find a list of further resources in Appendix C, "Further Reading."

About the Sidebars

Throughout this book, you'll find helpful text boxes that will make it easy for you to learn more about the popes. Here's what you'll come across as you read:

> **Pontifical ... but Mythical**
>
> Here you'll find the truth about common misconceptions and mis-understandings about the papacy.

> **Papal People**
>
> These boxes feature capsule bio-graphies of people who played important roles in the life of a given pope.

> **Vatican Vocabulary**
>
> These boxes include the definition of vocabulary words you may not be familiar with.

> **Bet You Didn't Know**
>
> Here you'll find extended case histories, anecdotes, explana-tions, or other tidbits of interest-ing information.

> **Pope Watch**
>
> These boxes give you tidbits of interesting information about an individual pope, or about the history of the papacy.

Acknowledgments

My editor Gary Goldstein was patient and supportive throughout the period of this book's creation, for which I am deeply grateful. Gene Brissie is the best agent an author could ask for. Jennifer Massa and Suzanne Lieurance helped in the research for this book; David Toropov and Judith Burros supplied invaluable administrative help.

Thanks to the entire Alpha team: Amy Gordon, development editor; Billy Fields, produc-tion editor; Amy Borrelli, copy editor.

Special Thanks to the Technical Reviewer

The Complete Idiot's Guide to the Popes and the Papacy was reviewed by an expert who double-checked the accuracy of what you'll learn here, to help us ensure that this book gives you everything you need to know about the popes and the papacy. Special thanks are extended to Joe Cece.

Trademarks

All terms mentioned in this book that are known to be or are suspected of being trademarks or service marks have been appropriately capitalized. Alpha Books and Pearson Education, Inc., cannot attest to the accuracy of this information. Use of a term in this book should not be regarded as affecting the validity of any trademark or service mark.

Part 1

When in Rome ...

In this part of the book, you'll learn the basics.

You'll find out about the distinctive beliefs of Roman Catholicism, the nuts and bolts of the office of the papacy, and some intriguing predictions related to the institution. You'll also get a quick overview of some of the most inspiring popes in history—and a look at some of the men who failed to meet the challenges of the office.

Roman Catholicism 101

In This Chapter

◆ Common questions about the faith

◆ Important Roman Catholic beliefs and traditions

◆ Where to find out more

In this chapter, you learn the answers to some of the most common questions about the Roman Catholic faith. You'll learn what the Roman Catholic Church is, what its adherents believe, and how to learn more about its central tenets.

What Is the Roman Catholic Church?

The Roman Catholic Church is the global Christian Church that operates under the authority of the Bishop of Rome, the pope. It is also known as the Holy Catholic and Apostolic Church. Roman Catholics regard the pope as the Vicar of Christ.

The phrase "Roman Catholic" is of relatively recent origin; it arose in England in the nineteenth century, and is now a standard way to refer to the Church.

The overwhelming majority of believers within this faith follow the set of traditions and rituals known as the Latin Rite; there are, however, some variations. Eastern Rite Catholics following the Byzantine, Antiochene, Chaldean, Alexandrian, and Armenian traditions, for instance, accept the authority of the pope, but follow ancient Christian patterns of observance that differ from those of the Latin Rite.

> ### Bet You Didn't Know
>
> In its *Decree on the Catholic Eastern Churches* (1964), the Second Vatican Council made a point of acknowledging the Eastern Rite traditions. It wrote in part: "The Catholic Church values highly the institutions of the Eastern Churches, their liturgical rites, ecclesiastical traditions, and their ordering of Christian life. For in those churches, which are distinguished by their venerable antiquity, there is clearly evident the tradition which has come from the Apostles through the Fathers and which is part of the divinely revealed, undivided heritage of the Universal Church."

In this book, when the word "Church" appears with a capital C and without further identification, it is the Roman Catholic Church that is being referred to. (Less formal references to this body are common in contemporary speech and writing; it is popularly—if somewhat imprecisely—known simply as the Catholic Church.) References here to the "Catholic faith" or "Catholicism" refer to the traditions and practices of the Roman Catholic Church; references to "Catholics" refer to members of the Roman Catholic Church.

The word "catholic" (which means "universal") is sometimes used to refer to all Christian believers. When Protestants use "catholic" (with a lowercase initial letter) in reference to Christianity, they are usually referring to the entire Christian spectrum of belief, observance, and history.

The term "Catholic" was first used in reference to the Church by St. Ignatius of Antioch in the early second century *C.E.* (Ignatius also emphasized the importance of the virgin birth of Jesus.)

Vatican Vocabulary

The term **C.E.** stands for Common Era. It means the period popularly associated with the time following the birth of Jesus Christ, and is a successor designation to A.D., which stands for *anno domini* ("in the year of our Lord").

What Do Roman Catholics Believe?

Roman Catholics, like many other Christians, embrace two ancient creeds—the Apostle's Creed and the Nicene Creed. Scholars believe the Apostle's Creed dates from the half-century after the composition of the later portions of the New Testament; it is traditionally associated with the Twelve Apostles of Jesus. The Nicene Creed was developed in the year 325 at the Council of Nicaea, and revised at the First Council of Constantinople in 381.

Two popular English translations of these creeds follow.

The Apostle's Creed

I believe in God, the Father Almighty,
the Creator of heaven and earth,
and in Jesus Christ, His only Son, our Lord:
Who was conceived of the Holy Spirit,
    born of the Virgin Mary,
    suffered under Pontius Pilate,
    was crucified, died, and was buried.
He descended into hell.
The third day He arose again from the dead.
He ascended into heaven
    and sits at the right hand of God the Father Almighty,
    whence He shall come to judge the living and the dead.

I believe in the Holy Spirit, the Holy Catholic Church,
    the communion of saints,
    the forgiveness of sins,
    the resurrection of the body,
    and life everlasting.

Amen.

The Nicene Creed

We believe in one God, the Father, the Almighty,
of all that is, seen and unseen.

We believe in one Lord, Jesus Christ,
the only Son of God,
eternally begotten of the Father,
God from God, Light from Light,
true God from true God,
begotten, not made,
of one Being with the Father.

Through Him all things were made.

continues

continued

For us and for our salvation
He came down from heaven:
by the power of the Holy Spirit
He became incarnate from the Virgin Mary,
and was made man.

For our sake He was crucified under Pontius Pilate;
He suffered death and was buried.

On the third day He rose again
in accordance with the Scriptures;
He ascended into heaven
and is seated at the right hand of the Father.

He will come again in glory to judge the living and the
dead, and His kingdom will have no end.

We believe in the Holy Spirit, the Lord, the giver of life,
who proceeds from the Father and the Son.

With the Father and the Son He is worshipped and
glorified.

He has spoken through the Prophets.

We believe in one holy catholic and apostolic Church.

We acknowledge one baptism for the forgiveness of sins.

We look for the resurrection of the dead,
and the life of the world to come.

Amen.

Roman Catholics also accept the Church as having a divine commission and acknowledge as definitive its teachings and interpretations regarding Christ's Gospel and the Bible as a whole.

They accept the doctrine of apostolic succession, which holds that the pope and the bishops of the Church exercise the authority assigned by Jesus Christ to the apostles.

They accept the Church's teachings and interpretations of Scripture as definitive.

There are, of course, many other distinctive aspects of Roman Catholic belief and practice. Some of them are examined in the questions that follow.

What Is Transubstantiation?

Transubstantiation is the doctrine holding that the bread and wine offered during the Mass are, when consecrated in the Eucharist, miraculously transformed in all but their external form to the body, blood, soul, and divinity of the crucified Jesus.

The teachings of the Orthodox Eastern Church take an analogous approach. Protestant denominations, which deny the element of sacrifice during Eucharistic celebration, have historically rejected, overlooked, or chosen not to address the concept of transubstantiation.

For Catholics, the key idea is that the nature of the bread and wine is fundamentally altered during the Mass. Christ is regarded as having assumed sacramental presence and substance through the *Eucharist*.

What Is Purgatory?

Roman Catholics believe in an intermediate realm after death between heaven and hell known as the Final Purification, or *purgatory*. Within Roman Catholic theology, the word "purgatory" also refers to the process by which those who die in God's grace are brought to the state of perfection necessary to enter heaven. Catholics view purgatory as a cleansing fire that dispenses with unpunished or unrepented sins. Purgatory is not to be confused with the eternal suffering of the damned in hell; to the contrary, it is understood as a temporary phase for those whose immortal souls are destined for union with the divine.

Souls in purgatory are regarded as benefiting from the prayers and efforts of both living human beings and saints who have concluded their earthly life. Prayers for the dead are thus an important part of Roman Catholic observance.

Theological explanations of purgatory and the communion of saints tend to be long and rather

Pope Watch

An enduring dispute between the popes and the patriarchs of the Eastern Churches involved the description of the Holy Spirit as proceeding "from the Father *and the Son*" in the Nicene Creed. The controversy centered on the phrase "and the son" (in Latin, *filioque*). Leaders of the Christian faith in the East argued that this formulation did not adequately reflect the unique nature of the Holy Spirit, and thus rejected this version of the Creed.

Vatican Vocabulary

The **Eucharist** refers both to the sacrament reenacting the actions of Jesus at the Last Supper (namely, the sharing of bread and wine as his body and blood), and to the consecrated elements of that sacrament.

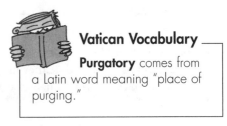

Vatican Vocabulary

Purgatory comes from a Latin word meaning "place of purging."

dense, but a brief summary of the Catholic position on biblical support for the Church's view of the matter can be offered here.

"Not a Thoughtless Word"

Here are important texts that Roman Catholicism regards as supporting its conception of the afterlife.

> "I tell you this; there is not a thoughtless word that comes from men's lips but they will have to account for it on the day of judgment. For out of your own mouth you will be acquitted; out of your own mouth you will be condemned."
>
> —Matthew 12:36–37

From this saying of Jesus, and from other passages, Catholic theology infers that only those who have attained perfection of the immortal soul are fated to see God in heaven. The condition of those who die in a state of grace, but with imperfections upon the soul, is seen as incomplete.

The implications of another passage in Matthew are also important:

> "No sin, no slander, is beyond forgiveness for men, except slander spoken against the Spirit, and that will not be forgiven. Any man who speaks a word against the Son of Man will be forgiven; but if anyone speaks against the Holy Spirit, for him there is no forgiveness, either in this age or the age to come."
>
> —Matthew 12:31–32

The great pope St. Gregory I (590–604) made a historic theological observation on this teaching of Jesus. Gregory's conclusion had to do not with eternal condemnation, but with the nature of heavenly judgment itself:

> "As for certain lesser faults, we must believe that, before the Final Judgment, there is a purifying fire. He who is truth says that whoever utters blasphemy against the Holy Spirit will be pardoned neither in this age nor the age to come. From this sentence we understand that certain offenses can be forgiven in this age, but certain others in the age to come."
>
> —St. Gregory the Great (Dialogues 4:39)

Support for the conception of the petitionary nature of prayer in general (and by inference, the effectiveness of prayers in aid of those whose souls are in purgatory) is understood from the following passage from the Book of Revelation:

> "Then another angel came and stood at the altar, holding a golden censer; and he was given a great quantity of incense to offer with the prayers of all God's people upon the golden altar in front of the throne. And from the angel's hand the smoke of the incense went up before God with the prayers of his people."
>
> —Revelation 8:3–4

The Roman Catholic conception of purgatory has been addressed here in some detail for three reasons.

First, it seemed appropriate to identify one of the distinctive beliefs within the faith. Eastern Christianity does not address these issues in the same manner as Roman Catholicism, and Protestants tend to reject the notion of purgatory altogether.

Second, the faith's emphasis on logical precision is worth noting. This is a variety of intellectual thoroughness that many feel carries a special theological beauty all its own. As Kallistos Ware observed in *The Oxford Illustrated History of Christianity* (John McManners, ed.; Oxford: Oxford University Press, 1990): "Latin theology has always made more use of juridical categories than the Greeks have done, and in its developed scholastic form it is much more systematic, more heavily dependent on logical argument, than is the predominantly mystical approach of the Christian East."

Finally, it seemed fitting to pinpoint an important Church doctrine whose expression owes a large debt to one of the great popes. As you will learn in the pages that follow, quite a few popes have made extraordinary theological contributions to the Church, and this is certainly true of St. Gregory I.

Bet You Didn't Know

St. Gregory I (ruled 590–604) was one of the greatest popes in history. He was a committed defender of Rome, a dedicated servant to the poor, and a brilliant writer. His immense intellectual gifts were accompanied by a deeply held belief that logical reasoning had its limits. In keeping with this belief, Gregory wrote, "If the work of God would be comprehended by reason, it would be no longer wonderful, and faith would have no merit if reason provided proof."

Why Do Catholics Go to Confession?

The Catholic practice of confession, like many other aspects of the faith, must be understood within the context of Gospel accounts that portray Jesus authorizing the apostles—the first priests of the Christian Church—to act with His authority and in His name. The doctrine of apostolic succession holds that the powers and authority granted to the apostles by Jesus have continued to be exercised, in unbroken succession, by the Church; these powers specifically include the forgiveness of sins.

Two relevant scripture citations are worth noting here.

On the Forgiveness of Sins

Jesus confers his authority to the Twelve Apostles.

"Truly, I say to you, whatever you bind on earth shall be bound in heaven, and whatever you loose on earth shall be loosed in heaven."

—Matthew 18:18

"Receive the Holy Spirit. If you forgive the sins of any, they are forgiven; if you retain the sins of any, they are retained."

—John 20:21–23

Two points sometimes overlooked by non-Catholics regarding confession are that God, rather than an individual priest, is regarded as hearing all confessions, and that dishonest or unfelt confessions are seen as spiritually meaningless, regardless of what a priest has to say about them.

Do Catholics Worship the Virgin Mary?

Mary is a saint, not a deity, and is not worshipped by Catholics.

Extraordinary love, pious regard, and veneration for the Mother of Christ have existed since ancient times. Acknowledgment of Mary's status as the blessed Mother of God and belief in her ability to intercede in human affairs have been strongly associated with Catholicism; it is, however, an ancient feature of Christianity in both the East and the West. Catholics believe Mary to have been conceived without sin, and to have been assumed bodily into heaven. Her special role in Catholic observance has been emphasized from time to time by reports of her appearance by means of visions to individual believers. Certainly, no one disputes that Catholics have a long tradition of glorifying and celebrating her unique role.

None of these facts, however, should lead one to overlook the clear teaching of the Church, which holds that no entity other than the Triune God is to be worshipped or adored. As a matter of theology, the Church understands Mary to be a saint in possession of special glory, not a deity worthy of honors to which God alone has claim. The distinction may seem to be a fine one to outsiders, but it has been in place for centuries and is a matter of settled understanding.

> ### Pontifical ... but Mythical
>
> Some non-Catholics mistakenly believe worship of the Virgin Mary to be countenanced by Catholic doctrine or by the office of the pope. Such worship is forbidden by the Church. Mary is honored, venerated, and celebrated, but she is not herself worshipped as a deity; statues and images of her (or of any saint) are not to be regarded as divine entities.

What Is a Catechism?

A catechism is a book containing basic instruction of the principles of Christian faith, the body of which is typically composed in a question-and-answer format. Many Christian churches have employed them as teaching tools for youngsters and recent converts over the centuries.

In Roman Catholicism, the introduction to the English-language version of the current official catechism features the following explanation:

"Building Up the Body of Christ"

"Quite early on, the name *catechesis* was given to the totality of the Church's effort to make disciples; to help men believe that Jesus is the Son of God so that, believing, they might have life in his name; and to educate and instruct them in this life, thus building up the body of Christ .... While not being formally identified with them, catechesis is built on a certain number of elements of the Church's pastoral mission which have a catechetical aspect, that prepare for catechesis, or spring from it. They are: the initial proclamation of the Gospel or missionary preaching to arouse faith; examination of the

continues

continued

reasons for belief; experience of Christian living; celebration of the sacraments; integration into the ecclesial community; and apostolic and missionary witness ....

"This catechism aims at presenting an organic synthesis of the essential and fundamental contents Catholic doctrine, as regards both faith and morals .... Its principal sources are the Sacred Scriptures, the Fathers of the Church, the liturgy, and the Church's Magisterium (teaching authority)."

—Catechism of the Catholic Church

In this chapter, I have given brief but—I hope—responsible answers to a few of the most common questions asked by outsiders regarding Catholic religious practice. Readers who are interested in pursuing any of these questions further, or who have other inquiries, will find a detailed summary of fundamental Catholic principles at the following Web site, which features the complete text of the current catechism: http://www.vatican.va/archive/catechism/ccc_toc.htm

This is certainly among the most important resources for resolving questions concerning the official positions and teachings of the Roman Catholic Church. It is an essential supplement to this brief introductory chapter.

The Last Word

Under Pope John Paul II, the following overview of the Catholic faith was incorporated into the official catechism:

"God, infinitely perfect and blessed in Himself, in a plan of sheer goodness freely created man to make him share in his own blessed life. For this reason, in every time and place, God draws close to man. He calls man to seek Him, to know Him, to love Him with all his strength. He calls together all men, scattered and divided by sin, into the unity of His family, the Church. To accomplish this, when the fullness of time had come, God sent His Son as Redeemer and Savior. In His Son and through Him, He invites men to become, in the Holy Spirit, His adopted children and thus heirs of His blessed life."

If there is a better passage illustrating the Church's vision of itself and its mission, I have not yet come across it.

The Least You Need to Know

- The Roman Catholic Church is the global Christian church that operates under the authority of the Bishop of Rome, the pope.
- Roman Catholics, like many other Christians, embrace two ancient creeds, the Apostle's Creed and the Nicene Creed.
- In addition, Catholics accept their Church as having a divine commission and as being in possession of the Christian revelation; they also accept the doctrine of apostolic succession.
- Catholics believe in an intermediate realm after death between heaven and hell known as the Final Purification, or purgatory.
- Mary is a saint, not a deity, and is not worshipped by Catholics.
- For more on Catholic belief and observance, visit http://www.vatican.va/archive/catechism/ccc_toc.htm

Chapter

The Papacy: Nuts and Bolts

In This Chapter

- ◆ Key concepts
- ◆ Essential summaries
- ◆ Terms to know

In this chapter, you get a quick overview of essential terminology and key concepts that will help you understand the simultaneously ancient and modern institution known as the papacy. What follows will give you an introduction to important terms, ideas, and traditions associated with the popes.

Terms of particular importance have been placed in **bold type.** You will also find a timeline that offers a general outline of the development of the office.

You may wish to refer to these resources as you make your way through this book.

The Hierarchy

A **bishop** is the senior pastor (literally, "shepherd") within a given geographic area. The pope is the preeminent bishop of the Roman Catholic Church. He serves as **Bishop of Rome.**

The region over which a bishop exercises authority is known as a **diocese;** his seat (or central location) of authority is known as a **see.** A superior bishop within a certain area is known as an **archbishop,** and the (larger) zone of authority encompassing those bishops under him is an **archdiocese.** The title **metropolitan** is sometimes conferred by the pope upon an archbishop; it signifies authority within a given region.

All bishops, under modern practice, are required to make **ad limina** ("unto the threshold") visits to the pope every five years to discuss goals and challenges within their dioceses with the Holy Father.

A **cardinal** is a senior adviser and special aide to the pope. The process of being elevated to the office of cardinal is sometimes referred as being "raised to the purple." Notwithstanding, the color primarily associated with cardinals is red, thanks to the mantle and hat traditionally associated with the office.

Since 1179, cardinals alone have elected popes, and Pope Paul VI (reigned 1963–1978) saw to the institution of a formal policy permitting only bishops to be elevated to the office of cardinal. For centuries, the office of cardinal has been associated with such elevated bishops, but, before Paul VI's pontificate, some of the most prominent cardinals were neither bishops nor priests, but rather in "*minor orders.*"

Vatican Vocabulary

The term **minor orders** refers to the vows taken in the lower degrees of the hierarchy within the Roman Catholic Church.

A **consistory** is a gathering of cardinals presided over by the pope.

Collegiality refers to the joint responsibility of bishops, "in communion with the pope and with each other," for the conduct of Church affairs.

A **priest,** in Roman Catholicism, is a person who is ordained to conduct the rites of the Catholic Church, and who is a member of the hierarchy below that of bishop. A **deacon** is a person within the rank below that of priest. In centuries past, the deacons in Rome were skilled administrators and, for a time, quite powerful; a good number were elected pope.

A gathering of **ecclesiastics** (persons in the clergy or members of religious orders) in accordance with Church law to address Church affairs is known as a **synod.**

How Popes Are Chosen

The process by which the earliest bishops of Rome were selected is lost to history; there is nevertheless an ancient tradition of selection involving church elders. Since 1271, the pope has been elected by a **conclave** of cardinals. Conclave means "with a key," and refers both to the meetings conducted by the **Sacred College** of Cardinals and to the closed quarters in which these men are kept until they select a pope by a two-thirds majority (plus one vote).

The burning, in a small stove at the Vatican, of the papal ballots is a sign of successful completion of the conclave's deliberations. The resulting puffs of white smoke serve as a signal to the world that a new leader of the Roman Catholic Church has been selected.

Since 1831, every man elected pope has been a cardinal first. (Historically, most popes have been cardinals.)

As a practical matter, popes can expect to serve for life once elected, although precedent exists for resignation.

The cardinal who oversees Church affairs and presides over the conclave that gathers following the death of a pope is known as the **camerlengo.**

Pope Watch
Scandalous delays in the election of popes have led to a number of electoral reforms over the centuries.

Papal Authority Within the Church

The pope is, in the realm of faith and morals, the final enunciator of the Church's official teaching (or **magisterium,** a term that also refers to the teaching authority of the Church itself). The pope issues **decretals** (letters meant to resolve disputes or clarify precedent) that are an integral part of **canon** (Church) **law.** He may negotiate **concordats** (agreements with heads of state regarding religious matters within their country) and name **legates** (representatives who act in his name and with his authority). He also appoints **nuncios** (envoys representing the pope to a sovereign state or a local church).

Popes, and those acting under the authority of the pope, have responded in various ways to those regarded as having deviated from or undermining the teachings of the Roman Catholic Church. Among the most extreme such measures are the **inderdict,** which cuts off an entire faction, group of people, or nation from the sacraments of the Church; and **excommunication,** which carries a similar isolation from the sacraments against an individual. In medieval times, excommunication also entailed severe political and social sanctions that have no real parallel in contemporary life; the loss of citizenship and most legal rights would perhaps be a fair approximation.

An **indulgence** is the remission of punishment associated with sins after confession and absolution; indulgences are associated with the Church as an institution and also with the popes.

The Papal Court

The court (and chief administrative arm) of the pope is known as the **Curia;** it is divided into subgroups, each of which operates under the direction of a cardinal known as a **prefect.**

The Pope and the Council

The First Vatican Council (1870) confirmed **papal infallibility,** and definitively settled a historically divisive question: Is the pope's teaching superior or inferior to that of the **General Council,** the formal (and rare) assembly of bishops gathered from time to time by the pope? (The First Vatican Council, by way of reference, was itself such an assembly.) The council's holding in favor of the pope, and its elucidation of the specific nature of the infallibility of his teaching, marked one of the institutional triumphs of the papacy.

Saints and Canonization

Since 993, **canonization** (declaration that a late Christian is a saint) has been linked to the papal office; since the twelfth century, the power to name saints has been exclusively the pope's.

Beatification, also bestowed by the pope, is an intermediate step toward sainthood, a formal acknowledgment that a deceased Christian enjoys the blessings of heaven and is a worthy subject of certain public honors.

A number of popes have themselves become saints.

Popes Who Have Become Saints

St. Peter	St. Zephyrinus	St. Marcellinus
St. Linus	St. Callistus I	St. Marcellus I
St. Anacletus	St. Urban I	St. Eusebius
St. Clement I	St. Pontain	St. Militiades
St. Evaristus	St. Anterus	St. Sylvester I
St. Alexander I	St. Fabian	St. Marcus
St. Sixtus I	St. Cornelius	St. Julius I
St. Telesphorus	St. Lucius I	St. Damasus
St. Hyginus	St. Stephen I	St. Siricius
St. Pius I	St. Sixtus II	St. Anastasius I
St. Anicetus	St. Dionysius	St. Innocent I
St. Soter	St. Felix I	St. Zosimus
St. Eleutherius	St. Eutychian	St. Boniface I
St. Victor I	St. Caius	St. Celestine I

St. Sixtus III	St. Gregory I	St. Zachary
St. Leo I	St. Boniface IV	St. Paul I
St. Hilarius	St. Adeodatus I	St. Leo III
St. Simplicius	St. Martin I	St. Paschal I
St. Felix III (II)	St. Eugene I	St. Leo IV
St. Gelasius I	St. Vitalian	St. Nicholas I
St. Symmachus	St. Agatho	St. Adrian III
St. Hormisdas	St. Leo II	St. Leo IX
St. John I	St. Benedict II	St. Gregory VII
St. Felix IV (III)	St. Sergius I	St. Celestine V
St. Agapetus I	St. Gregory II	St. Pius V
St. Silverius	St. Gregory III	St. Pius X

Papal Messages

Popes can issue messages of varying formality and authority. One of these is the **decretal**, discussed earlier in this chapter.

An **encyclical** is a teaching letter, once addressed exclusively to the bishops of the Church but more recently targeted to "all people of goodwill." (In the modern period, the encyclical has emerged as the vehicle of choice for the enunciation of papal teachings intended to be noticed and observed by Roman Catholics.)

A **bull** is a sealed pronouncement of great authority outlining a formal decision in a given matter; its contents are regarded as definitive. (Pronouncements of excommunication, for instance, may take the form of a bull.)

A **brief** is an official papal writing typically regarded as having lesser impact and formality than a papal bull.

The Papacy Through the Centuries

Each of the chapters in the main sections of *The Complete Idiot's Guide to Popes and the Papacy* (Chapters 6 through 23) addresses a particular historical period. As you make your way through these chapters, you may wish to refer to the timeline that follows. It offers a summary of some of the dynamic changes within the office over the centuries, as well as some sense of its enduring mission.

Here and in the main chapters, there has been a certain unavoidable compression of historical material for the sake of accessibility; there is a great deal more a volume such as this could cover. For more resources related to the fascinating (and endlessly analyzed) subject of the history of the papacy, see Appendix C, "Further Reading."

The Papacy: A Timeline

Here is a timeline showing the chief events in the evolution of the papal office.

Circa 55–300 c.e. (Chapters 6 and 7)

◆ Peter and his successors led the Roman Church during troubled times.

◆ Bloody persecution of Christians under the Roman Empire was common; increasing authority and reverence was accorded to the Bishop of Rome as missionary activity increased.

◆ Rome was the recipient of many gifts from converts; financial support of Christians from leaders of the Roman Church was increasingly important.

Circa 300–800 (Chapters 8 and 9)

◆ Following the conversion of Emperor Constantine, the leaders of the Roman Church assumed new prestige and power.

◆ With Rome in decline and the empire divided, the popes played a vital role in the defense of the city against foreign powers and barbarian invaders.

◆ After the fall of the Western Empire, the leaders of the Roman Church assumed many aspects of the (formerly) imperial role of guardian of civil culture, rule, and tradition.

◆ A donation of lands from the Frankish monarch Pepin the Short (756) left the popes with significant temporal authority over dominions later known as the Papal States.

800–1054 (Chapter 10)

◆ The pope's dual role (secular leader and supreme religious authority in the West) led to innumerable conflicts with lay princes.

◆ Corruption in the office of the papacy resulted in many scandals and in the cynical manipulation of the process by which popes were selected.

◆ Centuries of dispute and alienation between popes and patriarchs culminated in a formal split with Eastern Christianity.

1054–1276 (Chapter 11)

◆ The papacy itself spawned important and necessary reforms; these, however, were accompanied by increasingly bitter disputes over Church influence, notably the crisis over investiture, which began during this period.

◆ Disputes with European rulers continued; some popes emerged as extremely powerful figures, while others were no match for the political players of the period.

◆ Western Christianity's united efforts during the Crusades consolidated and reinforced the pope's potent transnational role.

◆ The papacy's high point of political influence in Europe came during the late twelfth and early thirteenth century.

1276–1484 (Chapters 12 and 13)

◆ Dominance of the papal office by the French crown was a characteristic of the early fourteenth century.

◆ A series of French popes moved the papacy to France in 1309, where it stayed until 1378. During this period, the Church's administrative and social presence in Europe reached a point of remarkable predominance.

◆ Shortly after the papacy's relocation to Rome, rival claims to the office resulted in the chaos of the Great Schism.

◆ Challenges to the pope's authority from the conciliar movement, which held that a general council was superior to the pope, were eventually overcome.

1484–1565 (Chapters 14 and 15)

◆ Meaningful political power for the popes was by now effectively limited to Italy.

◆ The popes declined to pursue a campaign of (long-overdue) religious reform. In part, this was because doing so would have entailed challenging both the dominant kingdoms and the local religious hierarchies of Europe.

◆ The popes focused on their own court affairs, and were notable patrons of the arts. Wealth, corruption, and worldliness in the papacy became matters of intense debate.

◆ Religious revolution swept Europe and challenged the papacy during the Protestant Reformation.

◆ The Jesuits, a religious order strongly associated with the pope, were founded.

◆ The popes opposed the Protestant movement; they eventually took an active role in the development of a new round of Catholic reforms, which were consolidated at the Council of Trent.

1565–1769 (Chapters 16, 17, and 18)

- ◆ Papal initiatives concerning foreign missions became increasingly important.
- ◆ In France, the emergence of Gallicanism, which promoted local resistance to the pope's authority, proved troublesome.
- ◆ Bitter disputes with European Catholic monarchs over control of local church appointments and practices resulted in many setbacks for the papacy, including the suppression of the Jesuit order.
- ◆ Many observers seriously questioned the papacy's ability to survive the eighteenth century.

1769–1846 (Chapter 19)

- ◆ The French Revolution and the rise of Napoleon brought further trials to the embattled institution of Roman pontiff.
- ◆ The papacy, however, emerged with a new moral standing in Europe, and secured some important diplomatic and propaganda victories in the period following the Napoleonic Wars.

> **Pope Watch**
>
> Since 1870, when political turmoil ended the status of the pope as a temporal ruler and forced his relocation, the pope has led the Roman Catholic Church from the Vatican, a complex located within Rome that includes St. Peter's Basilica and a number of other structures.

1846–1914 (Chapter 20)

- ◆ An enhancement of the pope's religious authority came when the First Vatican Council issued a decree of papal infallibility.
- ◆ The papacy contested (unsuccessfully) a series of setbacks in the secular realm. These reversals accompanied the rise of the modern Italian state, and ended the era of papal political authority over Rome and the Papal States.

1914 to Present (Chapters 21, 22, and 23)

- ◆ Since 1929, Vatican City has been recognized as a sovereign nation, with the pope as its head of state.
- ◆ In the latest period of the office's development, the pope's status as an ecclesiastical figure joins with his unique standing as a moral leader in a world frequently marred by tragedy and a lack of moral purpose.

An Enduring Institution

The papacy remains an institution accorded deep reverence, obedience, and respect by millions of Catholics around the world. It has outlasted schisms, suppressions, monarchs, empires, revolutions, and countless other upheavals.

It is still going strong.

The Least You Need to Know

- The pope is the preeminent bishop of the Roman Catholic Church. He serves as Bishop of Rome.
- The papacy, once a powerful temporal office, has evolved over the centuries.
- Today, the pope's status as an ecclesiastical figure joins with his unique standing as a moral leader in a world frequently marred by tragedy and a lack of moral purpose.
- Feel free to refer back to the terms and timeline in this chapter as you make your way through the book.

Chapter

Prophecies and Portents?

In This Chapter

- ◆ St. Malachy
- ◆ The predictions attributed to him
- ◆ Their many interpretations

Somewhere between revelation and conclave-sensitive parlor game fall the papal prophecies popularly attributed to St. Malachy (1094–1148), an Irish archbishop of the twelfth century.

What are the prophecies of St. Malachy? Did this Irish saint really predict a thousand years of Roman Catholic history? How many popes are "left" to lead the Church?

These and similar questions have a way of arising among Roman Catholics when a pope dies, falls ill, or reaches "a certain age"—namely, the age at which the prospect of a Vatican conclave to elect a successor becomes a realistic one.

In recent years, the aforementioned queries have been accompanied by another more urgent-sounding query: Is the pope who follows John Paul II really destined to be the next-to-last Bishop of Rome before the apocalypse? Answering such questions, of course, is a good deal more problematic than posing them. Posing them is, however, apparently habit-forming.

In this chapter is a brief overview of the writings attributed to Malachy, writings that have tantalized, intrigued, and, every now and then, terrified believers with an interest in the comings and goings of the papacy.

Vatican Vocabulary

The so-called **prophecies of Malachy** are a series of short mottoes that have been attributed to the reigns of popes from the year 1143 onwards. Their date of composition is a matter of controversy, but they are known to have been published in the sixteenth century.

Pontifical ... but Mythical

Some people believe that the prophecies of Malachy, because of their long association with the papacy, have attained formal acceptance or endorsement from the Church. They have not. The last prophetic work that the Church acknowledges as divinely inspired is the Book of Revelation.

In this part of the book, you'll take a look at these much-discussed prophecies, the man credited with their authorship, and the points of contact these brief mottoes share with the popes they have supposedly identified since the year 1143.

A word of caution is in order. The Church has never put much stock in these predictions. They have, however, captured the imagination and attention of believers (and nonbelievers!) for many centuries. They also make interesting reading, which is the reason I'm focusing on them here. In the end, the writings attributed to Malachy probably say as much about people's perceptions of the papacy as they do about the papacy itself.

Was St. Malachy a Real Person?

Malachy was indeed real, and his contribution to Roman Catholicism in Ireland has inspired a great deal of interest and scholarship over the years. So has speculation about the prophecies associated with his supposed visions of future popes.

Bet You Didn't Know

St. Malachy was a great reformer and defender of Catholicism in Ireland. In the face of challenges from indigenous religious practice, he established a clear Church hierarchy and imposed clerical discipline, and oversaw a great revival of commitment to Christianity in Ireland. Malachy was primate of Armagh; he was also a close friend of St. Bernard, who wrote his earliest autobiography. *The Catholic Encyclopedia* (1913 edition) reports that "(i)n 1139, (Malachy) went to Rome to give an account of the affairs of his diocese to the pope, Innocent II, who promised him two palliums for the metropolitan sees of Armagh and Cashel." Proponents of his authorship of the papal prophecies hold that he received a series of visions during this visit.

The Authorship Question

Malachy's authorship of the prophecies connected with the popes from Celestine II (1143–1144) forward is far from certain. These writings did not surface until 1559, more than 400 years after Malachy's death, and when they were made public, they were accompanied by an extraordinary and not entirely credible explanation.

Hidden Prophecies?

During a visit to Pope Innocent II in 1140, Malachy, having supposedly recorded a series of prophetic visions on paper, is said to have handed over the relevant documents to the pope.

For reasons purportedly having to do with their potentially explosive content, Innocent, we are told, chose not to circulate the Vatican prophecies. This caution ruled the day for four centuries, as the predictions remained the secret of the Vatican archive keepers until the time was ripe for their release.

So goes the legend. What is certain is that a Benedictine chronicler, Arnold Wion, oversaw the first publication of these writings in 1559. People have been arguing over their provenance ever since.

> **Papal People**
>
> St. Malachy appears to have told no one during his lifetime of any visions involving future popes that unfolded during a visit to Rome. No mention of these prophecies appears in St. Bernard's account of the saint's life.

What Form Do the Prophecies Take?

The predictions are a series of short Latin mottoes, typically three or four words in length, each attributed to a single pontificate not otherwise identified (beyond, of course, its position in the sequence).

The Catholic Encyclopedia refers to these mottoes as "mystical titles," and notes that "those who have undertaken to interpret and explain these symbolical prophecies have succeeded in discovering some trait, allusion, point, or similitude in their application to the individual popes, either as to their country, their name, their coat of arms or insignia, their birthplace, their talent or learning, the title of their cardinalate, the dignities which they held, et cetera."

If one bears in mind that this is an awfully wide net to cast, and comes to the realization that the connections that do arise are often fairly slim pickings in the prophetic-vision department, one can take a certain amount of entertainment from the predictions attributed to St. Malachy. There are indeed some interesting parallels between these short maxims and the traits, allusions, reigns, points, or likenesses of a number of popes.

Some nonexhaustive selections of such parallels follow.

Prophecies of Malachy That Attracted Early Notice

Here are some of the most celebrated of the early prophecies.

Regarding Pope Celestine II (1143–1144)

Motto: *Ex castro Tyberis*

Translation: "From a castle set upon the Tiber"

Interpretation: Celestine II's birthplace was the Citta di Castello, on the shores of the Tiber.

Regarding Pope Eugene III (1145–1153)

Motto: *Ex magnitudine montis*

Translation: "Out of the greatness of the mountain"

Interpretation: Eugene II was born in a castle called Grammont, the Latin version for which is *mons magnus*; his family name, Montemagno, also provides a close parallel.

Regarding Pope Adrian IV (1154–1159)

Motto: *De rure albo*

Translation: "From the field of Albe"

Interpretation: Adrian IV's birthplace was the town of Saint-Alban.

Regarding Pope Innocent III (1198–1216)

Motto: *Comes signatus*

Translation: "Signed count"

Interpretation: Innocent III was a descendant of the aristocratic Signy (or Segni) line.

Regarding Pope Gregory IX (1227–1241)

Motto: *Avis Ostiensis*

Translation: "Bird of Ostia"

Interpretation: Gregory IX was cardinal of Ostia prior to his elevation to the papacy.

Regarding Pope Urban IV (1261–1264)

Motto: *Hierusalem Campaniae*

Translation: "Jerusalem of Champagne"

Interpretation: Urban IV was from Troyes, Champagne; he served as patriarch of Jerusalem.

Regarding Pope Nicholas IV (1288–1292)

Motto: *Ex eremo celsus*

Translation: "From a hermit he is elevated"

Interpretation: Before his elevation to the papacy, Nicholas IV was a hermit in the monastery of Pouilles.

Regarding Pope Clement V (1305–1314)

Motto: *De fessis Aquitanicis*

Translation: "Ribbon of Aquitaine"

Interpretation: Clement V had been archbishop of Bordeaux in Aquitaine.

Regarding Pope John XXII (1316–1334)

Motto: *De sutore Osseo*

Translation: "Of the Osseo cobbler"

Interpretation: John XXII's family name was Ossa; his father was a shoemaker.

Regarding Pope Benedict XII (1334–1342)

Motto: *Frigidus abbas*

Translation: "Cold friar"

Interpretation: Benedict XII had been a priest at the monastery of Frontfroid, which translates as "cold front."

Regarding Pope Callistus III (1455–1458)

Motto: *Bos pascens*

Translation: "Grazing ox"

Interpretation: Callistus III's coat of arms featured an ox grazing.

The Scoffers Have Their Say

It's all fascinating, and perhaps even persuasive—*assuming* that one accepts the contention that the prophecies were composed in the twelfth century and cautiously hidden away in the papal archives.

But there is another viewpoint to consider. If there is merit to the claims of skeptics that the predictions in question were composed much later (say, 1559 or thereabouts), then what the above proves is not prophetic skill, but an ability to express known facts about dead popes in (seemingly) oblique Latin.

Of greater interest, perhaps, are the mottoes associated with popes who reigned *after* 1559. These, too, are fascinating.

Yet another word or two of skepticism, however, is worth sharing. The degree to which a given pope or his supporters may have consciously chosen to take steps aiding in the fulfillment of the (well-known) prophecies has, from time to time, been a matter of debate. That having been said, it is worth noting that many of the parallels between pontificates and the predictions attributed to Malachy offer interesting overlaps.

Selected Prophecies of Malachy Relating to Popes Reigning After 1559

Here are some of the more celebrated later prophecies attributed to St. Malachy.

Regarding Pope Sixtus V (1585–1590)

Motto: *Axis in medieate signi*

Translation: "An axis in the middle of the sign"

Interpretation: Author Peter Bander called this motto "a straightforward allusion to the pope's coat of arms."

Regarding Pope Clement IX (1667–1669)

Motto: *Sydus Olorum*

Translation: "Constellation of swans"

Interpretation: Clement IX reputedly occupied the Chamber of Swans in the Vatican upon his election.

Regarding Pope Pius VI (1775–1799)

Motto: *Peregrinus Apostolicu*

Translation: "Pilgrim pope"

Interpretation: According to *The Catholic Encyclopedia*, "(This) appears to be verified by his journey when pope into Germany, by his long career as pope, and by his expatriation from Rome at the end of his pontificate."

Regarding Pope Pius VII (1800–1823)

Motto: *Aquila rapax*

Translation: "A rapacious eagle"

Interpretation: It was Pius VII's fate to endure the assaults of Napoleon, whose emblem was indeed an eagle.

Regarding Pope Gregory XVI (1831–1846)

Motto: *De balneis Hetruriae*

Translation: "From the bath of Etruria"

Interpretation: At the time of his election as pope, Gregory XVI was a Camaldolese monk. (He was, in fact, the last monk to be elevated to the throne of St. Peter.) The order had been founded at Balneo, in Etruria.

Regarding Pope Benedict XV (1914–1922)

Motto: *Religio depopulata*

Translation: "Religion laid waste"

Interpretation: The ravages of World War I and the Russian Revolution took place on Benedict XV's watch.

Regarding Pope Pius XI (1922–1939)

Motto: *Fides intrepida*

Translation: "Unshaken faith"

Interpretation: Pius XI held firm, denouncing both Mussolini and Hitler as chaos descended and war loomed in Europe.

Regarding Pope Pius XII (1939–1958)

Motto: *Pastor angelicus*

Translation: "Angelic shepherd"

Interpretation: Contrary to popular belief (see Chapter 21, "The World in Flames"), Pius XII's pontificate nobly served Jews and others whose lives were thrown into turmoil, madness, and violence during World War II. His extraordinary efforts to help refugees (Jewish and otherwise) fleeing Nazi persecution were a recurrent subject of the eulogies pronounced after his death.

Regarding Pope John XXIII (1958–1963)

Motto: *Pastor et nauta*

Translation: "Pastor (shepherd) and mariner"

Interpretation: John XXIII had been patriarch of Venice (famous, of course, for its waterways) before his election as pope.

Regarding Pope Paul VI (1963–1978)

Motto: *Flos florum*

Translation: "Flower of flowers"

Interpretation: Paul VI's coat of arms featured three fleurs-de-lis.

Regarding John Paul I (1978)

Motto: *De medietate lunae*

Translation: "Of the half moon" or "in the middle of the month"

Interpretation: There have been several; the most intriguing involve the pope's birth in the diocese of Belluno ("beautiful moon") and his abbreviated pontificate, which lasted barely more than a month.

> ### Pope Watch
>
> In 1958, in the conclave that followed the death of Pius XII, Cardinal Francis Spellman of New York's ambitions for the papacy were something of an open secret. One joke of the day had it that Spellman, an eager student of the predictions of Malachy, had rented a boat, filled it with sheep, and sailed up and down the Tiber in an attempt to fulfill the prophecy that the next pope would be "pastor and mariner." The patriarch of Venice was eventually elected; he took the name John XXIII.

Regarding John Paul II (1978 to Present)

Motto: *De labore solis*

Translation: "Of the sun's eclipse" or "From the labor of the sun."

Interpretation: John Paul II was born during a solar eclipse (May 18, 1920).

Then What?

As of this writing, there are either two popes to go—or perhaps many more than that, depending on how one interprets the prophecies.

The final two predictions, subjects of intense debate and discussion, are as follows.

Regarding John Paul II's Successor

Motto: *Gloria olivae*

Translation: "The glory of the olive"

Interpretation: At present, there are so many proposed interpretations that they defy brief summary. Many of them manage to incorporate the tradition of the Order of St. Benedict, holding that the order will lead the Catholic Church in a final conflict with evil before the final days predicted in the Book of Revelation.

It is either worthy of note, or not, that the prophecies in question were first publicized by a member of the Order of St. Benedict.

Regarding Subsequent Events

The final prophecy in the sequence—the conclusion of which is itself controversial—reads as follows:

"In the final persecution of the Holy Roman Church, there will reign Peter the Roman, who will feed his flock among many tribulations, after which the seven-hilled city (Rome) will be destroyed and the dreadful Judge will judge the people. The end."

Interpreters have for years argued over the meaning of this passage. Does it predict that the successor of the *Gloria Olivae* pope will be followed directly by the last pope in history? Does it allow an indeterminate number of popes between the two? Is this final prediction even of the same provenance as the earlier ones attributed to Malachy? The only certainty, as is usual with these writings, is that detailed analysis and impassioned debate is likely to persist.

The Last Word

Fascinating, if not always meaningfully revealing, the prophecies attributed to Malachy may well be what they claim to be: long-suppressed evidence of a divine vision. Then again, they may represent a complex forgery that has happened to overlap with actual events in ways involving varying levels of ambiguity and chance. The smart money, as this book goes to press, is on the latter possibility.

On the predictions that have generated such heated discussions at the beginnings and ends of pontificates, the last and best word comes from Peter Bander, who accepted the theory that the writings were in fact created by Malachy and held secretly in papal archives.

Bander's analysis of the predictions is both thorough and thoroughly entertaining. His advice to his readers is equally important.

Simple Advice

"I have discussed the prophecies of Malachy with many friends, among them bishops, archbishops, and high prelates of the Roman Catholic Church .... We have always enjoyed our conversations and the tremendous sense of humor emanating from them. With no disrespect to the Saint, we have laughed at our personal idiosyncrasies in making certain Latin verses fit certain eminent dignitaries we knew, but most of all, we have realized that we shall still have to wait some time before we really know whether St. Malachy has once again foiled our speculations, or if, perchance, one of us has been right. My advice to the reader of the following comments on St. Malachy's prophecies is simple: Please, do not extend to them the same reverence you may extend to the Gospels, and remember that to err is human, but to err too often is foolish."

—Peter Bander, *The Prophecies of Malachy* (Rockford, Ill.: Tan Books and Publishers, 1973)

The Least You Need to Know

- St. Malachy was a real person, but he may or may not have written the papal prophecies popularly attributed to him.
- If you find yourself under compulsion, bet that Malachy isn't the real author of the prophecies.
- However they came about, many of the predictions are likely to have been written after the reigns of the popes they describe.
- Many more, however, offer intriguing parallels with the reigns of popes who lived long after the initial publication of these writings in 1559.
- Tantalizing as these predictions are, they are not to be mistaken as Scripture. The Church does not recognize them as divinely inspired.

Chapter **4**

Ten to Remember: Popes Who Made a Difference

In This Chapter

- ◆ Leo the Great
- ◆ Gregory the Great
- ◆ Gregory VII
- ◆ Pius VII
- ◆ John XXIII
- ◆ John Paul II

In this chapter, you learn about 10 of the most memorable popes in history.

What follows is not the *only* possible list of extraordinary pontiffs, of course, but it is one brief accounting of unforgettable men who made extraordinary contributions at fateful periods in Church history. Each of the men you're about to meet faced severe challenges—and rose to those challenges. They represent some of the indisputable high points in the history of the papacy, and any student of the office should be familiar with them.

The Right Men at the Right Time

A brief side note is in order. Any abbreviated discussion list of preeminent popes is problematic. If the aim is to construct a "10 best" list, some difficult questions arise. "Best" according to what? "Worthiest" by what yardstick? The standard by which the performance of a given pope can be measured or evaluated is a constantly changing one, just as the Church and the office of the papacy are subject to ongoing change. What was necessary or desirable in a Church leader in the fifth century is very different indeed from what was required during the Renaissance. What was required in a leader to help the Church fulfill its mission during the age of Napoleon was different from what was required at the dawn of the Nuclear Age.

Given that the roles of—and challenges faced by—the popes have changed dramatically over the centuries, the chief requirement for inclusion in this chapter is a willingness and ability to assume the job of furthering necessary change and growth. In this chapter, then, the aim is simply to discuss those popes who most obviously helped the Church to move forward in a positive way.

With that in mind, consider the following summary of 10 remarkable popes, each of whom inspired and transformed the Church he led, and each of whom, it can be argued, left the office better than he found it. Prepare to meet some giants in Church history. Remember them; they'll be coming up in later chapters as well.

Leo I

St. Leo I (440–461) ...

 ◆ Set and maintained a hard line against divisive and heretical doctrines.

 ◆ Enlisted the aid of Valentinian III, the Roman emperor of the West.

 ◆ Faced down *Manichaeism* and eradicated it from Italy.

 ◆ Established important institutional precedents regarding papal authority; served as an early and enthusiastic champion of the strength and power of the papal office.

 ◆ Established control over his own bishops and received the support of the emperor in this effort.

 ◆ Composed the *Tome of Leo*, a seminal text detailing Christ's dual nature and single person that was accepted at the *Council of Chalcedon*.

 ◆ Persuaded Attila the Hun not to ransack Rome in 452; similar diplomatic skills saved the lives of many Romans when the Vandals threatened the city in 455.

Vatican Vocabulary

Manichaeism was a religion founded by a prophet named Mani, probably a Persian, in the third century. It combined elements of other religious movements (including Gnosticism and Christianity). The religion postulated an ongoing battle between the forces of light and darkness, and saw darkness as inherent in all physical matter.

Leo is the first pope designated as "the Great." His abilities as a tactician, diplomat, writer, theologian, and advocate for the authority of the office of the papacy were extraordinary. He reigned during a time of Christian dominance in Rome, a period when he himself observed that Rome had become "greater through the apostles than it had as head of the world" (as quoted in *The Oxford Illustrated History of Christianity*, John McManners, ed. Oxford: Oxford University Press, 1990).

Vatican Vocabulary

The **Council of Chalcedon** (451) was the Church's fourth great ecumenical council. It is most widely remembered for its declaration that Jesus Christ possesses both a divine and a human nature, each of which exists inseparably within him. Leo's *Tome* was the basis of this pronouncement.

Gregory I

St. Gregory I (590–604) …

♦ Became the first monk to hold the office of the papacy.

♦ Maintained the primacy of the pope in the face of challenges from the patriarch of Constantinople.

♦ Negotiated a settlement with the attacking Lombards that forestalled complete ruin in Rome—and established a precedent that the pope could act to defend Rome in the absence of imperial initiatives. This enlarged Gregory's own temporal, or political, authority.

♦ Supported and extended the monastic movements.

♦ Proved a superb administrator and reformer.

♦ Emphasized the importance of celibacy in the clergy.

♦ Extended Christianity's reach and influence, specifically in England.

♦ Was known as "Gregory the Great."

After a distinguished monastic and administrative career, Gregory was elevated to the papacy, where he became a tireless promoter of the preeminence of Rome. His willingness to defend and negotiate on behalf of the city itself brought the office of the pope a measure of political authority that challenged even the emperor's power.

Gregory sent St. Augustine to England in 596 to launch what turned out to be a successful *proselytizing* campaign there. The pope may or may not have had a role in developing the liturgical songs

Pope Watch

Gregory the Great came from a wealthy Roman family. After his death in 604, his properties in Sicily became a significant financial asset for the papacy.

now known as "Gregorian chants." More significant is his record of sustained and masterful leadership of the Church in both the temporal and spiritual realms over a period of 14 years. Gregory's was a truly remarkable pontificate that is all the more notable because the man at its center initially tried to decline the job, claiming physical infirmity.

Leo III

St. Leo III (795–816) ...

◆ Traveled to the court of Charlemagne, where he recovered from physical injuries received at the hands of his rivals.

◆ Returned to Rome, where he confidently asserted his authority (based on, presumably, his new relationship with Charlemagne).

◆ Crowned Charlemagne emperor on Christmas Day 800, an act that set a precedent for the pope's authority, consolidated Leo's position, and set in place an important institutional relationship with the succession of rulers who would come to represent the Holy Roman Empire.

As the popes assumed greater authority in Rome, their rule became more and more a matter of secular concern. Violence became common in succession disputes, and instability was (and would, alas, remain for some time) a common feature of the office. Leo's authority, like that of many a pope before and after him, was challenged. We are told that his enemies sought to blind him; they failed, but he incurred serious injury. He responded to this hardship by building a powerful new alliance.

Leo III's pontificate is remembered chiefly for his decision to crown—and swear allegiance to—Charlemagne, who thus became the emperor of the West. This event is customarily regarded as the initiation of the Holy Roman Empire; it also strengthened Leo's secular position in Rome, and established a precedent for papal consecration of the emperor.

Leo also worked to promote unity between the Eastern and Western wings of the Church as they addressed doctrinal and liturgical controversies.

Gregory VII

St. Gregory VII (1073–1085) …

♦ Enforced rules mandating clerical celibacy and forbidding appropriating the sale of spiritual offices and advancements and privileges.

♦ Established groups of legates to enforce edicts across Europe.

♦ Entered into conflicts with European royalty over reforms related to the crisis of *investiture*.

Essentially, Gregory (one of the great reformer popes) claimed the power to strip royalty of its assumed right to fill the Church's clerical posts. As a result of his earnestness and commitment to this principle, Gregory suffered many hardships and was eventually exiled from Rome.

His reign is now seen by most historians as a valid reclamation of Church authority from secular forces who had come to a position of unhealthy dominance. Gregory's insistence on the Church's prerogatives (which eventually led to the invasion of Italy by Emperor Henry IV) are unlikely to be confused with modern democratic social reform, yet they established an important precedent in relations with secular rulers. He reinforced the moral foundations of the Church and the papacy.

Vatican Vocabulary

The **Investiture Controversy** was a conflict between the Holy Roman Empire and the papacy over the question of who had the right to invest bishops and abbots with their authority and office. In a larger sense, the controversy had to do with which institution—the monarchy or the papacy—had practical control over the Church.

Pius IV

Highlights of Pius IV's pontificate (1559–1565) include …

♦ Reconvening the Council of Trent.

♦ Accepting (and even welcoming) the reality of the break with the Protestants—and then charting a clear course for the Church in a new and unfamiliar world.

Pius IV was one of the great figures of the Catholic Reformation. By reconvening the seemingly endlessly delayed Council of Trent for its final and decisive session (1562–1563), and by marshaling his considerable diplomatic skills in

Papal People

Pius's nephew was St. Charles Borromeo. To learn more about these two remarkable men and their role in concluding the Council of Trent, see Chapter 15, "Rift and Reformations."

helping that body overcome its many logjams, he made important reforms possible and pointed the Catholic Church resolutely toward the future.

In so doing, Pius won back a considerable measure of the prestige and esteem that had often been absent in the papacy during its long period of conflict with the Protestant movement.

Sixtus V

Sixtus V (1585–1590) ...

- ◆ Returned the chaotic Papal States (over which the pope served as secular ruler) to a period of order, although his methods were occasionally fierce.
- ◆ Restored the Church's finances to a position of solidity after a period of lax administration.
- ◆ Implemented the edicts of the Council of Trent.
- ◆ Consolidated and extended institutional reforms initiated by popes who had preceded him, including Pius IV.

Not all of Sixtus V's initiatives seem noble in hindsight, but it is impossible to overlook the energy, insight, and effectiveness he displayed in the office he assumed from the frequently tactless, ill-briefed, and short-sighted Gregory XIII. Sixtus helped put into practice the edicts of the Council of Trent, reorganized the papal bureaucracy, improved the Church's financial position, rebuilt or built anew vast portions of Rome, and in general proved that a zealous man bent on reinvigorating Catholicism after the Protestant Reformation could actually do so.

Gregory XV

Gregory XV (1621–1623) ...

- ◆ Reigned for only two years, but made the important contribution of reforming the procedure for papal elections.
- ◆ Reinvigorated the Church's commitment to missionary work.
- ◆ Significantly expanded the Vatican archives.

If there is such a thing as an underrated pope, Gregory XV is that pontiff. His insistence on the reform of the papal election process ushered in changes that were quite literally centuries overdue; they were well thought out, they worked, and they have persisted with very little change for nearly four centuries. No serious student of the papacy can fail to be impressed by his achievement in this historically chaotic and bitterly divisive area of Church practice.

Slow, corrupt, or divisive conclaves have been common in Church history. These transitions were frequently halted in place; stretches of months (or, not infrequently, years) dragged on as cardinals deliberated on the selection of a new pope. The possibilities for abuse and delay often seemed endless.

Gregory's consolidation of reform in this area is all the more notable when one considers the number of failed attempts to reform the election system that preceded his reign.

His contributions to Catholic missionary work were also remarkable, as were his efforts to enlarge the Vatican archives.

Pius VII

Pius VII (1800–1823) ...

- ◆ Concluded an agreement, or concordat, with Napoleon in 1801, and then in 1804 submitted to intense political pressure to consecrate him as emperor.

- ◆ Engaged in a series of tense conflicts with the emperor in the coming years, which culminated in Napoleon's annexation of the Papal States and imprisonment of the pope.

- ◆ Returned triumphantly to Rome in 1814 when Napoleon fell.

- ◆ Showed extraordinary concern for the former emperor in the following years, advocating lenient British treatment of him and extending protection to members of his family.

A fascinating historical figure, Pius was revered for his resilience in the face of hardship, imprisonment, and dishonor, and for his evident compassion toward Napoleon, who had so clearly abused him. With Pius we encounter a number of hallmarks of what most observers would consider the modern papacy: personal examples of faith, persistence, strength, and kindness—all combining to forge a strong moral example that somehow appeared to render the office's decline in temporal political power irrelevant.

Bet You Didn't Know

It was during Pius VII's pontificate that two distinctly "non-political" elements of the papacy began to be noticeable. These were an increasing emphasis on the papacy's spiritual obligations (allowing the pope to play the part of an advocate of conscience to more powerful world figures), and a deep reverence among Catholics for the pope that was rooted, at least in part, in perceptions of his personal moral and ethical character. Both trends have endured.

John XXIII

Highlights from John XXIII's pontificate (1958–1963) include ...

- The decision to convene the Second Vatican Council in 1962.
- An ongoing commitment to support reforms affecting working people, the poor, and those whom society had appeared to have left behind.
- Explicit and unapologetic anti-Communism, combined with a deep concern for the rights of workers and for victims of social injustice.
- A number of initiatives designed to promote communication and emphasize the shared beliefs among Christians of all denominations.

One of the most beloved modern popes, John XXIII was a former World War I chaplain whose pontificate embraced the downtrodden, initiated remarkable reform, and celebrated the dignity of the human species in a way that surprised and enchanted the world. His crowning achievement, of course, was calling the historic Second Vatican Council, which brought about modernization of Catholic worship and organization, and emphasized the improvement of relations with other Christian churches.

Among the most notable achievements of the council, which did not conclude its work until after John's death, were its efforts to bring lay people into closer contact with Church rituals. The most obvious result: the acceptance of vernacular (that is to say, non-Latin) language in celebration of the Mass. Like other elements of the council popularly known as Vatican II, this was controversial to say the least, but it remains a symbol of the council's—and John's—determination to bring the Church into the modern era.

John's resilience, his energy, his commitment to Catholic renewal, and his undeniable love for people was intoxicating. His pontificate has come to be seen as an explosion of possibility and optimism.

John Paul II

Highlights from John Paul II's pontificate (1978–present) include ...

- A series of high-profile journeys spreading the Gospel message throughout the world. John Paul is the most traveled pope in history; the huge crowds he draws in foreign lands have sometimes seemed less like special occasions, and more like his standard and preferred mode of pastoral communication.
- Evident anti-Communism, combined with clear limits reining in those who would politicize the Gospel message itself. It's worth noting here that John Paul's anti-Communism is part of a larger distrust of a number of exploitative philosophies that he sees as eroding spiritual values; he includes among these materialism and consumerism.

◆ An ongoing effort to make Catholic practice and administration reflect its status as a global faith. (John Paul II, the first non-Italian pope in over four centuries, has significantly expanded the representation of South America, Africa, and Asia in the College of Cardinals and in the Church administration as a whole.)

◆ Emphasis on Marian devotion. This pope frankly credits the Virgin Mary with his survival of an assassination attempt in 1981.

Truly a force to be reckoned with, John Paul II has used high-profile pilgrimages beyond Rome to establish the modern, media-centered papacy.

His conservatism and deep conviction on matters of faith probably would not, on their own, entitle him to be reckoned among the most influential popes of all time. His masterful use of modern communications to spread his message, however, is unparalleled in the office, and has led to a visibility and prominence for the Catholic message that most of his predecessors could scarcely have imagined. He has led the first truly global pontificate.

The Least You Need to Know

◆ Leo the Great was an important early proponent of the primacy of Rome; his diplomacy saved many Roman lives, and his theological writings assumed extraordinary importance to the Church.

◆ Gregory the Great briskly assumed responsibility for securing the defense of Rome and was a superb reformer and administrator.

◆ Gregory VII is known primarily for his efforts to reform the Church and for his role in the Investiture Controversy.

◆ Pius VII pleaded for compassion for Napoleon after having been imprisoned by him, and thus helped to establish a distinctly modern role for the pope.

◆ John XXIII convened the Second Vatican Council, which eventually promulgated a host of modernizations, reforms, and initiatives for improved communication with other Christian churches.

◆ John Paul II used extensive travel and extraordinary media skills to launch the first truly global pontificate.

Ten to Forget: Popes Who Shouldn't Have Been

In This Chapter

- ◆ Moving beyond the "bad popes" label
- ◆ Popes who obtained their office by underhanded means
- ◆ Popes whose personal lives were less than exemplary
- ◆ One pope who didn't want the job (and said so)
- ◆ The truth behind the Pope Joan story

In the previous chapter, you met 10 outstanding popes—men who had an undeniable and lasting positive impact on the Church they led and the world in which they lived. In this chapter, you'll encounter ten popes who never should have taken the job in the first place, as well as one infamous pope (or is that popess?) who didn't reign, or even exist, in the first place.

Beyond the "Bad Popes" Label

Far more heat than light has been generated in debates over whether to call disreputable Church leaders *bad popes*.

Like any institution, the papacy has had its share of misguided, intemperate, and downright incompetent leaders. In the pages that follow, you'll meet a number of representatives of this group, whose members stand in sharp contrast to those popes you met in Chapter 4, "Ten to Remember: Popes Who Made a Difference."

Vatican Vocabulary

The label **"bad pope"** has been frequently applied to popes who clearly failed to set a high moral or leadership standard for the Church. Noting that there is no similar vernacular for the equally striking group of historical "bad monarchs," "bad emperors," or "bad politicians," many Roman Catholics object to the label, preferring to evaluate each pontificate on its own merits (or lack thereof).

What follows is certainly not intended as a list of *every* pope who scandalized the faithful as a result of worldliness, incompetence, corruption, or a simple inability to meet the demands of his job. The portraits that follow are, however, meant to give a taste of the most common ways in which some of St. Peter's many successors have, over the centuries, gone about demonstrating that the papacy was not always free from sin or error.

Out of His Depth: Vigilius Overreaches

Reportedly, Pope Vigilius (537–555) accepted, before his elevation to the papacy, a healthy bribe from the Empress Theodora that was meant to secure his loyalty. The sum in question: 700 gold pieces.

The bribe is a matter of controversy, as historical sources are not flattering in their accounts of Vigilius's reign, and cannot always be taken at their word. What is more certain is that, having either taken a leading role in or complied with the arrest, banishment, and starvation to death of his predecessor St. Silverius, Vigilius was manifestly ill-suited to the challenges of his pontificate.

He found himself overwhelmed by a political and theological crisis of incredible complexity, one that got worse with time, infuriated the faithful in Rome, alienated the Emperor, and left the pope—to use a modern expression—between a rock and a hard place. (The crisis was known as the "Three Chapters" controversy, and it is covered in Chapter 9, "Rome Reemerges.") Vigilius made his own problems worse in addressing the challenges he faced by issuing disingenuous pronouncements and acting on poor political calculations.

It is enough to say here that this misplaced aristocrat, who had apparently devoted his energies to obtaining the wealth and privilege he associated with the papacy, was no leader. He certainly learned quickly enough that the office he had coveted and schemed for carried practical demands that he had not anticipated, and few popes in history appear to have more richly deserved the intricate diplomatic and political burdens they inherited.

This may seem a harsh pronouncement, but it squares with the facts. If Vigilius was not a murderer, he was something very close to it; he was, at the same time, a careerist very far from possessing the gifts required to embark on the career he claimed for himself.

Money, Money: Sabinian Takes the Low Road

The papacy of Sabinian (604–606) contrasts sharply with that of Gregory the Great, who appeared in Chapter 4.

Gregory pointed the wealth and power of the Church toward the people, giving out free grain from his storehouses. Sabinian, the pope who followed him, made a point of *selling* the grain to famine-stricken citizens, and at exorbitant prices.

Our sources on the events of Sabinian's pontificate may well be biased in favor of the beloved, recently departed Gregory. They constitute, however, most of what we know about Sabinian, and their bitterness in describing his conduct following the disastrous winter of 604–605 is hard to dismiss.

His funeral was supposedly disrupted by angry mobs. Legends arose after his death that Gregory himself punished Sabinian for avariciousness.

Pope Watch
Sabinian is said to have re-placed many of the monks appointed by Gregory the Great with members of the secular clergy.

Dirty Business: Sergius III

Sergius III (904–911) set a new (and low) standard for personal morality in the papacy.

He had been legitimately elected to the office in 897, but had been forced to step aside because he lacked the support of the emperor. Understandably, perhaps, he viewed the popes that followed as frauds, and resented them deeply.

The violence he employed upon his own election, however, was beyond excuse. It was, unfortunately, not without precedent. Both the antipope Christopher and the legitimately elected Leo V (a humble priest in well over his head, who had been imprisoned by rivals) died at Sergius's orders.

Sergius's personal life was equally disquieting. His mistress, Marozia, was the daughter of Theodora; Marozia and her mother were both extremely powerful figures in Rome.

Papal People
Sergius III's mistress, Marozia, and her mother, Theodora, held positions of remarkable influence in matters of Roman politics and papal succession. The period that began with Sergius's rule and extended until Marozia's death in 932 came to be referred to as the "rule of the harlots."

We are told that Sergius was the father of Marozia's child. Regardless of whether that's true or not, the child eventually served as Pope John XI, whose election Marozia engineered.

Sergius died in 911. His had been a horrific, lurid, and bloody papacy, but it was only a hint of things to come. As it turned out, the tenth century was a pretty rough stretch in terms of papal morality and succession.

Bet You Didn't Know

Violence was common during many of the papal succession crises of the Middle Ages. A number of popes assumed the throne after the murder of the previous pope; often, pontificates were quite brief. The worst period may well have come in the century and a half following the papacy of John VIII, who, it is said, was clubbed and poisoned to death in 882. John appears to have been the first papal victim of assassination. Between his death and that of Clement II in 1047, who was also poisoned, some of the worst excesses occurred. Consider the case of Pope John XIV, who was seized by his rival, the notorious antipope Benedict. John was placed in prison and forced to endure starvation and poisoning; he died in 984. When Benedict himself died the following year, citizens of Rome flayed his body, mutilated it, and dragged it along the public thoroughfare. Not a pretty time.

The "Popess" Who Wasn't

There was no Pope Joan, though that fact has never seemed to stop people from talking about her.

The popular legend, which may have arisen in response to the influence of Marozia and Theodora in the tenth century, centered around an Englishwoman disguised in male attire who was so widely praised for her learning that she was eventually elected pontiff. The unforgettable mental image of the "popess" unexpectedly giving birth during an official procession helped the tale persist and spread.

None of it ever happened, although Joan's "papacy" does serve as an interesting example of an enduring, perpetually revised account that might today be classified as an urban legend. It is likely that the story was intended as the ultimate "bad pope" story, a cautionary fable reflecting widespread insecurities about women who played important behind-the-scenes roles in Church politics.

Bad Beginnings and Bad Ends: John XII

John XII (955–963), who became pope at the tender age of 19, apparently still had some wild oats to sow. During his pontificate, the papal residence was derided as a brothel; he was accused of conducting fantastic sexual escapades, and whether or not the most lurid accounts of these (seducing his father's mistress, cavorting with his own niece, castrating a Church official) are accurate, there is unanimity on the pope's general moral depravity.

John was a poor diplomat. He executed an amateurish double-cross of the powerful King Otto I of Germany that led to his own deposition.

John managed to return to the papal throne, but soon died of a stroke. The popular legend had it that the fatal attack came about when Satan himself struck the pope on the head during one of his amorous encounters.

Qualification Issues: John XIX

A layman with no clerical experience whatsoever, John XIX (1024–1032) offered sufficiently large bribes to secure his own election.

John is one of 40 or so popes to have been succeeded by his nephew. Many critics of the papacy have viewed both the uncles and the nephews with some skepticism.

Devoted to Pleasure: Benedict IX

Benedict IX (1032–1045) appears to have been only 20 or so when he assumed the papacy. He was described as "devoted to pleasure … (one who) preferred to live like Epicurus rather than like a pope" by Desiderius, a contemporary who later assumed the papacy himself as Victor III.

Benedict's personal degeneracy actually appears to have been the cause of a riot in Rome, and his hold on the office was always tenuous. He abdicated in favor of Gregory VI, who was accused of having purchased the papacy from Benedict outright.

> **Pope Watch**
>
> Vatican records report a remarkably high number of nephews who succeeded their uncles as popes in centuries past. One suspects that a fair number of these nephew pontiffs—often tactfully referred to by modern historians as "relatives" of earlier popes— were actually illegitimate sons. An alarming number of cardinals and popes made a habit of bestowing wealth, privilege, and position on sons who could not be acknowledged openly as such.

Why Did I Take This Job, Anyway?: Celestine V

Most accounts of the so-called bad popes leave out pontificates led by good men who simply weren't up to the job. Such is the sad story of St. Celestine V (1294), an 80-ish hermit who was elected against his will. This pious but ineffective man was not avaricious, lustful, or power-obsessed; to the contrary, he was persecuted—in large measure—as a result of his simplicity. His chief aims were solitude and communion with God. It is not surprising that he was eventually canonized; what is surprising is that he became pope in the first place.

The given name of this simple Benedictine priest was Pietro del Morrone. In 1294, the Church had been without a pope for a protracted period (a not uncommon state of affairs); del Morrone was concerned that the conclave had allowed the papal selection process to drag on for over two years. What horrible consequences, he must have wondered, would accompany further inaction? He resolved to write a letter encouraging the cardinals to evade God's wrath by settling on a pope expeditiously.

It was the biggest mistake of his life.

Del Morrone's letter did indeed have a galvanizing effect. The cardinals, apparently sick of their own perpetual deferrals and political maneuvering, showed how eager they were to be done with the selection process by electing the ancient hermit *himself* to the throne of St. Peter. Appalled at the news, del Morrone planned a quick escape, but was intercepted by Charles II, king of Naples, who pleaded with him to accept the office. Against his own better judgment, del Morrone became Pope Celestine V.

Pope Watch
Pope Gregory X (1271–1276) set down procedures requiring cardinals to select a new pope within 10 days of the death of the previous one. This resulted in the prompt election of the next pope, but meaningful reforms took many years to become established tradition.

He was a saintly man who proved a weak and pliable pope, and after five months he had succeeded only in two things: serving as a puppet for Charles and undermining his own authority. At this point he appears to have realized that he had been placed in an impossible situation, and he abdicated the office. The manner in which he did so constituted his only substantive accomplishment as pope, for he instructed the next conclave to follow the procedures designed by Gregory X to ensure the rapid selection of a new pope. This they did.

It would be nice to report that Celestine's problems ended there, but the truth is that he was still seen as either a threat or an opportunity by various political factions. He tried again to escape Italy, but the subsequent pope, Boniface VIII, had Celestine imprisoned while questions regarding the legality of his abdication were still dangerously prominent.

The "hermit pope" who never wanted the office died a prisoner in 1296. Perhaps the austere surroundings actually suited him, but his last days could not have been pleasant ones. He suffered from a painful abscess, and his prison doctors may well have worsened his condition.

Philip's Pawn: Clement V

Clement V (1305–1314) was promoted after a nearly yearlong struggle between French and Italian cardinals following the death of Benedict XI. Bertrand de Got, the French candidate, was archbishop of Bordeaux, and essentially a tool of the powerful French king, Philip IV. As Clement V, the new pope eventually moved the papacy from Rome to France, initiating the long period known as the Avignon Exile or the Babylonian Captivity.

This move proved disastrous, and eventually led to rival claims to the papacy that culminated in the Great Schism (1378–1417), one of the most chaotic periods in the history of the Church. Sensitive first and foremost to Philip's interests, Clement made the short-term appeasement of French political interests his priority. He set the Church that he (supposedly) led on the road toward discord and turmoil.

The Matchmaker: Innocent VIII

The son of a powerful Roman politician, Innocent VIII (1484–1492) was a compromise candidate under the control of the powerful Cardinal Giuliano della Rovere, and among the most shameless of the disreputable popes. Innocent's illegitimate children lived with him in the Vatican, and he succeeded in marrying them off to highly placed families.

His response to the fiscal crisis he inherited was to step up the sale of ecclesiastical offices. He thus serves as a representative of the group of popes guilty of the sin of *simony*.

Other notable events during his pontificate were an increase in the persecution and murder of supposed witches in Germany, and an agreement under which Innocent received ransom payments for holding prisoner the brother of the Turkish sultan Bayezid II. Innocent more or less ignored opportunities to mediate violent conflicts in Rome, and was preoccupied with finding new ways to finance his own opulent lifestyle. He reached one notable low point when he pawned his papal tiara.

Vatican Vocabulary

Simony is the sin of accepting worldly goods or honors in exchange for spiritual acts, church offices, or ecclesiastical advancement. The word derives from a passage in Acts (8:18–24) in which a magician named Simon attempts to purchase the power to perform miracles from the Apostles. The poet Dante consigned popes guilty of simony to terrible punishments.

Family Man: Alexander VI

Perhaps the most notorious pope of them all was Alexander VI (1492–1503), born Rodgrigo Borgia. Yes, you read right—Alexander was a prominent member of *that* Borgia family.

Papal People
The Borgias were a Spanish noble family of the fifteenth and sixteenth centuries whose reputation for greed and deceit was (and remains) extraordinary. Two popes were Borgias: Calixtus III and Alexander VI.

Pontifical ... but Mythical
Alexander VI's illegitimate daughter, Lucrecia Borgia, was known for centuries as a vicious poisoner given to sexual excess, but the unflattering legends about her appear to be unfounded. (Her brother, Cesare, on the other hand, actually earned his reputation as a ruthless, deadly prince best not crossed.)

Rodgrigo Borgia was a brilliant diplomat and fiercely ambitious family patriarch. He represents, for many, the most compelling example of the corruption, ruthlessness, and worldliness in high Church circles that helped bring on Martin Luther's Protestant Reformation. A shrewd tactician, experienced negotiator, and eager protector of the Church's material interests, this was a pope whose chief interests were, shall we say, temporal in nature. (Certainly, he had a few too many children than seems appropriate for the head of a supposedly celibate clergy.)

Borgia, who bought his pontificate from a corrupt conclave in 1492, had by that time built up an extensive and impressive portfolio of experience, as well as a powerful network of allies within the highest circles of the Church. He was an accomplished administrator and a superb politician, but his many mistresses, his numerous illegitimate children, his boundless greed, his ruthlessness, and his openly dynastic ambitions seem to undercut his credentials as a committed practitioner of the Catholic faith.

As Pope Alexander VI, he conducted a pontificate that placed his illegitimate son, Cesare Borgia, squarely at the center of the Church's power structure. Cesare, who became a cardinal at the age of 19, was the recipient of seemingly incalculable wealth and political favor. His ascent to manhood was marked by a twofold obsession: first, further accumulation of political power for himself and his family, and second, the accumulation of knowledge about the most effective ways to kill people. For Cesare and for much of the Borgia family, the two areas overlapped from time to time.

Able administrator or no, Alexander VI has deservedly become a symbol of personal and institutional corruption. Even people who don't like the term "bad pope" may find themselves tempted to apply it to this one.

So What's the Lesson Here?

There are two ways to look at the popes who shouldn't have been popes.

One school of thought (predominantly non-Catholic) holds that the least impressive papal officeholders dramatically showcase the limits and imperfections of the papacy, and even undercut the legitimacy of the office itself. This is certainly an understandable opinion, but mainstream Catholics find it unpersuasive. Does the fact that there have been corrupt presidents, they ask, mean that the administrations of Harry Truman or Ronald Reagan were not legitimate?

The other school of thought (predominantly Catholic) runs as follows. Even underqualified popes played a role in the Church's evolution, if only to demonstrate behavior that should not be repeated. Greedy, avaricious, feckless, or lustful pontiffs, the argument goes, did not alter central points of Catholic doctrine; and while Christ was born without sin, the Church itself hardly makes the same claim.

Human Failings, Human Lessons

An obsession with recounting the errors of the many disreputable popes can become something of a personal spiritual obstacle. As the author John Norton wrote: "I have read of many wicked popes, but the worst pope of them all remains Pope Self."

Translation: Don't get so distracted by the excesses of religious leaders, past or present, that you neglect your own spiritual growth. If it's time to take your own moral inventory, the sins of others, high or low, are immaterial.

The Least You Need to Know

- Sabinian suffered in comparison with Gregory the Great—but then again, who wouldn't?
- Fascinating combinations of violence, dynastic pretension, licentiousness, and/or political corruption accompanied the pontificates of many popes, including (but certainly not limited to) those of Vigilius, Sergius III, John XII, John XIX, Benedict IX, Innocent VIII, and Alexander VI.
- There was no Pope Joan; the myth promulgating her pontificate may have been a response to the "rule of the harlots" of the tenth century.
- Celestine V was a perfect example of someone who shouldn't have been elected pope—and knew it.
- Clement V neglected the long-term interests of the Church in order to fulfill the dictates of the powerful King Philip IV of France.

Part 2

The Ascent of Christianity

In this part of the book, you'll learn about the dawn of Christianity—and the beginnings of the papacy.

These chapters offer a review of the history of the Church and the papacy from the time of St. Peter to the conversion of the Emperor Constantine, from the rise of Constantinople to the bitter and corrupt struggles of tenth-century Rome, and from the violent conflicts over papal succession to the rupture with the Eastern Church.

The Rock: Peter and His Immediate Successors

In This Chapter

- Rome's leadership role
- A look at St. Peter
- Leadership within the early Church
- The first men who followed Peter
- Initial persecution
- Gnosticism: Early voices

In this chapter, you learn about the apostle Peter and those who followed him as leaders of the Church in Rome. You'll also find out about the first challenges faced by Peter and his successors, and how they prefigured events to follow in later years.

Warning: Conjecture Ahead

Any discussion of the very earliest leaders of the Christian Church poses something of a challenge. This is because there are often significant knowledge gaps about leadership and doctrinal questions that faced the Church in the first century or so after Jesus's crucifixion.

Even St. Peter, a figure of extraordinary importance in Christian history, presents an imposing array of historical question marks.

We really don't know exactly when or how these early Church leaders assumed prominence, or under what circumstances they did so. And as you will soon see, the many traditions concerning St. Peter that have come down to us are followed by nearly complete silence when it comes to meaningful information about his successors.

The Early Years

Three points about the earliest period of Church history are worth bearing in mind:

- Peter was regarded as preeminent among Jesus's Twelve Apostles. (Judging by the Gospel texts that took their final form after his death, he was also seen by many believers as Christ's representative on earth.)

- The apostles Peter and Paul, both strongly associated with Rome, were revered figures in the early Church.

- Rome came to play a special role in the growth and development of the brand-new faith.

Bet You Didn't Know

In Rome and elsewhere, the rise in influence of bishops, whose authority and doctrines could be handed down from successor to successor, appears to have been a response to teachers who made radical alterations to the teachings inherited from the apostles. However, scholars believe that the very first groups of Christians in Rome—who predated Peter's arrival in the city—at first embraced a more informal Church structure.

The last point is of particular interest, of course, to those who follow the institution today known as the papacy. A number of writings from the Church's early period support the notion that the group of believers in Rome held a preeminent position, served as the head of other early Christian churches, and took special care in administering and regulating the growth of the faith in other cities. Relevant authors whose work helps us to establish Rome's leadership role during this period include Hermas, Ignatius of Antioch, and Clemens Romanus (also known as Pope Clement I—more about him later in this chapter).

Why Rome?

The reasons for Rome's unique role in the development of the early Church appear to have included the following:

- Christianity's increasing appeal to non-Jews, specifically Greeks and Romans.

- The social impact of the initial persecutions faced by Christian groups who earned the enmity of the authorities. (In Rome, such episodes may have drawn believers into ever more tightly knit groups.)

- Peter's critical decision to assume a leadership role within the Roman Church, which he appears to have guided from roughly the year 55 until his apparent death as a *martyr*, often dated to the year 64.

- The apostle Paul's association with the city. He was imprisoned there and was probably executed during the persecutions of Nero.

- Jerusalem's fall at the hands of the Romans in the year 70 following a Jewish revolt.

Add to these points the compelling fact that the city itself was the center of the civilized world—the sort of place one went to learn what new movements and ideas were on the horizon—and it's not that hard to see why Rome came to predominate.

> ### Pope Watch
>
> Today, when we apply the term "pope" to Peter and his successors as an exclusive title reflecting leadership of the Roman Church, we do so as a matter of retroactive tradition. In fact, the title seems not to have been used in this sense until the sixth century.

Vatican Vocabulary

A **martyr** is a person who consciously chooses death rather than renouncing his or her religious beliefs. The term also refers to a person who endures persecution, suffering, and death because of his or her spiritual principles.

Bet You Didn't Know

In the year 70, the Roman emperor Titus responded to a revolt from the Jews by ruining the holy city of Jerusalem and destroying the Jewish Temple. The fall of Jerusalem may have made the enclave of Christians in Rome more important than ever to Christian believers elsewhere. Those who regarded Jesus as the Messiah foretold in the Jewish Scriptures probably looked to the Roman ministry (which had been guided by the apostle Peter, and was now maintained by his successors) for leadership and direction during the first century of the Church's existence.

So much for the role of the city in the early years. What about Peter himself, the man we think of today as the first pope?

Who Was St. Peter?

When he first encountered Jesus, Peter was a fisherman living in Capernaum. The Gospels tell us that he made a sudden, life-changing decision to follow the teacher who said to him and his brother Andrew: "Come with me, and I will make you fishers of men" (Mark 1:17).

> ### Pope Watch
>
> Among the New Testament Scriptures often seen as supporting "Petrine supremacy"—Roman authority over the Christian Church—are Matthew 16:13–20, in which Jesus calls Peter the rock on which the Church will be built, and promises to give him the keys to heaven. Peter is frequently pictured holding keys.

> ### Pope Watch
>
> Peter is consistently portrayed in the New Testament as the most prominent of Jesus's apostles, and historically speaking there is no reason to discount this view of him. Roman Catholics consider Peter the first Bishop of Rome, and regard papal authority as descending directly from him.

Peter appears, by all accounts, to have been the foremost of the original Twelve Apostles. The Gospels give the picture of a man who—with James and John, the sons of Zebedee—was a member of the Lord's inner circle. When, in the Gospels, Jesus addresses the apostles, he is frequently speaking to Peter. In another key Gospel passage, we read that Jesus plainly informs him that "upon this rock I shall build my church" (Matthew 16:18).

Which brings us to the subject of the saint's name. Peter's given name was Simon. Jesus nicknamed him Cephas, an Aramaic word meaning "rock." This word translates into Greek as "Peter," the name by which the apostle would come to be known through the centuries. The name reflects Peter's status as the foundation of the Christian Church.

He is reported as having been present at the Transfiguration (Matthew 17:1–13), and as having received special instructions from Jesus himself regarding his future role in the propagation of the faith. He is told by his master to "feed my sheep" (John 20:1–10, 21).

Although portrayed as a pillar of strength and a trusted insider, the Peter we meet in the New Testament is at the same time a man whose humanity, limitations, and imperfections are often evident. The Book of Matthew, for instance, depicts him attempting but—apparently because of his fear—failing to follow Jesus's example of walking on water (Matthew 15:28–33).

When Jesus prophesies his own betrayal, execution, and resurrection (Matthew 16:21–23), Peter reacts harshly to this and vows that such events will not come to pass. Jesus's rebuke is extraordinarily harsh: "Get thee behind me, Satan."

Shortly before the crucifixion, we are told, Peter draws his sword in Jesus's defense, but eventually denies even knowing Jesus, just as Jesus himself had foretold that he would (Matthew 26:30–35, 51–55, 69–75).

The image of Peter that lingers after a thorough reading of the Gospels is that of a distinctly human being—one who has been sent on a very difficult mission indeed.

Bet You Didn't Know

As recounted in the New Testament, Pentecost is the day of the Holy Spirit's descent upon Jesus's disciples in Jerusalem: "There appeared to them cloven tongues, like as of fire, and it sat upon each of them, and they were all filled with the Holy Spirit and began to speak with other tongues as the Spirit gave them utterance" (Acts 2:3–5). Shortly thereafter, the book of Acts reports, Peter made an impassioned speech to participants in the harvest festival Shavuot and converted many of them to Christianity. Peter's special role in the emerging Church is clear in this and many other portions of the Book of Acts.

After Pentecost

Peter appears to have headed the young Church at Jerusalem; we are told that he traveled elsewhere (Samaria, Lydda, Joppa, Caesarea, and Antioch) in support of the faith. He may well have founded the Church at Antioch before taking on responsibilities in Rome. He may also have played some kind of role in the creation of the work that became the Gospel of Mark, although scholars disagree on this, as on countless other questions of New Testament scholarship.

Two New Testament epistles are popularly attributed to Peter, although contemporary scholarship suggests that each was written by someone else. The Book of Acts gives particular emphasis to Peter's miraculous powers, to his unstinting defense of the faith, and to his abilities as a leader in the early days of the Church. It does not, however, provide us with an account of the end of Peter's life.

An apparent reference to the manner of Peter's death in the Gospel of John (John 21:18–19) is ambiguous to many modern readers; the prophecy that appears there may have to do with crucifixion, or may simply connect with existing knowledge among early believers about hardships Peter suffered in old age.

Ancient tradition holds that Peter was martyred at Rome under the reign of Emperor Nero. We are told that he arranged to be crucified upside down, so as not to die in a manner identical to that of Jesus.

Vatican Vocabulary

St. Peter's Basilica (the world's largest structure of Christian worship, located in the Vatican in Rome) is built over the site believed to be the tomb of St. Peter. Bones exhumed from beneath the structure were acknowledged as those of St. Peter by Pope Paul VI in 1965; modern scientists have been less definitive in their identification of these remains.

Bet You Didn't Know _____

Peter was probably among the Christians put to death by Emperor Nero, who (rather implausibly) held members of the sect responsible for the burning of half of Rome in the year 64. His campaign against the followers of Jesus marks the first in a long series of Roman persecutions. The prophecy in the Gospel of John that makes reference to Peter's arms being stretched out, and to his being bound fast and led where he does not wish to go (John 21:18–19), may refer to crucifixion.

A Tough Act to Follow

St. Peter stands with the apostle Paul as one of the two towering figures of the early Church. His role as leader of the Roman community of Christians carries a resonance and authority that is unique among the fathers of the Christian Church.

We move now to the leaders who followed him, pausing only to wonder, as they must have, at the enormity of their task.

Through a Glass, Darkly

At this point it is best to be straightforward: We know far less about most of these men than we know (or can safely assume) about the apostle Peter.

Papal People
Many of the first- and second-century leaders of the Christian community at Rome who are listed as Peter's immediate successors are obscure. The periods of time assigned their ascendancy are often completely conjectural.

Following is a summary of the main facts we do possess about the men now associated with very early Roman Church leadership—the formal structure of which should probably be regarded as "in transition" during this period.

St. Linus, tradition tells us, was the joint choice of Peter and Paul to lead the faithful. If the traditional dating of his reign (66 to roughly 78) is accurate, he would have been the head of the Roman Church when the Romans assailed Jerusalem in August of the year 70. We are told that he, like Peter, died a martyr.

St. Anacletus is also said to have died as a martyr. The dates of his guidance of the Church are an open question.

St. Clement I is an early apostolic figure whose period of prominence is equally uncertain. Tradition holds that he was one of Peter's disciples. A number of epistles have been circulated and attributed to him; only the first (his *Epistle to the Corinthians*) is regarded as authentic by contemporary scholars. A series of homilies attributed to him have been declared inauthentic. Whether or not he was a relative of the emperor, as some stories hold, he was certainly an important early figure in the history of the Church and a leader during its fateful first century; he, too, is said to have been martyred.

St. Evaristus is an early Church father about whom little is known.

The same can be said of **St. Alexander I.**

And Then There Was Sixtus

St. Sixtus I is of interest for two reasons. First, consider his name, which (one assumes) he chose for himself upon taking office. It means "the sixth one," a title that would seem to be out of keeping for a Church father occupying the seventh position in the succession. The very earliest lists of the leaders of the Roman Church, however, *do not* list Peter as the first in sequence. Perhaps their authors held the apostle in special regard and did not wish to appear to equate later leaders with him. In any event, these lists begin with Linus, a fact that would make Sixtus sixth.

The second reason Sixtus stands out is the period of time that tradition—perhaps reliably, perhaps otherwise—has assigned to his reign. Supposedly, he led the Roman Church for the decade following the year 115, although, as noted, the time references hereabouts are anything but reliable. The point is that Sixtus may have been head of the Roman Church in the fateful year 120, which was the period during which a man named Basilides began to come to prominence in faraway Alexandria.

Basilides claimed to represent a secret tradition that originated with St. Peter, a tradition that offered a radically new belief structure to the emerging Christian community. He was a very early *Gnostic*, and as such, a harbinger of a period of change, disruption, and testing that was to follow for the Christian Church.

In the rise of the Gnostics (whose best-known teacher, Valentinus, would come under fire in Rome in later years), the Church had the beginnings of its first doctrinal crisis. The first rumblings of that crisis may well have occurred on Sixtus's watch. The gravity of the challenge, and the nature of the orthodox response to it, would only become clear later in the century.

Bet You Didn't Know

Gnosticism incorporated elements from Christianity and a wide range of earlier traditions, including Hinduism and Greek religious and philosophical practice. The Gnostics emphasized the transmittal of secret wisdom to the initiated as a means of liberation; they both influenced and challenged orthodox Christian beliefs in the second and third centuries C.E.

In the 1940s, the discovery of a collection of Gnostic texts in Egypt led to an explosion of scholarly and lay interest in Gnostic practice.

Rome, a Century After Christ

Sixtus's leadership, if it took place anywhere near the period attributed to it, brought the Church within sight of its first 100 years. This was a momentous period that had seen both persecution from the authorities and the first internal challenge of sharp deviation from orthodox teachings. The early leadership in Rome, whatever its formal duties or succession structure during this period, had more than its share of challenges.

There were, of course, other centers of worship, notably that headed at Smyrna by the Greek bishop Polycarp, a disciple of St. John the apostle. Rome's decisive role during these early years appears hard to dispute, however. From its very early days, the Church as a whole looked to the *bishopric* of Rome for leadership, authority, and guidance—or, in the case of the Asian churches, for a harmonious approach to shared problems.

Some fateful questions, however, were emerging as the Church looked forward to its second century. Should Rome's predominance merit simple expressions of formal deference and honor to Roman leaders from representatives of other centers of Christian worship? Or was acquiescence required from all sides in Rome's desire to provide active, energetic, and ongoing leadership to the growing Church?

This, as it turned out, would become a central problem of Christianity.

Vatican Vocabulary

A **bishopric** is the office or jurisdiction of a bishop.

The Least You Need to Know

- Rome played a unique role in the development and growth of the early Christian Church.
- The New Testament paints a memorable picture of Peter as the most prominent of the apostles.
- Roman Catholics consider Peter the first bishop of Rome, and regard papal authority as descending directly from him.
- Peter probably died a martyr in the first wave of Roman persecutions against the early Christians. More persecutions would follow in the years ahead.
- We know considerably less about the six men regarded as Peter's immediate successors in Rome than we do about Peter.
- Doctrinal challenges during this period—specifically, the first appearance of Gnosticism—were a precursor of things to come.

Chapter 7

Tough Times: Persecution and Challenge in the Early Church

In This Chapter

- Gnosticism, continued
- Montanism
- The Church's reaction to early heretical teachings
- Questions of leadership
- Intensification of the persecutions

In this chapter, you'll learn about the leaders of the Roman Church in its second century following the crucifixion of Christ. During this period, Peter's successors dealt with persecutions and were forced to take a stance on alternative visions of the faith.

The Saints Come Marching In

Like all the men recognized as early successors of St. Peter, **St. Telesphorus** (ca. 125–ca. 136) was canonized. This step appears to have been taken in

Canonization is the process of being officially declared a saint. Each leader of the Roman Church from Peter to Julius I (337–352) has been canonized.

deference to the guiding role of the first Church fathers as a group, rather than as a result of the acts of specific individuals. (As you've seen already, a number of the men in question are fairly shadowy figures.) Tradition accords Telesphorus a reign concluding in the year 136.

This is approximately two years before the next man in the sequence. In other words, there is an unexplained gap between Church leaders. The gap is perplexing—at least for those who are skeptical of the ancient accounts of very early leadership sequences in the Roman Church. If the dates and names of the first- and second-century Church fathers are "suspiciously tidy" (as one writer of the modern era suggests), how do we explain the presence of an awkward, wholly unflattering gap in the early succession?

The traditional break between leaders may have been the result of persecution (which is certainly the explanation for some of the later gaps); it may have had some other cause that arose within the Church; it may have been the result of a clerical error of some kind; or, given the tenuousness of the historical record during this period, it may have had no connection whatsoever to actual events. It remains, however, the first reported instance of an interval during which the Church lacked even a nominal leader. There would be many more.

Doctrinal and Other Challenges

St. Hyginus (ca. 138–ca. 142), the next man in the sequence, is reported to have headed the Roman Church at a fateful time, the period when the Gnostic Valentinus first made his way to the city.

Bet You Didn't Know

Valentinus was the most prominent and probably the most important of the Gnostic teachers from the Church's early history. Contemporary writers tell us that he was born in Egypt and trained and educated in Alexandria. He appears to have spent about a decade and a half in the city, initially developing close ties to the community orthodox believers. It quickly became clear, however, that his main goal was to spread a new version of Christianity hard to reconcile with orthodox belief, based supposedly on a secret tradition of teaching revealed to him by Theodas, who had been a disciple of St. Paul.

The Gnostic religious worldview drew on a number of disparate Greek, oriental, and Christian elements, and featured an elaborate array of male and female spiritual entities, one of which was Christ and the Holy Spirit. It may well have looked, to the early leaders of the Roman Church, just a little like making Christianity up as one went along.

Valentinus was excommunicated for his efforts and he died in the neighborhood of the year 160. Like many Gnostic teachers, he was attracted to the concept of *dualism*.

Under **St. Pius I** (ca. 142–ca. 155), the challenges of unorthodox teachings would continue. The heresies of Marcion appear to have arisen on his watch.

St. **Anicetus** (ca. 155–ca. 166) held an important meeting with Polycarp, the bishop of Smyrna, to discuss questions relating to the proper observance of Easter. (This was to prove a divisive issue in later years.)

Vatican Vocabulary

Dualism is any principle of philosophy or religion attempting to explain the world by means of two contrasting principles (such as dark and light).

Bet You Didn't Know

During the period attributed to the reign of Pius I, the ship owner Marcion gave a great deal of money to Christians in Rome. This money was desperately needed for relief work on behalf of distressed Christians throughout the empire and for the propagation of the faith. Marcion, however, attempted to promote a version of Christianity that more or less deleted the Hebrew Scriptures. He was excommunicated in 144; Church fathers returned his donation.

St. **Soter** (ca. 166–ca. 174) is remembered for his assistance to Christians who had fallen on hard times in Rome and elsewhere in the empire. During this period, new heretical variations on Christianity were becoming prominent in Rome and elsewhere.

We think that under **St. Eleutherius** (ca. 174–ca. 189), the Church came into conflict with a movement as troubling as that of the Gnostics. It became known as Montanism.

This was an ecstatic variant on Christianity led by a man named Montanus. He attracted an energetic (and apparently quite noisy) following. His

Pope Watch

"It was in the time of Anicetus that the earliest attempts were made to compile a succession list of the Roman bishops, drawing on the remembered names of leading presbyters .... It was probably under Anicetus, too, that the shrine monuments to Peter and Paul were first constructed at the Vatican and the Via Ostiensis."
—Eamon Duffy, *Saints and Sinners* (New Haven: Yale University Press, 1997)

doctrines, beyond the encouragement of frenzied prophetic speech among his elect, sound something like this:

♦ Judgment Day is imminent.

♦ Ecstatic, impromptu pronouncements from highly regarded Montanists are divine in nature.

♦ Such pronouncements can reconnect believers to the minimalism, power, and vitality presumed to have existed in the very earliest Christian communities.

♦ People who have fallen from God's grace do not ever return to it.

The sect took this strikingly simple "insider" approach to what appears to have been fairly chaotic extremes, and Montanism won many followers.

Eleutherius was initially inclined to look with favor on the energetic Montanists, but there came a point where he appears to have taken stock of the danger they represented to Christianity as a whole. He denounced the sect.

Why the Hard Line on Heresy?

It may be tempting for someone who has lived only in a pluralistic social system to see the early Church fathers as high-handed in their dealings with teachers of variant doctrines (like Marcion, Valentinus, and Montanus). We must understand, though, that those who led the Church during this period lived in times that had no established tradition of religious tolerance. To the contrary, this was a period when fierce and indiscriminate slaughter could accompany periods of imperial disfavor against groups defined, however loosely, as Christians. It was sometimes impossible to predict those periods of imperial disfavor.

Bet You Didn't Know _____

During the first two and a half centuries of Christian worship and observance, believers were subject to fits of sudden and violent persecution from the Roman authorities. Often, these arose because Christians refused to render homage to the emperor or to state-recognized deities. Bloody and sustained persecutions of the remarkably resilient Christian sect took place under the emperors Nero, Domitian, Trajan, Maximin, Decius, Valerian, and Diocletian. Some of these campaigns were the result of official pronouncements; others were less formal.

Perhaps, in a perfect world, a Church elder could have calmly outlined to the authorities the various doctrinal differences among the sects, and added, for good measure, an appeal in support of the concept of religious diversity. This, however, was definitely not a perfect world. It was a world in which breaches of perceived propriety, suspicions of undue influence, or even whispered rumors could bring about grim consequences for all believers.

In such an environment, what may seem to modern observers to be simple "divergences" of Christian practice carried grave risks indeed. Consider, for instance, the implications of the Montanists' belief that it was praiseworthy to bring about official persecution—the better, perhaps, to hasten the end of the world!

"How's the Emperor Feeling Today?"

When the emperor was tolerant of Christian practice and beliefs, or even distracted from it, times were good. When the emperor took it into his head that the Christians were a destabilizing influence, or a blot on tradition, or in any way responsible for acts of disobedience or general social instability, times could be very frightening indeed. One major challenge for the earliest Bishops of Rome, then, must certainly have been the reining in of ecstatic believers likely to boast, proselytize too eagerly, or otherwise draw undue attention to themselves.

So the insistence of the early Church fathers on things like doctrinal and organizational cohesion arose from a fear that Christianity itself could be eradicated in a wave of bloody, state-sanctioned murder and terror. That meant essentially improvisatory or anti-intellectual movements (such as that of the Montanists) were condemned by Christian leaders. They seem to have held a conviction that the faith's survival depended on sound administration, the continuity of established traditions of worship, and, last but not least, a certain tactful ability to avoid attracting negative attention.

A Conflict over Easter

St. Victor I (ca. 189–ca. 198), who was born in Africa, advocated for the standardized celebration of the Easter holiday, a point on which there was disagreement from some Eastern Churches. This early conflict was a precursor to centuries of dispute between East and West.

Papal People
Montanus was the founder of Montanism, an early and heretical sect of Christianity. He promoted the oracular pronouncements of two priestesses, Prisca and Maximillia. The sect was eventually opposed by Eleutherius.

Pope Watch
Under Eleutherius, the Montanists were denounced. The sect eventually died out. The Montanist episode demonstrated that fervent (and, apparently, chaotic) spasms of individual spiritual experience would not dominate or guide the Christian Church as it grew.

Bet You Didn't Know _____

In the time of Victor I, the Eastern and Western wings of the Christian Church entered into their first serious power struggle. When the churches of Asia Minor refused to follow the Roman lead with regard to the timing of the celebration of Easter, Victor excommunicated them. The act was a controversial one (St. Irenaeus, for one, disapproved), but it did demonstrate vividly that Victor's vision for the Christian Church was one in which Rome played a dominant role.

Dark Times

St. Zephryinus (ca. 198–ca. 217) was less effective than his predecessors in combating heretical movements; contemporary reports describe him as too concerned with money and generally lacking in the sophistication required to lead the Church.

St. Callistus (ca. 217–ca. 222) was apparently a protégé of Zephyrinus. He was killed by angry Roman mobs in 222. Riots blaming Christians for various problems in the city were common by this point.

Vatican Vocabulary

An **antipope** is someone who assumes or lays claim to the papal office without the legitimate right to do so.

Pontifical ... but Mythical

The various waves of repression unleashed against Christians during this period did not carry, as some believe, an exclusively religious justification. Many of the Christians who died during the Roman persecutions perished because their refusal to do homage to the gods of the state religion left them looking suspiciously unpatriotic.

St. Urban I (222–230) appears to have been the first leader of the Church to be associated with what would eventually be known as an *antipope*. The respected scholar Hippolytus contested Urban's selection and fashioned himself as a rival Bishop of Rome.

St. Pontian (230–235) led the Church during one of those dark periods when not just the mobs but also the emperor had it in for prominent Christians. Pontian was arrested and exiled to Sardinia. With no prospect for a return to Rome, he resigned and eventually died as a result of the harsh treatment he had faced as a prisoner.

The brief reign of **St. Anterus** (235–236) falls under the same Roman emperor (Maximin) who had tormented Christian leaders like Pontian. We know little of Anterus, but the odds seem high that he, like his predecessor, led the faithful during a tense and difficult period.

Surviving records indicate that **St. Fabian** (236–250) arranged for Pontian's body to be returned to Rome. It was during Fabian's period as Bishop of Rome that the Roman emperor Decius came to power, an event that led to a new and vigorous cycle of butchery of the Christians after a period of tolerance. Fabian's grave indicates that he died a martyr's death. The bloody suppression was so intense that no one was named to succeed Fabian for some time.

Novatian, an antipope who held that those who had recanted the faith during periods of oppression could never be readmitted to the church, challenged **St. Cornelius** (251–253). Cornelius believed that those who had denied their faith could in fact be welcomed back to the fold after having performed due penance. The status of lapsed believers who sought to regain the favor of the Church was a particularly divisive issue.

Papal People
Fabian found himself leading the Church during the reign of the Roman emperor Decius. A merciless persecutor of Christians, Decius demanded, in 250, written declarations from each citizen confirming a routine of regular sacrifice to Roman gods. He was particularly enthusiastic in ordering the murder of Christian bishops.

Bet You Didn't Know

St. Cyprian gave us an early glimpse of what would become the papal election process:

> "He (Cornelius) was made bishop (of Rome) by the decree of God and of his Church, by the testimony of nearly all the clergy, by the college of aged bishops, and of good men." (Quoted in *The New Catholic Encyclopedia*.)

Cornelius's election and the key role played by the senior bishops were probably not without precedent.

St. Lucius (253–254) must have endured his share of trials. He reigned during yet another wave of officially sanctioned violence against Christians, this one under the emperor Gallus.

St. Stephen I (254–257), not to be confused with the early Christian martyr whose name he assumed, made the most of a lull between state-sponsored massacres. He energetically promoted the primacy of Rome, and engaged in a number of disputes with the powerful Carthaginian bishop Cyprian over the validity of Roman edicts concerning baptism. He is notable, too, because he is the first Bishop of Rome known to have appealed explicitly to the 16th chapter of Matthew ("Upon this rock I will build my church") in support of his authority.

We know that at least one leader of the early Church, **St. Sixtus II** (257–258), was murdered while actually leading Christians in worship. His epitaph, composed by the man who would lead

Papal People
St. Cyprian was the bishop of Carthage (ca. 248–258); he helped the Church avoid division by supporting Cornelius against the attacks of those who supported Novatian.

the faithful himself as Damasus I, recounts Sixtus's arrest by the emperor Valerian's forces. They interrupted his preaching to behead him.

St. Dionysius (260–268) led the Church during another period when the Roman authorities had tired (for the time being) of murdering and terrorizing Christians. He renewed efforts to support Christians throughout the empire. Financial support from the Roman Church continued to be important.

St. Felix I (269–274), **St. Eutychian** (275–283), and **St. Gaius** (283–296) all led the faithful, but none of them appears to have left much of a legacy. All three men remain enigmas to modern scholarship.

More is known about **St. Marcellinus** (296–304) but none of it is flattering. He may well have been the weakest leader to emerge during the Church's many periods of persecution. Summoned to repent by the forces of the emperor Diocletian, he obediently passed the Holy Scriptures over to the secular authorities and burned incense to the state-sponsored gods.

Papal People
The Roman emperor Diocletian, who ruled from 284 to 305, launched a particularly fierce series of persecutions against Christians.

It is impossible to know precisely what pressures Marcellinus faced. It is likely, however, that the threat of physical violence played a part in his capitulation.

As the fourth century dawned, it would have been entirely understandable for Marcellinus, or any other survivor of the campaigns of suppression, to pray for a miracle. The prayers might have appealed for an end to the official sanction of bloodshed and mistreatment, for a final rejection of the terrifying and constantly repeated cycle of either ignoring or callously slaughtering Christians.

If there were such prayers, they were about to be answered.

The Least You Need to Know

◆ The early Church fathers faced and rejected a number of heresies, including those of Gnosticism and Montanism.

◆ Heretical doctrines were rejected for a number of reasons, including that of survival in the face of government-ordered violence against Christians.

◆ Victor I's conflict with the churches of Asia Minor over the observance of Easter was a sign of trouble to come between the Eastern and Western wings of the Church.

◆ Divisive questions regarding the status of lapsed believers who sought to regain the favor of the Church were prominent during this period.

◆ Stephen I energetically promoted the primacy of Rome.

◆ Roman persecution of the Church was periodic, violent, and intense, and many of the early Roman Bishops died as martyrs.

Chapter

"In This Sign Shall You Conquer"

In This Chapter

- The Emperor Constantine I
- An end to Roman persecution of Christians
- The councils of Nicaea and Chalcedon
- The founding of Constantinople (and its consequences)
- Leo the Great

At a fateful point in the Church's history—the rise of Constantine—two fascinating things happened. First, the conversion of Europe began. Second, the chronicler's job became somewhat easier.

This is the point when, broadly speaking, the surviving Christian records and chronicles about the papacy seem to take on a stronger "present-tense reliability." The relevant writers are no longer simply discussing long-held traditions; accounts of contemporary personal experience begin to predominate. In fact, the dating and sequencing of events from the beginning of the fourth century forward in the Christian Church *as a whole* becomes noticeably less ambiguous now, compared to many events from earlier years.

With the dissipation of some shadows, and with the emergence of a contemporary chain of Church events, a change in narrative approach seems worthwhile in this book. Starting here, each chapter will begin with a brief summary of the most important verifiable events in Church history for the period in question.

What Happened When

The Rise of Constantine and the Years Following (306–461)

- **306:** Constantine's claim. Upon the death of his father, Emperor Constantius, Constantine was hailed by his soldiers as emperor of Rome. However, the succession was contested, and a period of political chaos and struggle followed.

- **312:** The Battle of the Milvian Bridge. After reporting a divine vision of a cross of light, Constantine defeated his rival Maxentius (who held a strong numerical advantage). Constantine consolidated his position and became sole emperor.

- **313:** The Edict of Milan. Constantine officially recognized the Church, formally initiating the ascent of the once-persecuted religion in the Greco-Roman world.

- **325:** The Council of Nicaea. Church fathers formulated the Nicene Creed ("I believe in one God, the Father Almighty, maker of heaven and earth, and of all things visible and invisible, in one Lord Jesus Christ …"), addressed questions relating to the observance of Easter, and resolved doctrinal questions, denouncing heretical teachings.

- **330:** Founding of Constantinople. Constantine proclaimed an imperial capital at the former Byzantium, a fateful choice that would eventually result in the division of the empire into Eastern and Western halves.

- **381:** First Council of Constantinople. Church fathers addressed the challenges of unorthodox teachings and added new material to the Nicene Creed.

- **431:** Council of Ephesus. Church fathers affirmed Mary's status as Mother of God (*theotokos*), thus resolving a doctrinal dispute with the bishop of Constantinople, and renewed the condemnation of certain heretical teachings.

- **451:** Council of Chalcedon. Church fathers maintained Jesus's possession of both divine and human natures in a single person, and excommunicated Eutyches, who had taught in opposition to this viewpoint.

A New Kind of Emperor

Uncertainty was the order of the day for the Bishops of Rome who succeeded the skittish Marcellinus (the fellow who had, under compulsion, burned incense to the pagan gods). Both **St. Marcellus I** (ca. 306–ca. 309)—who appears to have led the Roman Church at the time of Emperor Constantine's first claim to rule—and **St. Eusebius** (ca. 310) had been exiled from the city by previous emperor, Maxentius.

It was during the period of **St. Miltiades's** leadership (311–314) that the most extraordinary news yet about a Roman emperor reached the Christian community. The historian Eusebius of Caesarea (269–ca. 339; not to be confused with the pope of the same name) reported that, before the Battle of the Milvian Bridge (313), Constantine had a vision of an illuminated cross hovering above the sky and the words, "In this sign shall you conquer." He did, and the Church would never be the same.

After two and a half centuries of persecution, Emperor Constantine invoked a policy of official toleration of Christianity. It was a breakthrough that must have seemed like a miracle to fourth-century Christians.

Constantine and the Christian Church

There are four main points to consider about Constantine and his relationship with the once-reviled Christian Church.

- First, Constantine broke precedent and formalized an official policy of tolerance towards Christians; imperial persecution or obstruction of Christian religion observance ended here.

- Second, it's likely that he did this not only because of his own conversion, but also because his mother, St. Helena, was a Christian (and, from what we can tell, a particularly pious one).

> **Papal People**
>
> Constantine is regarded as the founder of the Christian Empire in Rome. Empires, however, rise and fall, and the one launched by Constantine turned out to be no exception to this rule.

> **Bet You Didn't Know**
>
> Emperor Constantine I (ca. 288–337), whose conversion to Christianity marks such a critical moment in Church history, later moved the headquarters of the empire to the city once known as Byzantium. He renamed it Constantinople in his own honor.

> **Pontifical ... but Mythical**
>
> Many people believe that Constantine made Christianity the official religion of the Roman Empire. Actually, what he did was issue imperial *recognition* of Christianity, a significant step that ensured formal tolerance of the religion, signaled the end of its bloody period of suppression under Roman rulers, and served as the first step in the conversion of Europe.

Vatican Vocabulary

Arianism was a heretical movement in Christianity that held that God existed before his Son and thus that the Son was not equal to the Father. It was condemned at the first Council of Nicaea, but proved hard to eradicate, resurfacing in the fifth and sixth centuries. (It was the primary cause for the convening of the council.)

Pope Watch

Sylvester was leader of the Roman Church at the fateful time Constantine founded the new imperial capital at Constantinople in the year 330. (Today we call this Turkish city Istanbul.)

◆ Third, he appears to have granted imperial favor to various groups of Christian believers, which led to a rise in power and esteem for the religion across the empire.

◆ Fourth, with Pope **St. Sylvester I** (314–335), Constantine summoned the First Council of Nicaea (324–325). This gathering of bishops formulated the initial rendering of what is today known as the Nicene Creed, and denounced the heretical movement known as *Arianism*. Sylvester himself did not attend, but was represented by a legate, Hosius, the bishop of Cordova.

Constantine Giveth, Constantine Taketh Away

Constantine's favor towards Christianity and Christian groups was clearly a turning point in the history of the Church, and without this event it is certainly hard to see how Roman Catholicism would have emerged as Western Europe's dominant (and, eventually, sole) religion over the next 12 centuries. It is also true, however, that Constantine unwittingly dealt a setback to the Church—albeit one that would not be felt for centuries—when he moved the imperial capital from Rome to the ancient city of Byzantium, which he renamed Constantinople.

Constantine's momentous decision to move the capital had implications that would play out for centuries to come. This choice led, eventually, to a divided empire, and with the fall of Rome in 476, the empire in the east, centered at Constantinople, remained a major power. It was the successor state to the Roman Empire. Constantine is therefore reckoned as the first Byzantine emperor.

His aim in moving the capital appears to have been to address more efficiently the administrative demands of the sprawling Roman Empire. As a practical matter, however, his decision to relocate the capital resulted in the eventual *division* of the empire; the separate bureaucracy spawned separate emperors in the years after his death. This would leave the Church and the leaders of its five primary Christian centers (Rome, Constantinople, Alexandria, Antioch, and Jerusalem) in an awkward position.

To understand why, we have to consider the position of the men who led the faithful at Constantinople. They resided in the imperial capital, and because of the city's special status, they would eventually come to consider themselves to be the equals of the Bishops of

Rome. Extraordinarily long-lived division, hostility, and conflict arose from this state of affairs. In fact, after centuries of mutual mistrust, a complete split would eventually occur between the Western and Eastern churches.

Formal separation, however, lay seven centuries in the future. For now, Christianity was vigorous, on the ascent, and, if not always perfectly unified, capable of closing ranks when the times demanded.

After the Council at Nicaea

The Church was growing in influence and authority, and had demonstrated an ability to establish a common front against heretical teachings. The men who led the Church during the period after Sylvester and the Council of Nicaea were …

- ◆ **St. Mark** (336), a figure about whom we know very little.
- ◆ **St. Julius I** (337–352), who engaged in what were quickly becoming routine disputes with Eastern bishops over recognition of the authority of Rome.
- ◆ **Liberius** (352–366), whose historical standing suffered as a result of his conciliation with the heretical movements of the Arians.

This brings us to the reign of **St. Damasus I** (366–383), a Spaniard notable for his bitter conflicts with followers of the Arian heresy. An Arian antipope opposed him unsuccessfully; the rival was exiled by the Roman emperor.

The First Council of Constantinople—which reaffirmed the position against Arianism and accorded the Holy Spirit the same status as that recognized in the Father and the Son at the Council of Nicaea—took place on Damasus's watch; he himself did not attend. A vigorous defender of the primacy of Rome and an energetic administrator, Damasus supported St. Jerome in his work on the *Vulgate*, the official Latin version of the Scriptures. He also memorialized the tombs of the early Christian martyrs.

St. Siricius (384–399) followed Damasus's lead and forcefully advanced the supremacy of his

> **Pope Watch**
>
> Sainthood denied! Liberius, whose dealings with the denounced Arian sect appeared to ignore the pronouncements of the Council of Nicaea, was the first leader of the Roman Church not to be canonized.

> **Bet You Didn't Know**
>
> Siricius was the first Bishop of Rome to apply the term "pope" to himself. From this point forward in the book, we'll follow Siricius's lead and refer to the leaders of the Church at Rome as "popes," even though the meaning of this word would continue to evolve for some time before it referred exclusively to the successors of St. Peter.

office. He was the first pope to issue decretals—formal rulings, with binding legal precedent, on disputes within the Church.

St. Anastasius I (399–401) took part in a notable dispute over the teachings of the influential third-century scholar Origen, whose willingness to synthesize Christianity with pagan teachings and elements of Greek thought was now seen as suspect. Under pressure from various parties, Pope Anastasius went along with the movement to condemn a number of Origen's writings.

Rome Drifts Toward Chaos

The pontificate of **St. Innocent I** (401–417) coincided with the sack of Rome at the hands of Alaric and the Visigoths (410), who took full advantage of a weak Western emperor. Alaric, a Christian himself, is said to have spared Christian structures and ransacked pagan ones. Innocent did his best to care for residents of his ravaged city after the catastrophe.

Bet You Didn't Know

In 402, during the papacy of Innocent I, Emperor Honorius selected Ravenna, in northwest Italy, as the capital of the Western Empire. Rome had declined in political importance, and its period of dormancy would continue until the rise of the Papal States in the eighth century. In the absence of a strong political center, anarchy became the norm in Western Europe.

St. Zosimus (417–418) found himself caught up in a series of intricate doctrinal and political disputes with the African bishops, and the same can be said of **St. Boniface I** (418–422), who also faced a number of serious challenges to his authority from Roman rivals.

St. Celestine I (422–432) engaged in the first notable conflict between the pope and the bishop of Constantinople. This one involved the movement known as Nestorianism (see the box summarizing the heresies of the period that appears following). The dispute culminated in the denunciation of both the bishop and the doctrine as heretical at the Council of Ephesus in 431. There would be many, many more such disagreements between Rome and Constantinople in the centuries to come.

Doctrinal Challenges

Heresies that divided the Christian Church during this period include:

Arianism: Held that God existed before his Son and thus that the Son was not equal to the Father. (Condemned at the Council of Nicaea, 324–325)

Donatism: Held that the delivery of the sacraments was invalid if the priest administering them was spiritually compromised. (Condemned at the Synod of Arles, 314)

Pelagianism: Rejected the notion of original sin and the view that humans must rely exclusively on grace for salvation. (Condemned at the Council of Ephesus, 431)

Nestorianism: Conceived of Jesus Christ as two separate persons, one of whom was divine. Regarded Mary as the mother only of the human person, and rejected her role as "Mother of God." (Condemned at the Council of Ephesus, 431; Christ's divine and human natures in a single person were affirmed at the Council of Chalcedon, 451)

St. Sixtus III (432–440) held, in general, to the leading principles followed by Celestine I in dealing with challenges to orthodox teachings. His reign is notable primarily for the fact that it produced a promising deacon, Leo, who displayed extraordinary skill as an ambassador and as a bulwark against unorthodox teachings. He was to become Pope Leo I.

Leo I

St. Leo I (440–461) is regarded as the greatest leader of the Church during this period (see Chapter 4, "Ten to Remember: Popes Who Made a Difference").

Leo was a tireless advocate of unity and doctrinal orthodoxy during a period when these were essential to Christianity's continuity and survival. He formed an alliance with Emperor Valentinian III against the spread of Manichaeism, and succeeded in ejecting that sect from Italy. In later years, Leo fiercely defended orthodox Catholic doctrines against the Nestorian-Monophysite challenge.

His vision of the office he held was both simple and clear: Rome was to lead. In a conflict with St. Hilary of Arles, Leo enlisted the emperor's help in establishing order among, and control over, other bishops—a key moment in the establishment of papal supremacy in Western Europe.

Leo's passionate conviction was that each leader of the Church in Rome was the successor, not of his immediate predecessor, but of St. Peter, whose power and authority were vested in the office. This was an essential (and, for the bishops of the East, a controversial) distinction.

> **Papal People**
>
> St. Hilary of Arles (d. 449) engaged in—and lost—disputes with Pope Leo I, conflicts that served as early precedents for the principle of papal supremacy in Church administration.

Bet You Didn't Know

In his *Letters*, Leo approvingly quoted the following pronouncement of Emperor Valentinian III:

> "(B)ecause the preeminence of the Apostolic See is assured by the merit of the prince of the bishops of St. Peter, by the leading position of the city of Rome, and also by the authority of a sacred synod, let none presume to attempt anything contrary to the authority of that see .... (T)he peace of the churches will be preserved everywhere if the whole body recognizes its ruler."

—Quoted by P.G. Maxwell-Stuart, *Chronicle of the Popes* (London: Thames and Hudson, 1997)

Leo's pontificate was not limited to defending the faith and promoting the primacy of his office. He was also an attentive pastoral leader (texts of surviving sermons demonstrate his genuine concern for the poor) and a superb diplomat. In 452, Leo persuaded Attila the Hun not to invade Rome; in 455 his negotiations with the Vandal raider Gaiseric also saved the lives of many Romans. He was also a vigorous promoter of Christian missions.

Pope Watch

Among the most notable missionary efforts of Leo's reign was St. Patrick's in Ireland, which began before Leo's elevation in 432. One high point was Leo's approval of Patrick's see at Armagh, ca. 444. When Patrick arrived, Christianity thrived only in parts of the island; before Patrick died in 461, it was virtually entirely Christian.

The long-term impact of Leo's inspired direction of the early Church is hard to overstate. Consider, for instance, the conversion of Ireland, which took place on his watch and with his encouragement, or the now-famous *Tome of Leo*. In this letter, Leo held that Christ had both divine and human natures in a single person. The position was accepted as ecumenical at the Council of Chalcedon.

In the long list of popes extending from the first successors of St. Peter to the current resident of the Vatican, Leo's name carries special distinction. He is the first to be designated as "great," and it is difficult to quarrel with this honorific.

A Time of Change

Leo was the great leader of the Roman Church in this era. He was also an important transitional figure for Europe as a whole.

As the final phase of disintegration of the Western Empire began, the popes themselves had been forced to do what the empire, increasingly, could not do—play a key role in the defense of Rome.

The decline in the West, which would leave Constantinople as the major center of political power, resulted in a chaotic period of diplomatic and military instability. It also brought on a series of increasingly intense disputes with the patriarchs and emperors of the East for the popes who followed Leo. As to the emperors of the West, they were on their way out; Ravenna was about to fall decisively to the Goths, and the last Western emperor would soon be deposed.

The Least You Need to Know

- ◆ Emperor Constantine is regarded as the founder of the Christian Empire in Rome.
- ◆ His decision to move the imperial capital to Constantinople (the former Byzantium) carried fateful implications for the empire and the Christian Church.
- ◆ Doctrinal challenges and disputes between East and West were common during this period.
- ◆ The first great pope, Leo I, was an accomplished theologian, diplomat, and politician passionately committed to the notion that the papacy was inherited, not from the previous pope, but from St. Peter himself.
- ◆ As the final phase of the Western Empire's disintegration began, the papacy did what the empire could not—play a key role in the defense of Rome.

Chapter 9

Rome Reemerges

In This Chapter

- ◆ The end of the Western Empire
- ◆ The fragmentation of the Early Middle Ages
- ◆ The Second and Third Councils of Constantinople and the Second Council of Nicaea
- ◆ Gregory the Great
- ◆ The Donation of Pepin
- ◆ Leo III and Charlemagne

In the period following the collapse of the empire in the West, Christianity became the focal point of European civilization.

Left to their own devices and lacking the protection and favor of a Western emperor, the popes frequently found themselves in conflict with Constantinople, with marauding invaders, or with both at the same time. In the tumultuous period that followed the fall of the empire in the West, the popes eventually gained secular authority, and extended that authority with the founding of the territories that came to be known as the Papal States. In time, the popes emerged as vigorous defenders of Rome, practitioners of statecraft, and initiators of political alliances that furthered their interests.

What Happened When

The Fall of the Empire and the Rise of the Papal States (461–800)

- ◆ **476:** Visigoth victory in Rome. The final Western emperor was deposed by Odoacer, a chieftain of the Visigoths. The event is often cited as the beginning of the Early Middle Ages (also known as the Dark Ages).

- ◆ **527:** The Rise of Emperor Justinian. The Byzantine emperor reclaimed Italy, pursued an aggressive agenda with regard to Church dogma, and promoted a policy of caesaropapism (supremacy of the emperor over the Church). His powerful wife, the empress Theodora, earned a reputation for cruelty and a strong will.

- ◆ **553:** The Second Council of Constantinople. Church fathers acted to rectify past doctrinal errors and condemned writings known as the Three Chapters. They also reaffirmed the authority of the Church's first four ecumenical councils.

- ◆ **568:** Lombard invasion of northern Italy. Persecutions of Christians in Italy took place in the late sixth century.

- ◆ **622:** Founding of Islam. Muhammad's *hegira* (flight) from Mecca marked the initiation of the Islamic calendar.

- ◆ **680–681:** The Third Council of Constantinople. Church fathers resolved doctrinal questions related to heretical teachings and clarified other positions relating to the human and divine nature of Christ's will.

- ◆ **754:** The Donation of Pepin. This grant of lands laid the foundation for what would later be known as the Papal States.

- ◆ **787:** The Second Council of Nicaea. Church fathers addressed the fateful question of the role of holy images in Church practices.

- ◆ **800:** Founding of the Carolingian Dynasty. Charlemagne was crowned emperor in Rome.

The Western Empire Disintegrates

St. Hilarus (461–468), a protégé of Leo I, was not shy about confronting the Western emperor, Anthemius, for his lenience towards heretical teachings. As it turned out, Hilarus was one of the last popes to *have* a Western emperor to confront. The Western Empire, which had been fraying since the beginning of the fourth century, was about to collapse.

St. Simplicius (468–483) was pope during the period when the last Roman Western emperor, Romulus Augustulus, was deposed and replaced by a German raider named Odoacer. With the dissolution of the western half of the Roman Empire, the office of the papacy took on renewed importance in regulating Rome and its environs, and was the clearest apparent successor to the authority of the Roman state. The period that followed, however, was nevertheless a fragmented one in Western Europe.

Bet You Didn't Know

The so-called Dark Ages that followed the disintegration of the Western Roman Empire is simply another (melodramatic) name for the Early Middle Ages (ca. 450–750). The period in question is certainly "dark" in that nothing resembling the spectacular advances of Roman culture, literature, and politics was to be seen. The Roman Catholic Church, however, would play a leading role in maintaining ancient scholarly traditions, and in the perpetuation of a Christian-centered culture in Western Europe.

Disputes with Antioch and Constantinople

Divisions between Rome and other centers of Christian worship were becoming more serious.

St. Felix III (II) (483–492) continued efforts to establish Rome's predominance when he excommunicated Antioch's *patriarch* Acacius, who had named as bishop an adherent of the Monophysite sect. Felix's bold act was understandable, given that the sect had been condemned at the Council of Chalcedon over three decades earlier, but Acacius acted as though nothing whatsoever had happened, and a rift between East and West ensued.

St. Gelasius I (492–496) reigned during a period when divisions arising out of the conflict with the East initiated under Felix III (II) were still simmering. On the home front, the Visigoth Odoacer was overthrown by Theodoric (an Ostrogoth king); Gelasius got along well with the new ruler and used this friendship to expand his own control of Church matters in Rome.

Pope Watch

Because of the now-discounted claim of a previous antipope, there is some confusion in the numbering of two popes (483–492 and 526–530) who took the name Felix. Most lists refer to these popes as Felix III (II) and Felix IV (III), and make no reference to Felix II.

Vatican Vocabulary

In the fifth century, the title of **patriarch** was accorded to each of the bishops exercising authority within the major sees: Alexandria, Antioch, Constantinople, Jerusalem, and Rome.

Bet You Didn't Know _____

The doctrinal dispute around Monophysitism was the pretext for a series of conflicts between the Eastern and Western wings of the Church. Monophysitism, which held that Christ had a single divine nature—rather than a divine nature and a human nature within a single person—had been condemned at the Council of Chalcedon (451), but remained a divisive and influential teaching for several centuries thereafter.

St. Anastasius II (496–498) attempted to end the rift between the Eastern and Western wings of the Church by making appeals to the Eastern emperor. Anastasius's efforts to win broader Christian unity, however, succeeded only in making him appear to have dealt weakly with the heretical Monophysites. The result: a split in the Roman Church, and a fruitless series of diplomatic efforts.

The reign of **St. Symmachus** (498–514) disrupted the claims of an antipope, Lawrence, whose supporters denounced Symmachus for corruption and shameful personal behavior. King Theodoric vacillated between Symmachus and his rival Lawrence, for some years. Bloody internal disputes between followers of the two men were the order of the day for the Roman Church until Theodoric finally settled on Symmachus in 506. Little of consequence was accomplished during his pontificate, and the schism with the East over Monophysitism continued.

St. Hormisdas ruled from 514 to 523. During his reign, a new emperor, Justin I, explicitly upheld the pronouncements of the Council of Chalcedon, thus rebuffing the East and, theoretically at least, concluding the squabble that had begun under Felix III (II). Having done this, however, Justin (confusingly) followed a policy of toleration toward the Monophysites.

The next pope was **St. John I** (523–526), whose primary challenge was a resurgence of the third-century heresy known as Arianism. There is a belief, not particularly credible, that the Arian king Theodoric arrested John and had him executed.

John was followed by **St. Felix IV (III)** (526–530) who appears to have been a loyal supporter of Theodoric. After Theodoric's death, Felix received two ancient structures in Rome as gifts from Theodoric's daughter Amalasuntha, who was inclined to look upon the Church sympathetically; these structures became the Church of Sts. Cosmas and Damian. The reign of **Boniface II** (530–532) was briefer, and was marred by questions regarding the legitimacy of his selection.

Intense behind-the-scenes maneuvering seems to have accompanied the selection of **John II** (533–535), who is reported to have taken a conciliatory line to the East in the seemingly endless controversy over Monophysitism. The long-running dispute was clearly a battle for primacy in the universal Church, as well as a falling out over specific points of doctrine.

The scholar **St. Agapitus I** (535–536) journeyed to Emperor Justinian to attempt to dissuade him from invading Italy. While on this (unsuccessful) diplomatic mission, he died. Before expiring, however, he succeeded in convincing Justinian that the patriarch of Constantinople should be deposed for heretical adherence to Monophysitism.

St. Silverius (536–537) conducted a pontificate that was as troubled as it was short. He was forced into abdication and exile by Belisarius—a general representing Justinian—on not entirely plausible (or consistent) charges of treason. This cleared the way for the election of a new pope sympathetic to Justinian's wife, the empress Theodora, which appears to have been the point of the whole exercise.

> **Pope Watch**
>
> After an appeal to the emperor from a concerned bishop, the deposed Silverius was ordered to Rome in order to stand trial. His successor, Pope Vigilius, however, had the rival pope arrested upon his return to the city and instantly dismissed to another, harsher exile on the island of Palmaria. The trial never took place. Silverius died within months.

The Puppet

Vigilius (537–555) came into office as a puppet of the emperor and empress. His standing was low from the beginning with the Roman people, who knew that he had acquired the papacy by underhanded means—namely, the seizure, persecution, and starvation to death of a legitimately elected predecessor. Matters promptly went downhill from there. Vigilius squandered the prestige and moral authority of his office in an unprecedented display of inconsistency and frequently incomprehensible double talk, and he proved not only a poor pope, but also a poor puppet. His mixed messages to the Eastern wing of the Church, to the Monophysites, to the people of Rome, and to Emperor Justinian (whose bloody invasion of Italy and defeat of the Goths occurred during this period) all yield a picture of a man whose mission was simply to cope.

One of the least accomplished papal diplomats, a poor tactician, and an epic equivocator, Vigilius was an unfortunate and shortsighted man whose gross ambitions did not prove equal to the demands of his difficult times. Papal historians usually conclude that he deserved the headaches and difficulties that he encountered during his chaotic and unpopular reign; the most notable of these challenges was the Three Chapters controversy.

Vigilius's defenders point out that he led the Church during a time of impossible external pressures. His detractors argue that he never really led it at all.

> **Pope Watch**
>
> During Vigilius's pontificate, in 553, the Second Council of Constantinople took place. Firmly under the control of the Emperor Justinian I, it condemned the Three Chapters. The council also confirmed the holdings of the previous four councils, specifically that of Chalcedon in 451, which had been contested by a number of Christian groups.

Bet You Didn't Know

During the reign of Pope Vigilius, Emperor Justinian denounced as heretical the so-called Three Chapters, teachings of three conveniently dead teachers accepted as orthodox by most Christians, but rejected by the influential Monophysite sect. Justinian's aim was to placate the Monophysites, who were becoming intractable. Actually, the Three Chapters affair only brought more chaos and division to the Church as a whole. Pope Vigilius tried, and failed, to satisfy both the faithful in Rome, who had no patience for compromise with the Monophysites, and the emperor in Constantinople, who wanted to reconcile them with Rome.

The Oxford Dictionary of the Christian Church (F.L. Cross and E.A. Livingston, editors; Oxford: Oxford University Press, 1997.) offers this explanation of the controversy that undid Vigilius: "(T)he Fifth General Council was convoked by the Emperor Justinian to decide the prolonged controversy over the Three Chapters: whether Theodore of Mopsuestia, Theodoret of Cyrrhus and Ibas of Edessa should be condemned as tainted with Nestorianism, or whether, following the attitude of the Council of Chalcedon, they should be accepted. The emperor, who wished to reconcile moderate Monophysite opinion, was opposed to any toleration of Theodore, Theodoret, and Ibas."

Justinian thought, erroneously, that by condemning dead teachers as Nestorian heretics he could win points with moderate Monophysites. In the event, he only worsened existing divisions.

Bad Times Get Worse

Pelagius I (556–561) stood by the findings of the recent General Council and made a brave effort to help Romans and others in the region recover from the grim destruction wrought by recent military campaigns. He also attempted to put the Church's finances on a sounder footing, and to institute necessary reforms among monks and clerics. Compared to the endless intrigues, miscalculations, backtrackings, self-absorption, and poor crisis management of Vigilius, Pelagius's papacy was a welcome change of emphasis. The times, however, were hard ones.

John III (561–574) reigned during yet another invasion of Italy. This time the attack came from the Lombards, an ominous new force who did not reach Rome, but who looked, for a time, as though they might. This prospect forced John to flee south to Naples, where he attempted to coordinate a defensive strategy. His journey seems to have led to instability in Rome, and a chaotic period of riots and bloody factionalism followed in the city. John chose to keep his distance. The stability and order of the holy city during the early years of Constantine I could not have seemed more remote.

Benedict I (575–579) was forced to deal with more incursions from the Lombards, with famine, and with the less-than-impressive troops furnished by Constantinople to defend Rome and its environs. His, too, was a grueling pontificate.

Pelagius II (579–590) thus assumed office during a period that can charitably be called a nightmare; unfortunately, it only got worse. Benedict had died while Rome was starving and poorly defended against the invasions of the Lombards. In 595, Constantinople negotiated a truce with the Lombards, but the period of famine in Rome was followed by a deluge and then a fearsome plague. Near the end, torrents of frogs and locusts and rivers of blood may well have seemed plausible predictions to Pelagius, who died a victim of the plague. Almost a year passed before a successor took his place.

One wonders how eager the members of the conclave could have been to follow in Pelagius's footsteps, as the last five pontificates in a row had unfolded under steadily more gruesome conditions.

> **Pope Watch**
>
> Pelagius II's pontificate witnessed the conversion of the Visigoths in Spain and the provocative adoption of the title "Ecumenical Patriarch" by the bishop of Constantinople.

Finally—a Man Big Enough for the Job

Whether or not his fellow bishops were actively avoiding the job, we know that the man who was elected to succeed Pelagius II wrote to Emperor Maurice to report that he himself did not wish to serve. Fortunately for Catholicism, Maurice ignored him, and the Church received **St. Gregory I** (590–604), one of her greatest popes (see Chapter 4, "Ten to Remember: Popes Who Made a Difference").

Gregory was the first monk to assume the papacy. His achievements have been the subject of many volumes, but can be summarized briefly as follows:

- Immediately organized a relief effort to assist the victims of famine; set up funds from the papal estates to provide food during future shortages
- Took responsibility for the defense of Rome by raising and paying for troops
- Used his considerable diplomatic skills to dissuade the Lombards from ransacking Rome—not once but twice—and stood fast in the face of criticism from Emperor Maurice that in doing so he had violated established lines of authority
- Spoke out against the Donatist heresy
- Launched the conversion of England by sending a representative to preach and minister there
- Argued for the strict implementation of injunctions mandating clerical celibacy, which had arisen under the leadership of Siricius two centuries earlier

- Demanded that members of the clergy serve as moral exemplars to the parishioners they served

- Wrote extensively and with lasting influence on theological matters

- Promoted and reinvigorated monastic practice, and continued to live as a monk while pope

- Reorganized the papal bureaucracy

Pope Watch
St. Gregory I is referred to as Gregory the Great.

That's a remarkable list of achievements, but it's not quite complete. Most important of all, Gregory made it clear that his reign would be dedicated to the fulfillment of important spiritual objectives outlined in the Gospels, specifically the ministry of the Church to the poor.

Pontifical ... but Mythical
The "Gregorian chants" popularly attributed to this pope are mislabeled. As John Howell writes on the Medieval Music and Arts Foundation site (www.medieval.org), "In about the year 800, two centuries after Gregory's time, the Emperor Charlemagne sent to Rome for authentic liturgical books and chants. Singing teachers were dispatched from Rome to teach the Franks by ear, but ... the Franks made major changes in order to adapt the chant to their taste and their ways of singing. The chant of the Franks is the style that eventually propagated. As a result, what we call Gregorian chant should probably be called Carolingian chant, but the easy way out is simply to use the term plainchant and leave it at that."

This was a high standard, and one that not all of his successors could boast of observing. It was a welcome break from the near-obsessive focus on doctrinal disputes with the East that had gone before and would reappear after his death. The constant, seemingly navigational return to the theme of service to the poor carried an important—and welcome—spiritual dimension, and made Gregory's pontificate one of the most esteemed in history.

"The Fear of God Restrains Them"

"The Britons, who formerly knew only their own barbaric tongue, have long since begun to cry the Hebrew Alleluia to the praise of God. The once restless sea now lies quiet before the feet of His saints, and its ungovernable rages, which no earthly princes could tame by the sword, are now quelled at the simple word of His priests in the fear of God. Heathen nations who never trembled before armed hosts now accept and obey the teachings of the humble. For now that the grace of the knowl-edge of God has enlightened them and they see His heavenly truths and mighty wonders, the fear of God restrains them from their former wickedness, and they desire with all their hearts to win the prize of eternal life."—Pope Gregory I, *Commentary on Job.* Quoted in *A Treasury of Catholic Reading*, edited and selected by John Chapin (New York: Farrar, Straus and Company, 1957).

In Gregory, we have an object lesson of sorts: the answer to the question, "What might a truly good, pious, capable, brilliant, and pious man accomplish if he were elevated to the papacy?" The answer: a great deal.

After Gregory

Few popes in history would stand up well in comparison with Gregory I, but **Sabinian** (604–606), his successor, came off looking very bad indeed—at least according to the chroniclers of the time, who appear to have devoted most of their efforts to recording Gregory's deeds. Supposedly, Sabinian charged exorbitant prices for grain during times of famine, a practice that stood in shocking contrast to his predecessor's incessant distribu-tion of free food to the poor. The price-gouging anecdote, whatever its level of credibility, has come to define Sabinian's pontificate (see Chapter 5, "Ten to Forget: Popes Who Shouldn't Have Been").

Boniface III (607) was pope when Emperor Phocus issued an important decree declaring the Bishopric of Rome's primacy. That this was necessary in the first place indicates the papacy's ongoing disputes with the Eastern churches.

St. Boniface IV (608–615) was, like Gregory, a monk. His residence, too, served as a monastery. During his pontificate, the pagan temple known as the Pantheon was dedi-cated to the Virgin Mary and the early martyrs of the Church.

St. Deusdedit (Adeodatus I) (615–618) served for three years, but little is known about him beyond reports that he saw selflessly to the needs of lepers and earthquake victims. Nor is much certain about **Boniface V,** who served even longer (619–625).

Honorius Launches an Argument

There is plenty on the record regarding **Honorius I** (625–638), and most of it has to do with heretical divisions engendered by his writings.

Monothelitism's capacity to serve as a pretext for distraction and division in the Church would prove extraordinary.

Bet You Didn't Know _____

Honorius wrote in support of the notion that Christ had a single will, as opposed to a divine will and a human will. A fine theological point, perhaps, but one that appears to have been raised as a compromise in the apparently ceaseless conflict over Monophysitism (which held that Jesus had a single, divine nature). The compromise, however, did not unite the parties in question, but had quite the opposite effect, serving as the excuse for more protracted debate and rancor between East and West. The school Honorius had embraced went by the name of Monothelitism; the emperor in Constantinople eventually embraced the single-will teaching.

Of greater practical significance was another event that took place during Honorius's pontificate: the death of Muhammad in Medina in 632. His followers would shortly launch challenges to Christianity in the name of a new and explosively popular religion, Islam. Over the next century, Christian churches in Alexandria, Jerusalem, and Antioch would succumb to the advances of the new faith.

As Islam flourished, astute believers in Rome and Constantinople may well have come to question the wisdom of the endless bickering between Christian leaders in the two great cities in the face of a common rival. If such doubts existed, they had no effect on the Monothelitist controversy, which continued to play itself out. The bickering continued under the popes **Severinus** (640) and **John IV** (640–642). **Theodore I** (642–649) continued the ongoing dispute with the patriarch of Constantinople. Emperor Constans ordered the pope to drop the issue entirely. **St. Martin I** (649–653) persisted in the argument, however, with the result that Constans had Martin deposed, arrested, convicted of treason, flogged, and exiled.

Small wonder, then, that **St. Eugene I** (654–657) initially took a more diplomatic approach. His attempts at compromise between East and West over the doctrinal dispute, however, met with opposition from the Roman clergy and the populace, and he fell into line with his constituents in Rome. From Constantinople, the emperor threatened reprisals, but Eugene died before they could be carried out.

St. Vitalian (657–672) managed to patch things up long enough to make possible a visit from Emperor Constans, but the long-running dispute over Monothelitism continued, resembling nothing so much as an annoying, protracted conversation carried on by an old married couple who have grown so used to arguing that they are incapable of communicating in any other way.

Adeodatus (II) (672–676) continued to press papal objections to Monothelitism, and with a new emperor (Constantine IV) in Constantinople, may have been testing how far he could go in agitating against the sect.

Donus (676–678) reigned for just under a year and a half—not long enough, apparently, to resolve the perpetual squabbling purportedly about the nature of Christ's will, but actually about primacy within the Church as a whole.

Half a Century of Squabbling Concludes

Finally, during the pontificate of **St. Agatho** (678–681), more than 50 years since the reign of Honorius I, Church fathers convened the Third Council of Constantinople, which resulted in a formal pronouncement that Monothelitism was heretical.

Over half a century of divisive debate and mutual suspicion had spun out; in that time, Islam had roughly quadrupled its geographical reach and had made inroads into some of the most ancient centers of Christian worship. What was needed in Rome, perhaps, was a seasoned hand who could guide the Church for an extended period and establish meaningful priorities that would unite the West.

Unfortunately, this didn't happen.

Turbulent Times

There followed four popes in quick succession, each of whom died before establishing much of a presence or consolidating the faith.

The papacy of **St. Leo II** (682–683) was delayed as the result of imperial negotiating tactics; the Eastern representatives of the emperor insisted on a formal condemnation of the views of Pope Honorius, whose writings had initiated the theological dispute, before allowing Leo to assume office. His successor, **St. Benedict II** (684–685), reigned for less than a year, and **John V** (685–686), a Syrian, had a similarly brief period in which to work. **Conon** (686–687) not only reigned briefly, but under a cloud of dispute, as an antipope contested his election.

Under **St. Sergius I** (687–701), there came proof (as if any was needed) that East and West had by now entered into a pattern of continual dispute. When the Eastern emperor, Justinian II, tried to dictate the policies of both halves of the Church and to promote an Eastern-dominated Church council, Sergius resisted. Justinian's attempts to win papal consent to his initiatives failed; shortly afterward, Justinian fell from power and was exiled. (Ten years later, Justinian would reclaim leadership of the Eastern Empire.)

John VI (701–705) endured another Lombard invasion of Italy; the constant incursions underlined the need for an alliance of some kind that could deter the marauders. No such alliance, however, was forthcoming.

Pope Watch
John V, a Syrian, was the first pope in more than 50 years to have been born outside of Italy or Sicily.

John VII (705–707) faced the resurgent Justinian II, who repeated, more or less, the ambitious demands for control of ecclesiastical affairs that he had made of Sergius. John's course of action was simply to return the documents Justinian had had delivered to him without signing them or appending any response. If this strategy was meant to buy Rome time, it appears to have worked, but John himself ran out of time when he died less than three years after his election.

Sisinnius (708) died even more quickly after taking office; we are told that he suffered from gout.

His successor, **Constantine** (708–715), was therefore left with the challenge of dealing with Justinian II. Constantine carefully negotiated a settlement with the emperor; each man was careful to observe appropriate ceremonial obligations during their meeting in 711 in Nicomedia. (Later in the same year, Justinian was assassinated.)

Tensions with Constantinople

St. Gregory II (715–731) faced new imperial decrees imposing a heavy tax burden—and had to endure another in the series of attacks from the Lombards. Both, to his credit, were repelled. More difficult was the next challenge to be issued from Constantinople. The emperor ordered Gregory to support the movement known as *iconoclasm*, which rejected the use of images and statuary in religious practice. This emerged as the latest point of disagreement between the papacy and Constantinople; it would be a matter of bitter controversy.

St. Gregory III (731–741) stood with his predecessor in opposing iconoclasm; the result was outright war with Constantinople. Adding to the sense of growing chaos was yet another invasion from the Lombards in the north. It was a dangerous time, and Gregory died before either conflict could be resolved.

Vatican Vocabulary

Iconoclasm (literally, "breaking of images," a frequent strategy of the movement) means opposition to the use of religious imagery in worship. Those who rejected religious use of paintings and statues considered reliance on images to be a stepping-stone to the sin of idolatry.

It fell to **St. Zachary** (741–751) to forge a peace with both attacking parties, which he did; a change in Eastern emperors meant a change in Constantinople's willingness to make war, but not a change in the nature of the conflict over iconoclasm. Rome remained, as ever, vulnerable to the Lombards. Zachary's support of Pepin III, who claimed kingship over the Franks, would have a number of extraordinary implications in later years, not the least of which was the Donation of Pepin.

Stephen II (752) died less than a week after his election.

Bet You Didn't Know _____

The Donation of Pepin led to the political entity eventually known as the Papal States, and secured a return to prominence for Rome, the capital of the States. The borders of the Papal States shifted over time, and they were at the center of many political and military struggles through the centuries. The popes ruled this territory from 754 to 1870. In considering the political events in Europe before 1870, think of the word "Italy" as representing a region, rather than a nation, and think of "Rome" as the capital of a grouping of states led by the popes.

The Donation of Pepin

Under **Stephen III** (752–757), who capitalized on Zacharias's work and forged an alliance with the Franks, came the Donation of Pepin. This grant of lands from Pepin III, which followed Stephen's recognition of Pepin's claims and Pepin's subsequent defense of Rome, transformed the papacy from a religious office in constant search of political favor to a true temporal power in its own right.

The alliance with the Franks alienated Constantinople, but that appears to have come as no surprise to Rome.

The next two popes, **St. Paul I** (757–767) and **Stephen IV** (768–772), faced an extremely complicated four-way diplomatic and military situation involving Rome, the Franks, Constantinople, and the Lombards. Neither mastered it.

It was left to **Adrian I** (772–795) to restore continuity and safety to Rome. He did so by strengthening his ties to the Frankish king, Charlemagne, who promptly routed the Lombards and destroyed their kingdom. The overture to Charlemagne was an exhilarating success, and this relationship would be the diplomatic centerpiece of both Adrian's papacy and that of his successor. With Adrian, the change in role that had been initiated by the acquisition of the territories of the Donation of Pepin was complete. The popes were now more than religious leaders; they were heads of state in their own right.

> **Pope Watch**
>
> Zachary's successor, Stephen II (752), died just three days after being elected pope. Some lists omit him.

Bet You Didn't Know _____

The Second Council of Nicaea (787) rejected iconoclasm and laid down guidelines for the veneration of holy images. More than 300 bishops attended the council, which occurred during the reign of Adrian I.

Leo III

After being subjected to a fierce physical assault in the streets of Rome at the hands of his enemies, Pope **St. Leo III** (795–816) was left for dead. He regained consciousness, and somehow made his way to Paderborn, to the camp of Charlemagne, king of the Franks.

Leo had been careful upon his election to request an envoy from Charlemagne so as to swear his (Leo's) loyalty. Now, in a time of crisis, he reaped the advantages of this decision, and of Pope Adrian's earlier connection to the king. He was received with honor, and he returned to Rome under royal guard. His opponents tried and failed to turn Charlemagne against Leo, and those who had conspired against him were conveyed to Charlemagne's custody.

> **Papal People**
>
> Charlemagne was the founder of the Carolingian Empire; he revived the title of Western emperor in 800 when he was crowned by Pope Leo III.

On Christmas Day 800, Leo III crowned Charlemagne as emperor of the West.

The successor state of the empire Charlemagne founded, the Holy Roman Empire, is identified today with the accession of the German king Otto in 936. Regardless of the name attached to Charlemagne's empire, its emergence in the year 800 placed at the center of European political history a powerful figure who saw it as his solemn duty to protect and reform Christianity. Leo's role in Charlemagne's ascent —and particularly his willingness to do the emperor homage—is worth noting. (See Chapter 4.)

The pope's relationship with Charlemagne solved a number of pressing problems. It further alienated the leaders of the Eastern Empire from their efforts to take the leading role in Church affairs; it secured vital military protection; and it formalized an alliance with a powerful Western ruler who embraced the faith. There were downsides, of course, including the imperial habit of meddling in clerical appointments. (This trend would carry repercussions for many later popes.) What mattered now was Leo's establishment of a distinctive papal role under the *suzerainty* of Charlemagne, which protected Leo himself, the office he held, and the Church he led.

> **Vatican Vocabulary**
>
> A **suzerain** is a political entity or state that maintains control over a dependent state. Charlemagne established suzerainty over the pope and his territories.

It was the right move at the right time—even if Charlemagne bustled a little more energetically into Church affairs than Leo might have desired. There were disputes, but Leo managed his balancing act well. Perhaps he comforted himself with the observation that the emperor at least recognized the authority of the pope, which was more than he could say for various representatives of the Eastern wing of the Church over the years.

The Least You Need to Know

◆ Nothing resembling the spectacular advances of Roman culture, literature, and politics was to be seen for centuries in Western Europe after the deposition of Romulus Augustulus.

◆ The popes would play a leading role in maintaining ancient scholarly traditions, and in the perpetuation of a Christian-centered culture in politically fragmented Western Europe.

◆ Ongoing conflict between the Eastern and Western wings of the Church (and the emperor of the East) took the form of disputes over Monophysitism, Monothelitism, and iconoclasm.

◆ The monk Gregory I (Gregory the Great) brought piety, focus, managerial skill, devotion to the poor, and great courage to the papacy.

◆ The Donation of Pepin, which took place under Pope Stephen III, established the territory that would become the Papal States.

◆ Pope Leo III crowned Charlemagne as emperor of the West on Christmas Day 800, and thus secured a measure of protection for the Catholic Church and its territories.

Chapter 10

Willing Spirits, Weak Flesh, and Fresh Division

In This Chapter

- ◆ Vicious struggles for power in Rome
- ◆ Marozia and the Rule of the Harlots
- ◆ The decline of the Carolingian line and the rise of Otto as Holy Roman Emperor
- ◆ The papal reform movement
- ◆ The final split with the East

In assessing the two and a half centuries after the reign of Leo III and before the final schism with the Eastern Church, we come face-to-face with the moral low point of the papacy as an institution.

While consolidating (and competing for) political power commensurate with their emerging role as secular rulers, many popes came to neglect the ethical and ecclesiastical dimensions of their duties. In particular, one shameful period known as the Pornocracy or the Rule of the Harlots served as a dark legacy of this corrosion of integrity at the Church's highest level.

The final rupture with the Eastern Church occurred, then, after a prolonged phase of corruption, violence, and intrigue in Rome. This timing may have seemed to some to be a kind of retribution for the errors and excesses of the period. Actually, the split with the East had been worsening for centuries, and had more to do with a profound, centuries-old, and essentially irreconcilable disagreement over the role of the see of Rome than with the behavior of any individual leading it.

What Happened When

◆ **Beginning of ninth century:** Eastern Church had given way to Islam in all of Asia, with the exception of Asia Minor.

◆ **Ninth century:** The iconoclastic movement continued to gain strength and supporters in the East, particularly in Constantinople.

◆ **849:** Papally organized naval forces defeated a Muslim force at Ostia, ancient "protector" city of Rome, located at the mouth of the Tiber.

◆ **869:** The Fourth Council of Constantinople was convened; acknowledged by the West but rejected by the East, this council condemned the work of an earlier council convened by Photias and rejected the status of Photias himself, whom the Roman Catholic Church regarded as an illegitimate patriarch. The resulting Photian Schism marked the beginning of the end of the period of nominal unity between East and West. (The Fourth Council of Constantinople was not, and is not to this day, acknowledged as lawful by the Eastern Church.)

◆ **888:** Decline of dominions once held by Charlemagne forces the Western Church to rely on Constantinople and on Western princes for protection.

◆ **962:** Otto I assumed the crown as emperor of the West.

◆ **1050:** Launch of the papal reform movement.

◆ **1054:** The Eastern and Western churches formally split.

After Leo III

Stephen V (816–817) immediately ordered Romans to swear their allegiance to Emperor Louis the Pious, Charlemagne's son and successor, then notified Louis of his election and asked to meet with him in Gaul. There the pope consecrated and anointed the emperor.

St. Paschal I (817–824) was a relatively humble abbot when he was elected pope. Although he acted to protect Romans from the persecutions of the still-vigorous iconoclasm movement, there was a backlash in Rome when he died, and a period of backhanded dealing preceded the election of the next pontiff.

Eugene II (824–827) was the Roman nobles' choice to succeed Paschal. He decreed that uneducated bishops and priests were to be suspended until they were knowledgeable enough to perform their sacred duties. Eugene also agreed that future candidates elected to the papacy should swear an oath of loyalty to the emperor of the West before being consecrated. It is worth noting, though, that he resisted Louis's pressure to embrace iconoclasm, which, though officially rejected, still challenged the Church and its flock.

Valentine (827) conducted a very brief reign, apparently just over a month.

Gregory IV (827–844) is remembered chiefly for his mediation in the struggle between Lothair I (co-emperor) and his father, Emperor Louis the Pious, when Louis granted part of his kingdom to Lothair's half-brother, Charles the Bald.

> ### Papal People
>
> Louis the Pious crowned himself co-emperor (with his father Charlemagne) in 813; Pope Stephen V's consecration of him in 817 was meant to secure his protection.

Sergius II (844–847) was consecrated without the acknowledgment or permission of the ascendant Lothair I, who sent his son Louis II with an army to rebuke the new pope. Sergius was able to pacify Louis, and his brisk resolution of the crisis was a sign of a new independence and political strength in the office. There were dark clouds over this pontificate, however. Sergius had been opposed by the people, he had embarked on a shockingly vast campaign of simony, and he had witnessed the worst sacking of the city of Rome in history. In 846, *Saracen* invaders had crushed their opposition, attacked Ostia, and made their way to the holy city, which they proceeded to ransack.

Conflict and Trial

St. Leo IV (847–855) restored Rome after it had been more or less devastated by the Saracens. To prevent a repeat of such an assault, he fortified the city and its suburbs by various means—most importantly the erection of what came to be known as the Leonine Wall. Leo also fortified his own office, making it known that there were limits to the behavior that would be

> ### Vatican Vocabulary
>
> **Saracens** is a medieval term for Muslims, regardless of their national origin. Originally, the word referred to nomadic tribes on the border of the Roman Empire.

tolerated from representatives of the emperor, establishing order within the Church on his own initiative, and still maintaining good relations with the imperial court.

Benedict III (855–858) was duly chosen as the successor to Leo IV, but his papacy was not a smooth one. Emperor Louis II, who opposed him, set up an antipope and did not immediately confirm Benedict's election. Benedict was imprisoned, but opposition to his election was later dropped in the face of support for his cause from the people of Rome.

Pope Watch

In 849, a naval effort organized by Leo IV defeated the Saracens.

Clearly, there were limits to imperial control over what was emerging as a very important office indeed.

Nicholas I (858–867) had no aversion to conflict. He faced down the Western emperor on questions relating to a royal divorce, briskly deposed bishops who opposed him, and, most memorably, rejected Photius's claim to the title of patriarch of Constantinople. Although Photius managed to repair relations with Rome during his second term, the ongoing discord with Constantinople was a preview of the formal rupture to come.

Bet You Didn't Know

Under Adrian II, the Fourth Council of Constantinople rejected the claims of Photius to the title of patriarch of Constantinople and condemned Photius's earlier council. The Fourth Council of Constantinople was, in turn, rejected by the East; no future council would be accepted as legitimate by both Rome and the Eastern wing.

Papal People

During the reign of Adrian II, Sts. Cyril and Methodius invented the Cyrillic alphabet.

Into this worsening breach stepped **Adrian II** (867–872), who had refused the papacy twice before. Finally in 867, at age 75, he accepted the office. Adrian supported the missionary works of Cyril and Methodius among the Slavic peoples. He is also remembered for the Fourth Council of Constantinople, which convened in 869.

Blood and Scandal

After Adrian's reign, the papacy rapidly spun into a cycle of seemingly perpetual violence, lechery, and scandal. It was a turbulent period for the office, and probably its low point. They may not always have been superb role models, but most of the popes of this period could not be accused of being boring.

John VIII (872–882) forged an alliance with Emperor Louis II against the Saracens. When Louis II died, John named and crowned Charles II the Bald of France as Western emperor. John was assassinated in 882, a sign of the growing power of the office he held … and the violence now likely to be employed by rivals and enemies.

Marinus I (882–884) was a deacon when Pope Adrian II made him a legate to the Fourth Council of Constantinople. When he became pope upon the assassination of John VIII, he absolved and restored the controversial Cardinal Bishop Formosus, whom John had deposed. It was not the last the Church would hear of Formosus or his opponents.

St. Adrian III (884–885) was pope during troubled and bloody times; he reigned for just under four months and may have been murdered.

The reign of **Stephen VI** (885–891) saw a famine caused by drought and locusts. There was no money to speak of left in the papal treasury, so he used his father's money to help the poor, repair churches, and ransom captives. His family background was of less help in addressing the larger questions raised by the complex political situation of the era; the empire built by Charlemagne was starting to come apart at the seams.

Formosus (891–896) had been excommunicated by John VIII for opposing John's coronation of Charles the Bald, but he was later restored by Marinus I, and his influence grew. He was an energetic diplomat, a balancer of various critical constituencies, and, from all appearances, a profoundly polarizing political force.

After his election as Stephen VI's successor, Formosus hatched a plan to free Rome from domination under the (declining) Western Empire by arranging for King Arnulf of the Eastern Franks to invade Italy. This plan collapsed, however, when Arnulf was suddenly stricken by paralysis and had to return to Germany.

Formosus's primary ability, however, appears to have been the creation of bitter political foes, some of whom, as will shortly become clear, nursed notable grudges.

Boniface VI (896) was pope for only 15 days. He either died from gout or was murdered by Stephen VII, his successor.

Stephen VII (896–897) was a member of the ruling family of Spoleto in Italy. When he was elected pope, the Spoletan party assumed political control of Rome. The Spoletans hated Formosus so much that they had his corpse exhumed to attend a trial at which Formosus's pontificate was declared void.

Romanus (897) was elected pope after Stephen VII was imprisoned and (probably) strangled by Formosus's supporters. Romanus was responsible for the retrieval of Formosus's body from the Tiber River, where it had been cast. Romanus was pope for only four months. We do not know whether he met his end as the result of foul play, but given the political tone of the era, the prospect seems, at the least, to be a significant statistical possibility.

Theodore II (897) continued the cycle of suspiciously short pontificates; he was pope for only 20 days. During this period he saw to the burial of the corpse Romanus had rescued from the Tiber.

John IX (898–900) continued the effort to restore the good name of Formosus by officially reinstating and acknowledging his reign as pope. He also reinstated Stephen VII's deposed clergy. Perhaps reacting to the bloody chaos of recent transitional periods, John confirmed a decree (*Constitutio Romana*) calling for the presence of an imperial emissary at all papal elections.

During yet another brief reign, **Benedict IV** (900–903) excommunicated Baldwin II, count of Flanders, for causing the assassination of Fulk, archbishop of Reims, France. Benedict crowned Louis II the Blind as emperor of the West in February 901.

Leo V (903), the next soon-to-be-vanquished pontiff, issued a bull exempting the canons of Bologna from the payment of taxes. Leo was later deposed and imprisoned by an antipope, Christopher. Some believe he was murdered by Sergius III (his successor)—others, that he died a natural death in prison. Then again, during this period, one would avoid placing wagers against the appearance of homicide during transitional periods.

Papal People

Marozia (ca. 892—ca. 937), reputed to be Sergius's mistress, appears to have enjoyed the company and prestige of other powerful men as well. She married three such men—Albert I of Spoleto, Guido of Tuscany, and Hugh of Provence—in order to secure her family's political position. (Albert and Guido both died while married to Marozia.)

Vatican Vocabulary

The Cadaver Synod was conducted by Stephen VII. The body of Pope Formosus was brought to trial for high crimes, found guilty, stripped of its papal vestments, mutilated, and dragged through the streets of Rome before being tossed into the Tiber. One senses that Stephen held a grudge against his dead rival.

With **Sergius III** (904–911), we encounter a figure often proposed as one of the worst pontiffs in history (see Chapter 5, "Ten to Forget: Popes Who Shouldn't Have Been"). An ominous whiff of credibility pervades the rumor that he had an illegitimate son by the noblewoman Marozia, of whom we learn more later in this chapter. That Sergius murdered his predecessor to attain office is a distinct possibility. That he was in other matters bloody, vengeful, and a deferential servant of the powerful nobles who supported his candidacy is beyond dispute.

The most resolute apologists for the excesses of the popes down through the centuries have found little good to say about Sergius. The bright spot of the pontificate may have been his forbearance from acting on any temptation he may have felt to exhume Formosus for a second time and put him on trial. Sergius, too, was a Formosus-loather, and had supported Stephen VII in the posthumous trial of Formosus to nullify Formosus's pontificate. He settled for issuing a formal confirmation of the *Cadaver Synod*.

Bet You Didn't Know

With Sergius III, the papacy entered a period known as the Pornocracy or the Reign of the Harlots. The critical figure was one Marozia, daughter of the Roman consul Theophylact. She was directed by her mother, Theodora. Marozia was said to be the mistress of Sergius III and the mother of John XI. She also contrived the selection of two other popes, Leo VI and Stephen VII. Of greater importance than attention-grabbing words like "harlot" is the trend during this period of popes being installed and removed more or less at will by the leaders of a series of three powerful Roman families: the Theophylacts, the Crescentii, and the Tusculani.

"Family Drama" Continues

Anastasius III (911–913) was dominated by the house of Theophylact, and thus exerted little personal authority.

Lando (913–914) reigned for only a little more than six months; he, too, presided during the time when the Holy See was dominated by the relatives and dependents of the nobleman Theophylact—father of the woman who reputedly bore Sergius III's child. Beyond his wealth, his nationality (he was a Lombard), and his pliancy, not much is known about Lando.

John X (914–928) joined with Byzantine emperor Constantine IV and Berengar I of Italy to defeat the Saracens. When Berengar was assassinated in 924, John X sided with King Hugh of Italy. Despite having conferred unprecedented honors on Marozia (he gave her the titles "senatrix" and "patricia"), she nevertheless had him deposed, imprisoned, and, in all likelihood, killed.

The only known act of **Leo VI** (928) was the approval of the decrees of the national synod held at Spoleto in 926. He decreed that the archbishop of Spoleto was to have jurisdiction over all Dalmatia. Leo appears not to have comported with someone's long-term plans, and he was murdered half a year into his pontificate.

Stephen VIII (929–931), we are told, reported directly to the ubiquitous Marozia. He had been a priest. His few recorded papal activities involved granting privileges to monasteries in France and Italy.

With the next pope came a more obvious sign of the resumption of the family melodrama: **John XI** (931–935), Marozia's son, assumed the papal throne. He was eventually arrested and sent to prison by his own half-brother (also Marozia's son), Alberic II. Since John had supported Marozia, he was deposed and confined to the Lateran Basilica until his death.

Pope Watch

In interesting contrast to his own stormy family history, John XI supported the work of the Cluniac monks, who were committed to reversing patterns of excess in monastic practice.

Leo VII (936–939) helped bring peace between Hugh of Provence, the king of Italy, and Alberic II, the duke of Spoleto. Leo VII named Frederick, archbishop of Mainz, as his vicar throughout all of Germany. He authorized the expulsion of the Jews if they would not accept Christianity.

Stephen IX (939–942) was under the domination of Alberic II, prince of the Romans, throughout his reign, so he had little chance to do much on his own. Under orders, he supported the last Carolingian, King Louis IV (Charles III the Simple's son). Stephen formally recognized Louis and threatened to excommunicate anyone who rebelled against him. He was mutilated by political opponents and left to die.

Marinus II (942–946) tried to work behind the scenes for Church reform and to devote himself to repair of Church property and to care for the poor.

Agapetus II (946–955), another choice of Alberic's, tried to restore ecclesiastical discipline. He is remembered for the spread of Christianity in Denmark, for settling a dispute over the see of Reims in France, and for supporting the German king Otto in his plans to bring Christianity to the heathens of the north.

John XII (955–964), the illegitimate son of Alberic (and thus the latest bearer of the legacy of Marozia), didn't have much choice about being pope. When he was less than 20 years old (some sources say he was only 18), his father ordered John's election.

John was called the "boy pope," but he appears to have been quite old enough to frequent brothels. Indeed, for many observers, houses of ill repute became the emblem of his papacy (see Chapter 5).

He crowned Otto I the first German emperor, and he and Otto pledged loyalty to stand against Berengar II of Italy. But when John grew to dislike Otto's influence in papal affairs, he sided with Berengar's party against Otto. In retribution, Otto invaded Rome and John was deposed. He was later restored but soon died under mysterious circumstances.

Otto Takes Charge

Leo VIII (963–965) was installed by Otto I. Leo didn't remain pope for long, however. As soon as Otto I left Rome, the Romans expelled Leo.

Benedict V (964) was chosen by the Romans to replace Leo VIII, on the theory that Otto's installment of Leo had been illegal. The act greatly angered Otto and he returned to Rome to see Benedict deposed and exiled, and Leo VIII reinstated. Benedict had reigned for just over a month.

John XIII (965–972) was another under the control of Emperor Otto I. Roman nobles opposed John, so they kidnapped him. Otto saved John and punished his enemies. Later, John crowned Otto's 12-year-old son, Otto II, emperor. Just before Otto II married the Byzantine princess Theophano, John crowned her empress. His connection with the royal family prevented further discord.

Benedict VI (973–974) was chosen to succeed John XIII, but his consecration was delayed pending the approval of Otto I. In the meantime, Benedict was imprisoned by the powerful Roman Crescentii family and replaced by an antipope, Boniface VII. Boniface, we are told, strangled Benedict with his own hands.

Count Sicco, representative of Otto II, expelled the antipope Boniface VII, clearing the way for **Benedict VII** (974–983). Benedict's rule was peaceful, but in an agreement with Otto, he dissolved the bishopric of Merseburg (in present-day Germany) in 981; this was considered a setback to missionary work in central Europe.

The Crescentii family opposed Otto's next choice, **John XIV** (983–984), supporting instead the murderer Boniface VII. Boniface and the Crescentii family imprisoned John and had him killed, at which point Boniface once again assumed the papal throne.

John XV (985–996) was supported by the Roman Crescentii family when Boniface VII died suddenly in 985. It was no surprise, then, that John's pontificate was dominated by Roman interests, though John somehow managed to remain friendly with the German court. In 993, Bishop Ulrich of Augsburg was canonized on John's orders, the first instance of canonization by a pope.

The New Millennium Dawns

Gregory V (996–999) was a young cousin of, and chaplain to, Otto II. Otto II promoted Gregory's candidacy as pope; a few weeks after Gregory was consecrated, he reciprocated by crowning Otto II emperor. When Otto II had to return to Germany, Crescentius II (a Roman aristocrat of, as his name suggests, the Crescentii family) caused a revolt in Rome and Gregory V was forced to flee. Crescentius then installed a rival, who was deposed when Otto returned to Rome. Crescentius was executed, and Gregory V was reinstated.

Sylvester II (999–1003) was a French scholar, teacher, and scientist. He became Holy Roman emperor Otto III's teacher and went with him to Italy. When Gregory V died, Otto supported Sylvester II for pope. During his reign, the millennium turned, and dire anticipations of the apocalypse were rampant among believers eager to connect the era's

Pope Watch

Sylvester II was the first French pope.

Pope Watch

There was no Pope John XVI, only an antipope bore that number. The sequence appears to have confused someone; the acknowledged line of Johns goes from XV to XVII.

often bloody and chaotic political situation with the prophecies of Revelation.

The last days were not, as it happened, imminent, and so **John XVII** (1003) was chosen by the Crescentii family to succeed Sylvester II. He served under their influence for the entirety of his short reign (from June to December 1003).

John XVIII (1004–1009) was, like John XVII, elected due to the influence of the Crescentii family. As pope, his main interest was in dealing with details of ecclesiastical administration. He was more independent of the Crescentii family than John XVII; he appears to have abdicated, perhaps after somehow having run afoul of their interests.

Sergius IV (1009–1012) continued the Crescentii family's chokehold on Rome and on authority in the Church. He was celebrated for helping the poor and for granting privileges to several monasteries.

The Tusculanis Assume Power ... for a While

Benedict VIII (1012–1024) was the first of the popes from the powerful Tusculani family. His election reflected the decline of the rival Crescentii clan, which had been overcome during a revolution in Rome.

Benedict, the son of the head of the Tusculani house, crowned Henry II of Germany as emperor, and quickly set out to earn a reputation as both an enforcer of discipline within the clergy and a model warrior pope, personally conducting battles against Saracen forces. He also secured an alliance with Henry to check Byzantine aggression in Italy, demonstrating, in his military campaigns against imperial Constantinople, how tenuous the link between the two halves of the Christian Church had become.

Benedict's brother **John XIX** (1024–1032) bribed his way into a papacy chiefly remembered for his willingness to be paid for recognizing the patriarch of Constantinople (see Chapter 5). News of the arrangement provoked popular fury, and he was forced to withdraw the agreement.

Benedict IX (1032–1044, 1045, 1047–1048) was the last of the popes from the Tusculani family, and his reign was an on-again, off-again affair that reflects the instabilities of the period. We are told that he sold the papacy outright in 1045 (see Chapter 5).

Sylvester III (1045) was elected pope by a Roman faction that had driven Pope Benedict IX out of Rome. Soon Benedict's supporters expelled Sylvester.

Gregory VI (1045–1046) was a Roman priest when Benedict IX abdicated and, apparently, sold him the papacy for a large sum. Gregory was himself accused of simony at the Council of Sutri; he eventually abdicated and retired to Germany.

The candidacy of **Clement II** (1046–1047) was promoted by the German King Henry III after Henry journeyed to Italy and found no fewer than three rivals (Sylvester III, Benedict IX, and Gregory VI) claiming to be the rightful pope. Henry had all three claimants deposed and saw to the installment of Clement II.

Clement immediately crowned Henry as Holy Roman Emperor. In 1047, Clement died suddenly. His death was attributed to poisoning by Benedict's supporters, who launched their man one last time before his own apparent abdication.

Damasus II (1048) was nominated by Henry III to succeed Clement II. Damasus died of malaria after reigning for only 23 days.

A Great Reformer, a Formal Break

Any doubt that the papacy was now strongly allied to the Holy Roman Empire was dispelled by the selection of **St. Leo IX** (1049–1054), who was a relative of Henry III. Under Leo, a necessary period of renewal and reform took place. He spearheaded a campaign that called for repudiation of simony and an end to the sensual lifestyle pursued by some members of the clergy, and spread the word himself by preaching throughout Europe.

The charismatic Leo's aim was not to "reform" the Church in any contemporary democratic sense, but to ensure that those who administered the sacraments of the Church were not defiled by sinful obsessions with sex or money. The reform movement he supported may be said to have rescued the papacy from endless factional violence and to have added to the undoubted political power of the papacy a spiritual dimension that had been too often ignored.

Leo's rule also was marked by a fateful dispute with the fiery Michael Cerularius, the patriarch of Constantinople. After leading an unsuccessful military effort in southern Italy against the Normans, Leo was cast into prison; during his captivity, Cerularius embarked on a campaign to shut down Latin churches in Constantinople.

The argument that followed had many ostensible topics, but only one issue was truly in dispute.

Pope Watch

Leo IX was the third successive German pope. Most of the men who had engaged in the divisive and bloody succession disputes of the ninth and tenth centuries had been from Rome; after Leo, however, no citizen of Rome would be elected to the papacy for nearly eight decades.

Was Rome to be acknowledged as Christianity's foremost see, or was it not? It was an old argument, and it had a predictable result: bitterness and mutual recrimination. Shortly after Leo's death, however (he had returned to Rome in April of 1054), the mutual condemnations took the form of mutual excommunication. And this time, there would be no turning back. The breach was final.

There was much to mourn, but also much to celebrate, as the Roman Catholic Church concluded the fateful year of 1054. Communion between the Eastern and Western wings of the Church was officially a thing of the past; military threats were just as daunting as they had ever been. On the other hand, the period of conversion initiated under Constantine was now unshakable and complete: Almost the whole of Western Europe embraced Christianity. The worst excesses of the papacy had given way to a spirit of reform and spiritual reinvigoration. And the Church had survived the fall of another imperial line.

It was the beginning of the High Middle Ages. New cultural and economic forces were emerging, forces that would spark a fresh series of alliances and conflicts between the lay rulers and the popes—and solidify the Catholic Church's position as the unifying social institution.

The Least You Need to Know

♦ A prolonged phase of corruption, violence, and intrigue in the papacy followed the death of Leo III.

♦ The low point of this period was probably the Rule of the Harlots.

♦ The papacy of the charismatic Leo IX brought about a healthy emphasis on reform, and reflected the emphasis of the Holy Roman Empire.

♦ Conflict during the reign of Leo IX with Michael Cerularius, the patriarch of Constantinople, resulted in the final breach between the Eastern and Western Churches.

Part 3

Consolidation and Challenge

Here, you'll learn about the complex series of challenges and conflicts the Church underwent between the years 1055 and 1563.

These chapters take you from the time of the Crusades to the turmoil of the Protestant Reformation—and the Church's momentous response to the challenge of internal reform, the Council of Trent.

Chapter 11

As Far as to the Sepulchre of Christ

In This Chapter

- ◆ The reform movement continues
- ◆ The Crusades
- ◆ Gregory VII and the Investiture Controversy
- ◆ Innocent III

Over a period extending from the eleventh century to the thirteenth, the popes took the leading role in the adoption of a newly popular application for the word *Christianitas*. Up to now, it had meant "Christianity." By the end of the period in question, it was widely used to express the notion of "Christendom"—the shared cultural and religious identity of the nation-states of Western Europe.

The popes accomplished this in two ways. First, they set about refining their own role, influenced by the vigorous reform campaign set in motion by Leo IX. Not infrequently, they came into conflict with secular forces as they did so; these often bitter disputes ended up reinforcing the centrality of the Roman Catholic Church. Secondly, the popes helped to lead a series of religious wars aimed at reclaiming the Holy Land from the Muslims. These battles had a religious theme, and their territorial aims corresponded with religious beliefs—but their practical political purpose and economic aims (including the acquisition of trade routes) did not escape the notice of secular leaders. What's more, the benefit of keeping powerful kings and emperors occupied overseas did not escape the notice of the popes.

This was a time of broad economic expansion, a time when royal governments, not always the most effective administrators at the local level, found themselves in conflict with the Church (which transcended national borders) in the regulation of society. During this period, the popes were not always successful in establishing better relations with lay rulers, or in securing military victory in the Holy Land. They were, however, successful in forging a distinctive (and potent) Christian self-image for Western Europe as a whole.

What Happened When

- **1056:** The Patarini reform movement began in Milan.
- **1059:** A decree was pronounced naming cardinal bishops as the electors of the pope.
- **1073–1122:** The Investiture Controversy (it was resolved at the Concordat of Worms in 1122).
- **1095–1099:** The First Crusade.
- **1123:** The First Lateran Council pronounced against the practice of lay investiture, addressed questions of discipline within the Church, and examined issues related to the campaign to recover the Holy Land.
- **1139:** The Second Lateran Council condemned Arnold of Brescia.
- **1147–1149:** The Second Crusade.
- **1179:** The Third Lateran Council denounced the Albigensians and Waldensians.
- **1182–1192:** The Third Crusade.
- **1202–1204:** The Fourth Crusade.
- **1212:** The Children's Crusade.
- **1215:** The Fourth Lateran Council repeated and enlarged the condemnation of the Albigensians, pronounced against other unorthodox teachings, and issued numerous reformatory decrees. This council was considered a high point in papal authority and prestige.
- **1218–1221:** The Fifth Crusade.
- **1228–1229:** The Sixth Crusade.
- **1245:** First Council of Lyons issued a formal deposition of Emperor Frederick II.

- ◆ **1249–1253:** The Seventh Crusade.
- ◆ **1270–1272:** The Eighth Crusade.
- ◆ **1274:** The Second Council of Lyons laid out rules for papal elections and attempted, in vain, to end the breach of 1054 between East and West. This council was rejected as illegitimate by Eastern Christians.

After the Breach—Business as Usual

A modern observer transported, via a time machine, to the early eleventh century might have expected **Victor II** (1055–1057) to have been preoccupied with what we, in hindsight, know to have been the final split with the Eastern Church. But he was not. To the contrary, he may well have considered the latest squabble with the Eastern patriarch to be another passing rainstorm, likely, as had every storm before, to clear eventually. Victor focused on the incursions of the Normans and on instilling new respect for the dictates and teachings of his own Church. He secured progress on the first front by means of an extremely close working relationship with his patron, the German King Henry III, as well as a talent for diplomacy with two powerful vassals, Baldwin of Flanders and Godfrey of Lorraine. With regard to internal matters, Victor followed Leo IX's reformist example and spoke up forcefully against those who had grown lax in the observance of Church law concerning clerical celibacy and simony.

Stephen X (1057–1058) led a brief pontificate— less than eight months—one highlight of which was his notification to the German court that he had been elected without its knowledge or approval. This gesture of independence, significant after a period of imperial dominance in the selection of the pontiff, may or may not have been followed by a scheme to crown Stephen's brother Godfrey of Lorraine as emperor of the West. If such a plan ever existed, it was never carried out. During his brief time in office, he established an alliance with the populist *Patarini movement* in Milan, thus confirming his belief in the spirit of papal reform associated with Leo IX and Victor II.

Nicholas II (1058–1061) had to contend with an antipope, Benedict X, who had gained ascendancy

> ### Pope Watch
>
> Victor was the last pope "nominated" (that is to say, selected) by the German King Henry III.

Vatican Vocabulary

The **Patarini** ("rag-pickers") **movement** in Milan was a boisterous grassroots effort to enforce existing decrees against simony and marriage in the clergy.

after Stephen X's death with the financial support of Roman aristocrats who opposed the reformers. Peter Damian, cardinal bishop of Ostian, smelled a rat and refused Benedict consecration. Nicholas was then elected; confusion in Rome was dispelled when the German imperial court, which supported Nicholas, drove Benedict from the city.

Presumably as a result of this unsettling experience, Nicholas sent out an important decree: From this point forward, cardinal bishops, and no one else, would have the duty of naming the pope. Nicholas made explicit provision for "cardinals, clergy, and devout laity, with weapons both spiritual and material" to rise up against men placed on the throne of St. Peter by unorthodox or sinful means.

Nicholas II's decision to form an alliance with the Normans raised hackles at the imperial court in Germany, and led to challenges to his authority and calls for his deposition. He ignored them.

Alexander II (1061–1073), duly elected under the provisions of the decree of Nicholas II, faced (of course) an antipope. Eventually, he consolidated his position and eclipsed his rival, but the struggle to secure the papacy for the canonically elected candidate had not commanded the unanimity envisioned by Nicholas. Rome tore itself to pieces before Alexander's claim was widely accepted.

The Papacy Takes a Stand

Alexander's successor, **St. Gregory VII** (1073–1085), had been an important adviser to the last three popes, and a promoter of the claim of Alexander II during times of uncertainty and dispute in Rome. It was under Gregory that the era's most significant conflict between secular power and the papacy would begin (see Chapter 4, "Ten to Remember: Popes Who Made a Difference").

Gregory was a reformer who demanded to see evidence of actual change. He set firm standards of comportment for the Church and sent representatives throughout Europe, not merely to pronounce his prohibitions of clerical marriage, simony, and the selection of bishops by lay authorities, but to enforce them. This made him extremely unpopular.

His insistence on the Church's right to invest (that is, authorize) bishops brought on a titanic conflict with the German king Henry IV that became known as the *Investiture Controversy*. Henry opposed reform and wanted to retain control of the German clergy; Gregory excommunicated him, an act that cost Henry vital political support.

In apparent recognition of the validity of Gregory's claim, Henry abased himself before the pope and for a time gained readmittance to the fellowship of the Church. But Gregory concluded that the display had not been accompanied by a change of heart, and excommunicated Henry a second time, adding a pronouncement of deposition for good measure.

Bet You Didn't Know

The **Investiture Controversy** was a dispute over the right of temporal monarchs to invest—transfer authority to—candidates for spiritual offices, but it was also more than that. The papal reform movement initiated by Leo IX stood little chance of success in matters such as clerical celibacy, simony, and misuse of power if clerics were selected by royalty, rather than by the Church itself. Investiture, Gregory VII decided, represented a line that had to be drawn—and observed—for the sake of reform.

The consequences were horrific. As soon as he had set aside a civil uprising in Rome, Henry invaded Rome, set up an antipope (Clement III), and forced Gregory to flee. Eventually, Gregory sought the protection of the Normans, but their campaign in Italy was unpopular, and Gregory was forced into exile. A period of instability followed in Rome.

Victor III (1086–1087) was abbot of the Benedictine monastery of Monte Cassino before his election. There he promoted writing, had many important manuscripts copied, and was responsible for improvements and reconstruction. Victor's reign as pope was short (due to poor health); it was also marred by tumult in Rome arising from the claim of Clement III.

Bet You Didn't Know

The abbey of Monte Cassino, heart of the Benedictine monastic order, had been obliterated by Lombards in the sixth century, and then rebuilt; it was destroyed by Saracens in the ninth century, and rebuilt again. By the time of Victor III, it had become a great center of learning and devotion, and a powerful reminder that the Church could commit itself to something enduring, something more than the management of political challenges. Monastic orders became the model for ordinary clergy in the eleventh and twelfth centuries; monk-popes, a comparatively uncommon phenomenon in Church history, reigned for nearly half a century beginning with Gregory VII.

Urban II (1088–1099) inherited not only the papacy but also the same German-installed antipope who had beset the pontificates of his two predecessors. He eventually consolidated his own position in Rome and agitated strongly in support of the positions of Gregory VII.

He is remembered primarily, however, for his support of the notion, gaining strength in Europe, that it was pointless for Christians to kill other Christians. At Clermont in 1095, Urban delivered a sermon that called instead for a holy war against Islam to reclaim the Holy Land, and he explicitly linked participation in this military exploit

Vatican Vocabulary

"Deus volt" was the great unifying battle cry of the Crusades. It means "God wills it."

with an attention-grabbing indulgence, granting participants in the campaign pardon for all sins thus far committed.

The response was extraordinary. Urban II's call to arms at Clermont was followed by a sudden (and doubtless welcome) strengthening of support for the pope after a period of challenge and instability. Urban may well have been surprised at the torrents of enthusiasm his offer set in motion. He had found the strategy for uniting and reinvigorating Western Europe behind the papacy.

A Cheat Sheet on the Crusades

The popes sanctioned all the Crusades, but secular figures actually led the troops into battle against the Muslims. What follows is a concise summary of all of the campaigns.

- **The First Crusade** (1095–1099) was led by Baldwin of Boulogne, Godfrey of Bouillon, and Peter the Hermit. Its high point was the capture of Jerusalem in 1099. It also established kingdoms on the coast of Syria. The crusades that followed were essentially reinforcement campaigns to aid those Westerners already in the regions.

- **The Second Crusade** (1147–1149) was led Louis VII of France and the Emperor Conrad III. It was repulsed by the Muslims.

- **The Third Crusade** (1189–1192) was launched in reaction to the loss of Jerusalem to the Muslims in 1187, and led by Philip II of France. The crusaders failed in their effort to recapture Jerusalem.

- **The Fourth Crusade** (1202–1204), headed by William of Montferrata and Baldwin of Hainault, was shamefully redirected by Venetians who focused their efforts on the destruction of cities outside the mission's formal authority, including Constantinople, which was sacked.

- **The Children's Crusade** (1212) is one of the low points of Christian history. Boatloads of boys left Europe for Palestine, on the tenuous theory that they could somehow redeem the military effort in the Holy Land. Most appear to have perished from starvation or disease, or to have been sold into slavery by those in charge of their transport. According to one chronicler of the period, the movement arose from the ranks of the children themselves, "without anyone (else) having preached or called for it." Accounts of survival levels are vague but ominously dark: "What their end was is uncertain. One thing is sure: that of the many thousands who rose up, only very few returned." See *Chronica Regiae Coloniensis Continuatio prima*, translated by James Brundage, in his *The Crusades: A Documentary History*, (Milwaukee, WI: Marquette University Press, 1962).

- ◆ **The Fifth Crusade** (1218–1221) was led by King Andrew of Germany and others. The crusaders took, but did not hold, Damietta in Egypt.

- ◆ **The Sixth Crusade** (1228–1229) was led by Emperor Frederick II and was marked by internal divisions among the crusaders. This mission regained Jerusalem by diplomatic means, but the city was lost again in 1244.

- ◆ **The Seventh and Eighth Crusades** (1248–1254 and 1270, respectively) were conducted under Louis IX of France. Both failed. Louis died on crusade in Tunisia.

- ◆ **The Ninth Crusade** (1271–1272) was led by Prince Edward of England, and resulted in a truce almost immediately.

The last Christian stronghold in Syria fell in 1291.

Under **Paschal II** (1099–1118) the long-simmering Investiture Controversy bubbled on. Paschal may have thought to settle the dispute by supporting Henry IV in his (successful) coup against his father, but in the end he won no meaningful concessions, and was even placed under arrest and compelled to crown Henry V as emperor. It was during Paschal's reign that the First Crusade climaxed in the seizure of Jerusalem.

The struggle over investiture continued during the pontificate of **Gelasius II** (1118–1119); Gelasius's disagreements with Henry V resulted in Gelasius's flight from Rome. Henry named an antipope; Gelasius escaped to France, where he was treated royally, but suffered poor health. The rightful pope died in France on January 29, 1119, having reigned for just over a year.

Nearly 10 months passed before the election of **Callistus II** (1119–1124), who excommunicated Henry V and declared him a heretic. The long controversy over investiture came to an end when Callistus II and Henry V reached an agreement called the Concordat of Worms (September 23, 1122). This ended the investiture battle by guaranteeing an end to imperial interference in the selection of the clergy.

Bet You Didn't Know _____

In 1122, the Concordat of Worms put an end to the bitter struggle over investiture. In exchange for acknowledgment of certain rights over the German Church, the emperor renounced his claim to invest bishops. Although the papacy was certainly not in any position to impose direct control over all aspects of Christianity in Western Europe, it had, in the fateful period following Gregory VII's election, emerged with a firm sense of purpose. It was a guardian of spiritual authority. It was a reforming institution that had taken a clear stand in the face of secular political power and reestablished the position of the Roman Catholic Church as a unifying international force.

After the investiture conflict, the papacy controlled the appointment of bishops … right? Actually, no. Although the resolution of the Investiture Controversy did demarcate an important area of authority for the Roman Catholic Church, the problem of clerical selection was to arise with distressing regularity in the Church's dealings with other secular rulers.

Honorius II (1124–1130) had been sent as a legate to the Concordat of Worms, and his diplomatic skills helped end the Investiture Controversy. His election was a particularly chaotic one. Once the tumult subsided, Honorius supported Lothair III in his successful claim to succeed Henry V, and approved the *Order of the Knights Templar*.

Vatican Vocabulary

The **Order of Knights Templar** was a monastic/military order initially founded to protect those journeying on pilgrimage to Jerusalem. They observed vows of chastity, shared property, and committed to fight "only infidels."

Vatican Vocabulary

An **interdict** is a punishment permitting an offender to remain in communion with the Church, but prohibiting participation in certain sacraments and activities.

Still greater electoral disarray attended the papacy of **Innocent II** (1130–1143), who was named pope by one faction of cardinals at the death of Honorius II, while another faction rejected him in favor of a rival. An eight-year period of divided rule ensued, and eventually Rome became dangerously unstable. Innocent fled the city and went to France, where he conducted an aggressive campaign promoting his claim. He was soon recognized as pope by the leaders of the major European nations. In league with Lothair III, he marched on Rome, and there crowned Lothair emperor. Violence, rival claims, and other assorted crises accompanied his reign, which stabilized, more or less, in the year 1138. The following year, as though to send a message to the Church about who, at long last, was indisputably in charge, he convened the Second Lateran Council, which condemned Arnold of Brescia, a priest who may have been a disciple of the theologian Abelard. Arnold's efforts to implement radical reform had shocked the hierarchy. (He had, for instance, demanded that members of the clergy renounce all secular authority and forswear earthly possessions; he had also called for believers to confess to one another, rather than to priests.) Condemnation or no, Arnold was to continue to be (from the point of view of the papacy) a very troublesome man.

Innocent also issued an *interdict* against King Louis VII of France because Louis refused to accept the pope's appointment to the archbishopric of Bourges.

Faced with a repentant King Louis, **Celestine II** (1143–1144) undid his predecessor's interdict. He also opposed the claim of Roger as king of Sicily.

Lucius II (1144–1145) forged an alliance with the same Roger, despite the fact that he had recently invaded papal lands. The reason for the strange union: a popular revolt in Rome. Lucius led an attack on the rebels, and died in the battle.

That left **Eugene III** (1145–1153) with a Commune to contend with. He did it mostly at long distance, having refused to renounce authority over secular affairs. His decision to promote the ill-fated Second Crusade may have been an attempt to secure union during a time of discord and political challenge, and to exert his own authority. In 1152, by the terms of a treaty with Holy Roman Emperor Frederick I, Eugene III regained his see and returned to Rome. He died before the imperial intervention that put an end to the Commune.

Anastasius IV (1153–1154) granted special privileges to the Order of the Hospitallers of St. John of Jerusalem. Anastasius is also credited with having the Pantheon restored. He was criticized for failing to take an aggressive approach to affairs in Rome, and for not showing enough initiative and shrewdness in his relations with Emperor Frederick I. Anastasius reigned for less than two years.

He was succeeded by the only English pope, **Adrian IV** (1154–1159), the former Nicholas Breakspear. Adrian was the only pope to place Rome itself under interdict; he did this in an attempt to force the exile of Arnold of Brescia, the troublesome priest who had by now emerged as a leader of the Commune in Rome. The interdict was withdrawn; Emperor Frederick captured Arnold and put him to death. Adrian's later decision to ally himself with the Normans in opposition to Frederick led to damage in relations with the emperor.

Bet You Didn't Know

The reformer priest Arnold of Brescia became the leader of the Commune movement in Rome; this movement had set aside (for a time) the political authority of the pope in Rome. The Commune was eventually overcome by Emperor Frederick I. Arnold was tried as a rebel, convicted, and executed.

Papal People

Adrian IV, the only English pope, bestowed overlordship of Ireland to King Henry II of England. His given name was Nicholas Breakspear.

Alexander III (1159–1181) fought off a number of antipopes and eventually secured a measure of tolerance from the German court. Finally secure in authority, he led the Third Lateran Council, which condemned two troublesome movements.

Bet You Didn't Know

The Third Lateran Council (1179), over which Alexander III presided, rejected the Albigensians and the Waldensians as heretics. The first group envisioned the material world as an inherently evil phenomenon, and the incompatibility of their teachings with Christian doctrine is difficult to dispute. The Waldensians, on the other hand, promoted a mission of poverty and simplicity for lay believers. Their unorthodoxy was their eagerness to preach and their rejection of the entire Church hierarchy. The Waldensians prefigured the Protestant Reformation; indeed, some elements of the group survived persecution and joined with German and Swiss Protestants in the sixteenth century.

Lucius III (1181–1185) issued a bull, *Ad abolendum*, which declared that unrepentant heretics, excommunicated by the Church, should be turned over to civil authorities. Lucius refused to crown Henry VI emperor while Henry's father, Emperor Frederick I Barbarossa, still lived.

> **Pope Watch**
>
> Lucius III lived in Velletri or Agnani during most of his papacy; the Romans had declared their city a republic free from papal interference.

Urban III (1185–1187) became pope at a time when the Roman people were hostile to his office, so he lived in Verona. Urban refused to grant Emperor Frederick I Barbarossa's wish that his son Henry be crowned co-emperor. Henry was crowned king of Italy by the archbishop of Aquileia. Henry used his armies to enforce his father's rule against the papacy. Urban died before he could excommunicate Frederick.

Word that the Muslims had captured Jerusalem galvanized **Gregory VIII** (1187), and inspired him to agitate for another crusade to restore the city to the Christians. He died while trying to establish cooperation between the ports of Pisa and Genoa, which could have helped him obtain supplies during the crusade.

Clement III (1187–1191) picked up where Gregory had left off, and at his urging the Third Crusade was launched; it was not, however, to succeed, and it would conclude in the year after his death. Clement changed the jurisdiction of the Scottish church from the English see of York in 1188 to direct rule by the Holy See. Clement continued the battle for papal independence against the power of Henry VI of Germany. Clement's most important accomplishment may well have been his diplomatic efforts at home, rather than abroad; he somehow managed to dissolve the long-held disdain of the popes held by the republican forces in Rome.

Celestine III (1191–1198) was the first member of the Roman Orsini family to become pope. The day after his consecration, he crowned King Henry VI of Germany as Holy Roman emperor and did not excommunicate him for keeping papal lands won on his way to the Holy See to be crowned. Celestine III also finessed the problems associated with Henry's kidnapping of Richard the Lionheart, a clear violation of a papal decree forbidding such actions against crusaders. The picture that emerges is one of a schoolyard bully (Henry) and a wily fellow-student (Celestine) who's smart enough to stay out of his way until the bully gets himself into trouble. The trouble, for Henry, came in Messina, in northeastern Sicily, where he succumbed to a fever while preparing to invade the Holy Land. The dispute over who would succeed him left conditions perfect for a pope willing to make the most of an imperial leadership crisis.

A Pope Willing to Make the Most of an Imperial Leadership Crisis

With **Innocent III** (1198–1216) we reach a major figure of the Middle Ages. Innocent …

- ◆ Propagated the doctrine that spiritual papal authority exceeds the administrative authority of monarchs and emperors, because the spirit is superior to the flesh.

- ◆ Served as mediator in disputes regarding primacy within the Holy Roman Empire, eventually holding for the claim of Otto IV as emperor.

Pope Watch

"(Under Innocent III), (t)he pope was presented as vicar of Christ on Earth and as Melchizedek, the Old Testament figure who was both king and priest; he was said to enjoy 'fullness of power,' in contrast with the partial authority of all other bishops; and it was argued that the Roman Church had shown its authority over the empire …."
—Colin Morris, *The Oxford Illustrated History of Christianity*
(Oxford: Oxford University Press, 1990)

- ◆ Cut short a quarrel over his authority to name the archbishop of Canterbury by excommunicating England's King John, who then relented and accepted his own kingdom as a fiefdom from the pope. Unable to bend King Philip II of France to his will in quite the same dramatic fashion, Innocent nevertheless effectively enforced canon law in France.

- ◆ Presided over the Fourth Crusade and prepared the Fifth.

- ◆ Attempted (in vain) to extend Roman Catholic rites into Constantinople, much to the dismay of the patriarch there. This overreaching, which amounted to a religious coup after the sacking of Constantinople during the Fourth Crusade, could not endure, and it embittered Eastern Christians.

◆ Led a vigorous new campaign against unorthodox religious movements, culminating in the Fourth Lateran Council, which held against the Trinitarians and the Albigensians (again). Innocent's repression of the Albigensian heretics in France was particularly bloody, and extended by association to many who had merely sympathized with the movement.

Innocent was a force of nature, and one of the extraordinary leaders of the era. His pontificate was a political success without precedent. Had he been an equally great religious reformer, his achievement would have been truly magnificent.

Honorius III (1216–1227) spent most of his papacy attempting to persuade Frederick II, the Holy Roman emperor, to join the Fifth Crusade. Frederick promised to go, but was preoccupied with more pressing political problems and somehow found reasons to avoid committing himself.

Bet You Didn't Know

Two exceptional monastic orders surfaced during this period. The Franciscans (or the Order of Friars Minor, their official name) were founded by St. Francis of Assisi, one of the most revered figures in the history of Christianity. Their emphasis on poverty, care of the sick, and simplicity reflected the spiritual gifts of their remarkable founder. The Dominicans (formally known as the Order of Friars Preachers) were founded by St. Dominic, and were an outgrowth of the preaching campaign in Spain to overcome the Albigensian heresy. Both orders received papal approval in the early thirteenth century.

Age 84 at his election, **Gregory IX** (1127–1241) commanded the Holy Roman emperor Frederick II to keep his long-neglected promise to go on crusade. When Frederick delayed, Gregory excommunicated him. But Frederick's failure to obey had not been mere procrastination this time; he had been sick. When he recovered, he embarked on a crusade. He had waited so long, however, that the Fifth Crusade had concluded in failure, and so Frederick's campaign was in support of the Sixth Crusade.

Celestine IV (1241), the nephew of Urban III, was old and sick when he became pope, and he died just over two weeks after the (extraordinarily long and divisive) election that produced him.

Innocent IV (1243–1254) felt unsafe in Rome after trying to negotiate with Frederick; he fled to France

Pope Watch

In 1233, Pope Gregory IX established the papal Inquisition by sending Dominican friars to southern France. Their initial aim was to overcome the spread of the Albigensian heresy, but other heretical views would soon come under papal scrutiny. Before this, bishops had led efforts to counter local heretical movements.

where he called the First Council of Lyons. Here, Frederick was condemned and then deposed. Innocent IV made his triumphant return to Rome after Frederick's death in 1250.

Alexander IV (1254–1261) followed most of the policies of Innocent IV: continuing war on Manfred, son of Emperor Frederick II, by excommunicating him and giving Edmund, son of Henry II of England, the Sicilian kingdom. But Alexander was not as strong as Innocent IV had been and Manfred was crowned king of Sicily in 1258 despite papal opposition.

Urban IV (1261–1264), who also opposed Manfred, helped restore order to the Papal States. He diminished German political influence and improved relations with leaders of other European kingdoms.

Clement IV (1265–1268) also resisted the German (Hohenstaufen) empire by giving Charles I the crown of Naples, and by raising an army for him.

Bet You Didn't Know

The papacy of Clement IV was followed by an absurd—and apparently record-setting—three-year internal logjam preventing the selection of a new pope. The leadership gap did not arise from military necessity or natural disaster; it was the result of an endlessly quarrelsome College of Cardinals. One of the least effective gatherings of high officials in the history of the Church (and perhaps in all of human history), the conclave that convened after Clement's death took decisive action only when they were locked in their stronghold by the local authorities of Viterbo and warned to prepare themselves for starvation.

Gregory X (1271–1276) was the compromise candidate who finally emerged from the chaos of the seemingly perpetual conclave. At the time of his election he was on crusade in the Holy Land. Gregory summoned and led the Second Council of Lyons in 1274, which attempted to undo the breach of 1054, but which was ultimately rejected by the Eastern Church. He was pope during the initiation of the eighth and final crusade, which ended in defeat in 1291.

Gregory also succeeded in promulgating a set of regulations ensuring the timely election of popes. This was a goal that had eluded many of his predecessors, and that was, historically speaking, surely among the most difficult of all of the Church's institutional improvements. Later popes undid much of his work in this area, but Gregory's effort stood as an important precedent for later reforms.

Having consolidated the powerful notion of Christendom, the papacy reached a position of remarkable dominance in Western Europe. In the centuries that followed, it would encounter unprecedented institutional challenges and a series of prolonged internal divisions that had no parallel in Roman Catholicism.

The Least You Need to Know

- Gregory VII, a passionate reformer, held his ground during the Investiture Controversy over nomination of Church officials, and was eventually driven from office because of this.

- The Investiture Controversy was resolved at the Concordat of Worms in 1122; the Church carved out a special niche of spiritual authority against the claims of lay rulers.

- Paschal II endorsed the First Crusade, which unified Europe and led to a number of later crusades in support of the campaign in the Holy Land.

- Innocent III was one of the preeminent leaders of the period.

Chapter 12

Who's Who? The Avignon Popes and the Council of Constance

In This Chapter

♦ The Babylonian Captivity

♦ The popes of Avignon

♦ Rival claims and the Great Schism

After an era that had seen both reform and social unity strongly associated with the popes in Western Europe, the tide turned.

In the thirteenth and fourteenth centuries, the reform impulse faded, and the popes left Rome for France. By the time they finally returned to Rome, rupture between the Roman and French factions had led to disputed leadership claims. The discord and confusion in papal succession was remarkable, even given the conflicts between rivals that had come in the years and centuries before. An unprecedented breakdown of authority followed.

What Happened When

- **1291:** Acre, the last of the crusaders' outposts in Syria, fell.
- **1305–1378:** Period of the Avignon popes.
- **1313:** Council of Vienne.
- **1378:** A bizarre dual papal election left deep divisions within the Church and began the Great Schism.
- **1409:** The Council of Pisa failed to resolve the divisions within the Church.
- **1414–1418:** The Council of Constance ended the Great Schism.

Stability in the Top Spot ... Not!

Innocent V (1276) was the first Dominican pope. He helped draft a rule of studies for the Dominican order, but did not have time to accomplish much more, as he died five months after his election. His papacy is seen first and foremost as a vindication of the electoral reforms of Gregory X: Innocent was the first pope chosen under the system Gregory promulgated, which worked smoothly the first time out.

Incredibly, however, **Adrian V** (1276), Innocent's successor, revoked these regulations. He died a little more than a month after his election. Fortunately, Adrian's act—the only significant one of his pontificate—was overturned before the end of the century, and Gregory's reforms gradually—but only gradually!—began to influence practice again. (The most meaningful electoral reforms would not be set out until Gregory XV.)

John XXI (1276–1277), a man of learning and medicine, was elected after the five-week reign of Adrian V, but he himself was pope for only nine months. During John's reign, the papacy tried to unite the Eastern Church and Rome, and launched initiatives to urge the major monarchs of Europe to put aside their disputes and unite in a new Crusade. These efforts were brought to an early end, however, when John died; the ceiling of the papal palace at Viterbo (in what we would call central Italy) collapsed, crushing him to death.

Pontifical ... but Mythical

Many people believe that the phrase "Great Schism" refers to the split with the Eastern Church in 1054. Actually, the term describes the split within the Roman Catholic Church that occurred between 1378 and 1417.

Pope Watch

Adrian V was consigned to hell by Dante in his *Purgatory*. The great poet portrays the pontiff (who was the nephew of Innocent IV, and who had not even been a priest when elected) as grieving over his avarice during his time on earth, and as observing "how great the mantle weighs."

Nicholas III (1277–1280) was a Roman from an aristocratic family. He worked hard to free the Papal States from foreign rule.

The Frenchman **Martin IV** (1281–1285) supported Charles of Anjou, unlike Nicholas III. Martin's adherence to Charles's policies occasionally appeared to run counter to the interests of the Church itself. French dominance and control of the papacy, as it turned out, would bring one of the most fateful challenges in the history of the office. For now, however, Martin was something of an aberration.

Martin IV should have been named Martin II, but he assumed the name Martin IV because popes Marinus I and II had been mistakenly read (presumably by some errant scribe) as Martin I and II in the thirteenth century.

The tilt toward France appeared to have been countered with the election of the next pope. **Honorius IV** (1285–1287) was from Rome, and was a grandnephew of Honorius III. The new pope favored the monks of the mendicant orders, who took vows of poverty. In hopes of effecting a reconciliation between the Western and Eastern Churches, Honorius encouraged the study of Eastern languages at the University of Paris.

Following Honorius's death, another of the protracted electoral stalemates ensued; this one lasted for 11 months. The need for re-implementation of Gregory X's policies regarding the selection of popes could hardly have been more obvious, yet it was ignored once again.

Nicholas IV (1288–1292) was the first pope from the Franciscan order. He sent missionaries to Ethiopia and was responsible for the founding of the first Roman Catholic outpost in China. He was also a notable patron of the arts.

The sad story of **St. Celestine V** (1294) has been recounted in Chapter 5, "Ten to Forget: Popes Who Shouldn't Have Been." Celestine was a Benedictine hermit whose fate it was to have written a passionate letter to the College of Cardinals urging them to put an end to their protracted deliberations and select a pope immediately. The letter inspired the hopelessly divided cardinals to name the hermit himself as pope.

Celestine V may well have been the most reluctant pope in history.

The choice was not a fortunate one. After having been persuaded with some difficulty to assume the papacy (his first instinct had been to leave Italy), the new pontiff turned over his duties to a group of three cardinals, realized the inadequacy of this approach, and abdicated after only five months. But extricating himself from the papacy would be more difficult than he imagined. Celestine, who had wanted nothing more than to put an end to political intrigues, was to become a prisoner of them.

This was because his successor, **Boniface VIII** (1294–1303), tracked him down and kept him in confinement until his death. That he did this after having advised Celestine on the legalities of abdication offers insight into Boniface's character and ambition. He was, like many of the most notable popes who would reign over the next few centuries, one part committed patron to arts and learning, and two parts ruthless politician.

Boniface is remembered for his bull *Unam Sanctam*, which aggressively outlined the duty of monarchs to subject themselves to the pope. He also engaged in a series of unsuccessful attempts to intervene in European political disputes.

Bet You Didn't Know

Boniface's bull *Unam Sanctam* was a powerful and influential proclamation of papal authority. The critical passage reads: "(W)e are compelled to believe and sustain one holy Catholic and Apostolic Church. This We firmly believe, and We make simple confession that outside the Church there is no salvation or remission of sins .... Therefore, We declare, affirm, and define as a truth necessary for salvation that every human being is subject to the Roman pontiff."

—Quoted by P.G. Maxwell-Stuart, *Chronicle of the Popes* (London: Thames and Hudson, 1997)

King Philip IV of France, a powerful and committed rival to the pope, sent a group to depose him, but their attack on Boniface roused popular sympathy and the emissaries were rejected from Rome. Stunned by the assault, the elderly Boniface fell ill and died shortly thereafter. The episode was a grim portent of crises to come.

Benedict XI (1303–1304) repealed Boniface's excommunication of Philip IV of France. He couldn't, however, reconcile himself with Boniface's enemies. He died of dysentery in Perugia (located in what we would call central Italy); there he had established quarters following a period of political upheaval in Rome. No one knew it at the time, but his decision to vacate Rome was the beginning of an unprecedented dislocation of the city's ancient identification with the papacy.

The Avignon Popes

Clement V (1305–1314) was a Frenchman promoted by Philip IV of France at Perugia. Clement created a majority of French cardinals, a circumstance that led to a succession of

French popes. During his pontificate, the papal residence was moved to Avignon, France, where it remained until 1377. Clement's subordination to Philip IV, his tendency toward nepotism, his fiscal recklessness in bestowing legacies, and his persistent promotion of French interests over the interests of the Church all combined to brand him as one of the feeblest and least visionary popes in history (see Chapter 5). His record is dominated by his successful efforts at the Council of Vienne to carry out Philip's wishes and dissolve the Order of the Knights Templar while ensuring that the Knights' property in France would be passed into French hands. (King Philip ultimately came into possession of the Knights' belongings.)

> **Vatican Vocabulary**
>
> The **Babylonian Captivity** refers to the period (1305–1378) when a series of French popes relocated the papacy in France. This period is also known as the **Avignon Exile.**

John Stays Put in France

John XXII (1316–1334) may have been a compromise selection. (His advanced years suggest as much.) Frequently, such elderly popes serve as transitional figures, leaders who will resolve the immediate question of succession, serve as caretakers, and allow the disputing parties to renew the selection struggle once again with fresh alliances and renewed hope of victory. If this was the plan, it didn't work out: John reigned for 18 years. He was committed to maintaining the papacy in France, and as the second successive pope to hold this view, he may be seen as a key figure in the perpetuation of the abandonment of Rome known sardonically as the *Babylonian Captivity*.

John's pontificate was marked by a series of unfortunate controversies. He took a hard line against elements of the Franciscan order that advocated an absolutist approach to the matter of personal poverty, and eventually persecuted the *Spirituals*, a wing of that order that wished only the formal right to follow the example of St. Francis. Later, an ill-advised dispute with the German King Louis IV led to an invasion and a German-dominated campaign from Rome that resulted in a notice of the pope's deposition. John paid no attention to it; when Louis departed Rome a year or so later, the antipope he had set up, Nicholas V, traveled to Avignon and abased himself, begging forgiveness. Demonstrating a capacity for magnanimity that would have served the Church well in his earlier dispute with the Fransciscans, John forgave his rival and sheltered

> **Vatican Vocabulary**
>
> The **Spirituals** were members of the Franciscan order who sought to observe a complete ban on personal possessions and maintain the original rule associated with St. Francis of Assisi. When they could not obtain papal support for this policy within the order, they tried to establish a separate group. Pope John XXII commanded that they abandon this effort and return to the authority of the main Franciscan order, persecuting those who refused.

him at Avignon. This is all the more striking when one considers that Nicholas was a Spiritual.

Near the end of his life, John XXII preached that the souls of the just are not granted a Beatific Vision (a vision of God) until Judgment Day. The position was highly controversial.

John was apparently in his late 80s or early 90s when he made this harsh and ill-conceived series of pronouncements involving the nature of the vision experienced by the faithful when they die. Despite their origination with the pope, these views were too extreme for the theologians of the day, and John came under attack. He died an isolated man. He had been condemned as a heretic, and only a conciliatory (but inconclusive) revision of his views kept him from dying as one.

A divisive pontificate that confirmed the pattern of removal from Rome, John's reign was filled to the brim with pronouncements, holdings, and attempts to exert authority over events in Rome without actually being there. Sizeable sums from the papal treasury were appropriated to maintain armies to defend, at some distance, the Church's holdings in Italy; bribery and dubious alliances were the order of the day. A sense of insularity from actual events isn't hard to detect, and this pattern reflects some of the chief difficulties of the Avignon period. There had been important administrative reforms and missionary work under John, but there had also been a tendency toward aloofness and narrow-mindedness. In the haughty and imperious figure of John XXII, we have a model as good as any for the intransigence and dislocation of the papacy in France.

Vatican Vocabulary

The **Hundred Years' War** was a bitter conflict between England and France that actually lasted 106 years (1337–1453). It was essentially a dynastic dispute; Shakespeare dramatized elements of it in his *Henry V* and *Henry VI* cycle.

Benedict XII (1334–1342) was the third French pope at Avignon. He attempted but failed to stop the hostilities between France and England, which became the *Hundred Years' War* (1337–1453). He issued the bull *Benedictus Deus*, which revoked John XXII's pronouncements regarding the Beatific Visions of the faithful.

Clement VI (1342–1352) was faced with many problems during his reign, and was incapable of addressing most of them. During his pontificate, the banks of Florence failed, war raged in Europe, and the Black Death swept across the continent. Clement's attempts to resolve Italian quarrels were ineffective, and he was criticized for maintaining a luxurious lifestyle during times of crisis. He supported Charles of Bohemia over Emperor Louis IV, who eventually died during a hunting expedition, with the result that Clement's man prevailed and was crowned king. Of greater moment for the Church was Clement's decision to appoint a large number of French cardinals, a move that was to have far-reaching implications in later leadership struggles.

Innocent VI (1352–1362) was a stern pope. He sent a number of Spiritual Franciscans to their deaths and reprimanded the Knights Hospitaller for their lack of discipline. He crowned Charles of Bohemia as Holy Roman emperor in 1355 but later argued with him regarding the requirement of papal assent to the emperor's coronation.

Urban V (1362–1370) was the sixth pope to reside in Avignon instead of in Rome. A year after his election, he preached a Crusade to be led by John II of France, but it did not win a great deal of support in Europe. He attempted to resettle himself in Rome, but unrest in the city forced him to leave, and he eventually landed back in Avignon.

And Back to Rome

Gregory XI (1370–1378) was the last French pope. He had a sense of the historical imperatives of his office, and tried to build his pontificate around them. Gregory wanted to make Rome the seat of the papacy, restore union between the Eastern and Western churches, and bring about a new Crusade. He could not have been happy with his lack of progress in each of these areas. His return of the papacy to Rome, for instance, was successful for a time, but was so disrupted by violence and upheaval that he had to leave the city. He never did manage to settle himself peacefully in Rome, the city so strongly associated with the history of the Church.

At Gregory's death, Avignon had been the papal seat for most of the past 68 years. However, the citizens of Rome, where the next conclave was held, wanted to hear nothing more of French popes.

Who's in Charge?

At this point, the institution of the papacy suffered what might charitably be called (to use a modern term) a nervous breakdown.

Urban VI (1378–1389) was the first Italian pope elected in 75 years, and a fateful figure in the history of Roman Catholicism. His behavior toward the French cardinals who chose him was apparently high-handed. Whatever the new pontiff's comportment, the cardinals later met at Anagni, where Gregory had died, to nullify his election, saying they had been intimidated into electing an Italian pope by an angry mob, which was probably true. In the same year that Urban had been elected, the very conclave that had elected him announced that it had elected Clement VII to replace him.

Thus started the Great Schism, or Western Schism, which lasted until 1417.

Bet You Didn't Know _____

The 1378 conclave's attempt to nullify the election of Urban VI and install Clement VII led to rival popes each elected by the same conclave. The implications were nightmarish and long-lasting. Whether what followed is to be attributed to the poor behavior Urban displayed after his election, or to the conclave's extralegal announcement of a new selection, the result was one line of popes in Rome, and another line of rivals in Avignon. Today, the Avignon figures are considered antipopes.

Boniface IX (1389–1404), the second Roman pope of the Western Schism, tried and failed to end the division. His forceful methods of obtaining money to support his cause earned him many enemies.

Innocent VII (1404–1406) was not a popular pope. In fact, his election was opposed in Rome and caused considerable unrest both there and in Avignon. King Ladislas of Naples went to Rome to settle the unrest over Innocent's election. In return, Innocent named Ladislas "defender" of the Church. He then promised the king he would only negotiate with Benedict XIII, the latest Avignon antipope, if he (Benedict) recognized Ladislas's claims to Naples.

Gregory XII (1406–1415) was the last of the Roman popes during the Western Schism. The Avignonese antipope Benedict XIII continued to challenge the Roman line.

Bet You Didn't Know _____

The Council of Pisa (1409) was meant to end the schism between Rome and Avignon; it only succeeded in muddying the waters further. By rejecting the claims of both the Roman and Avignon lines, and electing yet another pope, it upped the ante impressively. After Pisa, there were no less than three contenders for the papal throne: Gregory XII (of the Roman line), John XXIII (selected by the Council of Pisa when Alexander died, and thus considered an antipope today), and Benedict XIII (of the Avignon line and thus considered an antipope).

Tempting though it may have been to wait until the number of rival popes broke the double-digit barrier, reason finally prevailed in 1414. A council was called in Constance with the goal of putting an end to the complex divisions within the Church. Moving at a stately pace, the Council of Constance managed to resolve matters by 1418. Gregory XII resigned his office; John XXIII and Benedict XIII refused to step aside, and were officially deposed. The way was clear for a new pope, and **Martin V** was elected in a manner that finally commanded something resembling universal acceptance.

The Costs of the Great Schism

Leaving aside the remarkable amount of time and energy wasted, the Great Schism left deep wounds upon the Church. Needed reforms were postponed or ignored altogether, and the means of resolving this crisis—vigorous conciliar authority, of the kind exercised at Constance—would serve as the basis of the next one.

To put the matter plainly: Martin had been duly elected, but those who had elected him believed (or perhaps only hoped) that this pope would, for a change, follow the lead of the Council. Whether or not this would turn out to be true would be the next great question to face the Church.

The Least You Need to Know

- ◆ After the Babylonian Captivity (or Avignon Exile), the Roman Catholic Church was deeply divided between French and Roman factions.
- ◆ This division led to a rival chain of popes, and later to three competing claims for the papacy.
- ◆ The Council of Constance put an end to the divisions within the Church and finally produced a pope with an undivided mandate, Martin V.
- ◆ During the Great Schism, the Church had wasted time and energy, neglected reform, and sown the seeds of future conflict.

13

Showdown with the Council

In This Chapter

- ◆ The Council of Basel
- ◆ Another polarizing dispute
- ◆ A crisis of vision

Having survived one prolonged dispute, the papacy found itself face-to-face with another one almost immediately. The distraction was unfortunate, because the time was right for a housecleaning. Instead, the energy needed was diverted to resolving another challenge over leadership of the Church, one rooted firmly in the conclusion of the Great Schism.

Emerging from the rubble of the Great Schism, **Martin V** (1417–1431) was forced, like every other pope of the past four decades, to contend with challenges to his own right to hold the office. But Martin's problems with rivals were tame compared to the frenzied agitation of the period that concluded with the Council of Constance.

His reign's legitimacy was only vaguely and unconvincingly contested by the claims of two cardinals continuing, as it were, to hold their breath in protest, both of whom were allied with the Spanish wing of the Church. Of greater significance was the set-to he experienced with the council that selected him.

What Happened When

- ◆ **1417:** Election of a canonically legitimate pope marked the conclusion of the Great Schism.

- ◆ **1420:** Hussites (followers of the executed reformer John Huss) issued the Four Articles of Prague, which demanded freedom of preaching, reform of communion rites, limits on Church property holdings, and civil prosecution for simony. The movement results in war in Bohemia and Moravia. The calls for reform are regarded as heretical by the Roman Catholic Church.

- ◆ **ca. 1420:** Beginning of the Italian Renaissance.

- ◆ **1431–1449:** Council of Basel.

- ◆ **1453:** Ottoman Turks overtook Constantinople.

- ◆ **1479:** Initiation of the Spanish Inquisition.

- ◆ **1484:** The Colonna family perpetuated chaos in Rome, leading to violence and civil unrest during a darkly manipulative conclave.

A New View of the Papacy?

There was disagreement regarding the very nature of the papacy after the Great Schism. To the members of the Council of Constance, Martin was to be a new kind of pope, one who would acknowledge the preeminence of conciliar members and establish a grateful partnership with them. After all, didn't Martin owe the council some concession to the realities of the situation? In fact, didn't the ultimate authority in the Church reside with the council itself?

This was the conciliar theory, which had first been promoted at Constance. It gave rise to a number of practical political challenges, most of them distinctly unfavorable to an incoming pope.

As it asserted its authority, members of the council seemed to be raising, by implication, a number of additional questions. Wasn't the council a better representation of the Church as a whole? Hadn't the council been forced to take the lead in resolving the Church's most divisive challenge to date? Looking back, was it possible to imagine any other conclusion of the distracting and prolonged crisis that had just passed? Hadn't the schism been prolonged and intensified with each claimant's forceful restatement of the principle of papal authority? Looking back even further, hadn't seeds for the debacle been sown by popes who had unilaterally and unwisely relocated the papacy in France? Was it not, in short, time for a change in emphasis?

Martin Exerts His Authority

Martin was having none of it. He insisted that papal pronouncements regarding questions of faith were binding and definitive, and thus held for papal supremacy over Church councils.

Any suspicions that Martin would accept some form of rule by committee were dispelled when he called a halt to the Council of Constance in 1418. The adjournment must have been a tense one.

The outrages and disorder of the Great Schism were finally a thing of the past. That, at the time, was what seemed to matter most.

A Missed Opportunity

After years of chaos, the Church now had a single, broadly recognized leader, but in the face-off between pope and council it also had the beginnings of yet another internal crisis.

What was even worse, papal commitment to vigorous reform—a hallmark of great pontificates in years past—had been absent for some time and seemed unlikely to resurface anytime soon. It is true that Martin had initiated a new approach to the levying of papal taxes, but the energy of his pontificate, like that of most of this era, was dedicated to military and political questions, such as the exertion of authority over the Papal States.

The Church was in fact unwilling to consider upsetting existing relationships with monarchs and bishops, and this is what embracing meaningful internal reform would have entailed. Church leaders attempted, without much success, to put down a movement in Bohemia and Moravia, inspired by the executed reformer John Huss. The demands of the Hussites—which included punishment of simony and other sins and limits on Church holdings—may have seemed extreme at the time, but one wonders how Church history would have unfolded had some kind of an accommodation been reached.

> ### Pontifical ... but Mythical
>
> The Council of Constance did not, as one may be tempted to assume, include all the cardinals who had taken various sides during the Great Schism. A small number of (increasingly isolated) cardinals continued to support antipopes who opposed Martin V.

> ### Pope Watch
>
> "The ideology which had prevailed (to challenge Martin V) at Constance was that a general council, truly representative of the entire Church, had a greater authority than any of its members, including the head himself."
>
> —Patrick Collinson, *The Oxford Illustrated History of Christianity* (Oxford: Oxford University Press, 1990)

Vatican Vocabulary

The **conciliar theory** held that authority within the Church originated with the Church council, and considered the pope to be subject to the council.

Pope Watch

Martin V assumed residence in Rome in 1420. He had a keen sense of the importance of the symbolism of the structures of the city, and made restoring them a priority during his papacy. Erection and restoration of buildings in Rome, as well as patronage of the arts, were characteristic of the papacy during the Italian Renaissance (ca. 1420–ca. 1600).

The Pope and the Council, Continued

Under **Eugene IV** (1431–1447) came the papacy's great struggle with the Council of Basel.

At issue was the same divisive question that had faced Martin: Which institution is superior, the pope or the council? This time, the debate left the realm of theory and took on the brutal practicality of power politics.

Papal People

John Huss and John Wycliffe were important figures of the period. Wycliffe, an Englishman, argued that Christ was the only true of overlord to humanity, and that the Bible represented a supreme spiritual authority that transcended the Church. He was condemned twice as a heretic, but not executed. Huss relentlessly attacked abuses of clerical authority and was executed in 1415 for heresy. His death brought about still deeper opposition to Church authority in Bohemia and Moravia.

Why Basel?

The schismatic fiasco that followed the papacy's tenure at Avignon had strengthened the notion, first raised at Constance, that conciliar authority was supreme over the authority of the pope. The difference now was that the bishops that Eugene faced at Basel were willing to embrace this idea much more forcefully than those who had convened at Constance.

This left Eugene in a very difficult position indeed.

Eugene Tries to Follow Martin's Lead

Wary of the motives of the council, and preoccupied, perhaps, with his political problems (which included his own recent enforced flight from Rome to Florence in the face of political unrest), Eugene appears to have sensed trouble in the council's early sessions. He ordered it to disband.

Such a strategy had worked for Martin when faced with a similar challenge, but it did not work this time. The members of the council stood their ground and defied the pope, refusing to disperse, and a crisis atmosphere set in.

Bet You Didn't Know

The Council of Basel (1431–1449) ended up looking a great deal more like a rival Church government than an ecumenical council. Initiated by Martin V, who died shortly after its convocation, it owes its strange role in Church history to forces that had begun to coalesce at the Council of Constance—and to an accident of timing. (When Eugene IV was elected, the council had already begun its work.)

In 1433, despite the efforts of Sigismund, the Holy Roman emperor, to help resolve the conflict, the council declared itself superior to the pope. A struggle for control of the Church was underway. Desperate to avoid another schism, Eugene granted concessions and tried to feel his way through the crisis.

By the time Eugene died in 1447, he had secured the support of most of the temporal rulers of Europe, successfully convened and adjourned a separate council (known as the Council of Ferrara-Florence) to take up the work of the first, and generally outmaneuvered the enemies of his pontificate who had stayed at Basel.

After the Council

Under **Nicholas V** (1447–1455) there came an end to the protracted conflict between the council and the papacy. When the conciliar antipope abdicated and submitted himself to Nicholas's authority, the air went out of the ecclesiastical rebellion.

The Council of Basel finally voted itself out of existence in 1449.

Bet You Didn't Know

Between 1431 and 1437, the Council of Basel accomplished a good deal, especially in matters related to unorthodox teaching and the resolution of religious conflicts in Bohemia. In 1437, however, Pope Eugene IV finally lost patience and issued a bull condemning the council. Another period of rival claims to power ensued, complete with the election of a council-friendly antipope.

What Basel Cost the Church

The crisis of antipapal conciliarism, like the Great Schism before it, had been essentially a dispute over the acquisition and exercise of power for its own sake. These narrow, long-running crises at the highest level of the Church did not come without a price.

Division itself was not without precedent, of course. But similarly bitter struggles in Church history had often carried a spiritual dimension: Gregory VII's conviction that secular rulers must not control the dispersal of spiritual offices, for instance, or Leo IX's insistence on clerical celibacy. These battles, too, had been divisive, but they had illuminated a higher purpose, and they had strengthened the moral foundation of the papacy.

It was hard indeed to draw any high lesson about the Church's new spiritual goals from the last two epic conflicts it had endured. Taken together, the Great Schism and the dispute between the papacy and the council had consumed nearly three quarters of a century, and the negotiating skills of some of the greatest minds of the era. It was time and energy that could certainly have been better spent.

Dark misgivings about a number of issues were beginning to be felt in various corners of Europe. These issues included ...

- The abuse of Church power.
- Taxation for projects important to Rome but less so to the rest of Europe.
- The sale of indulgences.
- The personal excesses of certain members of the clergy.
- The appointment of relatives and political allies to positions of authority in the Church.
- The splendor and affluence associated with high Church office.

These were all issues meriting, if not open debate, at least a candid risk assessment from high Church officers. Nicholas, however, failed to promote significant reforms in any of these areas. To the contrary, he continued to persecute those who called for change, setting a pattern for the popes of this period and worsening a number of oversights that would steadily weaken the Church's claim to moral leadership in Europe.

Wanted: A Great Pope

What was needed was a great reviving figure, the kind who had arisen so often in the past to orient the Church to its "true north." That the conclaves of the fifteenth century failed to produce such a vigorous, visionary, and morally exemplary character must be accounted one of the failures of the papacy and of the Church.

A storm, bigger than any yet seen, was brewing. But one gets the impression that no one—or at least none of the popes of the era—understood its true dimensions.

Business as Usual

There followed a series of Renaissance popes whose capacity for growth, change, and renewal were not, as events came to prove, sufficient to the times.

A Spaniard of the Borgia family, **Callistus III** (1455–1458), was elected soon after the fall of Constantinople. In his late 70s at the time of his election, Callistus followed Nicholas's example and called for a crusade against the Turks to recover Constantinople. When this appeal drew no support from the temporal leaders of the day, Callistus launched a naval expedition himself. To fund it, he decided to levy a series of unpopular taxes. Callistus, like the rest of the Borgias, was well known for his nepotism and his concern for the interests of his family.

Pius II (1458–1464) tried and failed to unite Europe in a crusade against the Turks. He intended to lead one himself, but died before he could carry out the plan.

Paul II (1464–1471) installed the first printing press in Rome. He also successfully brushed off an attempt from the College of Cardinals to place his actions under the review of a general council, thus overcoming the lingering spasms of the malady that had beset some of his immediate predecessors. When Negroponte (in Greece) fell to the Turks, Paul, like his predecessor, called for a crusade, but he, too, was unsuccessful.

Clearly, by this point, Europe had had its fill of crusades. Another, entirely different kind of unifying initiative was required, along with a statesman to implement it. Instead of such a statesman, the cardinals, upon the death of Paul II, followed a familiar route and elevated to the throne of St. Peter the candidate who had undertaken the most extensive and well-planned campaign of bribery.

Sixtus IV's Two Legacies

Sixtus IV (1471–1484) is remembered today for two very different categories of achievements.

To heaven first: Sixtus, following the example of his predecessors, commissioned the creation of a great building in Rome. The structure, completed in 1473, was named after him: the Sistine Chapel. It would become world famous for its decorations, and specifically for its ceiling, which, after Sixtus's death, would be decorated with a transcendent masterpiece by Michelangelo. His central image of God imparting life to Adam would resonate powerfully for centuries. Like other popes of the era, Sixtus was also a renowned patron of the arts and a committed preserver of the intellectual legacy of the West. He founded the Vatican Archive and expanded its library substantially.

He was also, however, a man one did not want to turn into an enemy.

On the political front, Sixtus engaged in a bitter conflict with the French King Louis XI over Church matters in France and Naples, and found himself drawn into the violent intricacies of a protracted rivalry with the de Medici family in Florence. An infamous nepotist, Sixtus's elevation of six nephews to the rank of cardinal still stands as the high-water mark of papal weakness in this area.

> **Pope Watch**
>
> Sixtus IV engaged in a bitter struggle with the powerful de Medici family.

Sixtus was, however, a competent manager, an impassioned advocate of the importance of building and maintaining Rome beautifully, and an important supporter of the Dominican and Franciscan orders. He was, however, prone to stir up pointless, shortsighted, and bloody conflicts with the Italian overlords of the era. His standing in history is further muddled by his decision to launch the Spanish Inquisition, the most famous (or infamous) extension of the papally-sponsored campaign to deal with heresy that had begun in 1233.

Occasionally, modern writers have pointed out that the Spanish Inquisition was the subject of later propaganda efforts by opponents of the Church. This is true. It is also true that the tradition of the Inquisition as a whole brought to vivid life the worst nightmares of what would today be called a police state; secular authorities carried out the Inquisition's formal sentences. The campaign endorsed by Sixtus at the urging of Ferdinand and Isabella was by far the cruelest expression of that brutal authority.

If this was not a perversion of the Church's mission, nothing was.

Bet You Didn't Know

The Spanish Inquisition was the Church's most ruthless and excessive campaign of papal persecution of supposed heretics. The Spanish initiative was instigated at the urging of Spanish royalty suspicious of the intentions of recent converts from Judaism and Islam. (The institution of the Inquisition itself dated to the thirteenth century.) Torture was so liberally applied that Sixtus IV was forced to issue a brief chastising of the inquisitors for their excesses.

Tensions Build

The Church was wealthy, but it had descended to a lamentable moral low point, and it had been led there by precisely the kind of worldly, money-hungry cleric whom Gregory VII would have despised.

The papacy's excesses—narrow-mindedness, violence, avarice, nepotism, heedless taxation, neglect of the office's spiritual dimension—were leading to tensions in Europe.

Something had to give.

The Least You Need to Know

- Martin V's papacy led to a dispute with the Council of Constance over the supposed supremacy of a council over the pope.
- This notion of conciliar supremacy to the pope reemerged with vigor at the Council of Basel.
- Eugene IV tried and failed to adjourn the Council of Basel, and another protracted, energy-consuming period of struggle for leadership of the Church ensued. Eugene outmaneuvered and outlasted his opponents; the Council of Basel acknowledged his successor before dissolving.
- The failure of the conclaves of the fifteenth century to elect a great reformer as pope must be accounted one of the failures of the papacy and of the Church.

Chapter 14

The Earthquake

In This Chapter

- ◆ The Borgias and the papacy
- ◆ Arts and diplomacy
- ◆ Martin Luther and the Protestant Reformation

During the late fifteenth and early sixteenth centuries, the popes continued the pattern of promoting narrow familial interests; offering support to artistic, literary, architectural, and archival undertakings; and, all too often, virtually ignoring the spiritual dimension of their offices and of the Church as a whole.

This indifference to matters of piety and reform was to result in a shock treatment of sorts to the Church, and to the papacy, as a religious upheaval initiated by Martin Luther was felt across Europe. The movement would come to be known as the Protestant Reformation. (The term "Protestant" would not arise until 1529, when a minority group of reformists at the Diet of Speyer in Germany delivered a formal *protestatio* in opposition to the Catholic majority there.)

What Happened When

- ◆ **1497:** Italian reformer Girolamo Savanarola was excommunicated, having ignored orders from the pope to cease his public appeals for a return to morally vigorous leadership and practice within the Church.

- ◆ **1498:** Savanarola was hanged as a heretic and a schismatic by city officials in Florence; papal condemnation had helped to seal his doom.

- ◆ **1509:** Desiderius Erasmus launched criticisms against the excesses and moral laxity of the Church.

- ◆ **1517:** Martin Luther made a prominent attack against the sale of indulgences by nailing his 95 theses to the church door at Wittenberg.

- ◆ **1519:** Luther explicitly denied the authority of the pope and the General Council.

- ◆ **1521:** Luther was excommunicated; after having then intensified his attacks on the pope, Luther was condemned at the Diet of Worms.

Suspicion and Corruption

At precisely the time Europe desperately needed a new brand of moral and religious leader—someone who could sweep away the cobwebs and take a stand against the excesses of the era—the papacy produced more of the familiar white-knuckled suspicion and corruption.

Innocent's Dark Legacy

Suspicion came first. The paranoia that had blackened the Church and been given its full expression with the commissioning of the Spanish Inquisition continued under **Innocent VIII** (1484–1492). (See Chapter 5, "Ten to Forget: Popes Who Shouldn't Have Been.")

Innocent was elected at a time when Europe witnessed a wave of executions of people thought to be practicing witchcraft; he imparted papal authority to this belief and issued a bull in 1484 that formalized his condemnation of witchcraft and its supposed practitioners. He dispatched a fresh wave of inquisitors to Germany to try people thought to be witches. Many of these "witches" perished.

Innocent addressed pressing financial problems by various means, including an agreement to hold under imprisonment the brother of a Turkish sultan. The grateful sultan reciprocated by arranging for payments to the pope and forwarding a lance believed to have been used to pierce the side of the crucified Jesus.

Alexander Steps In

Stark corruption followed; in the election of **Alexander VI** (1492–1503) we encounter what can only be described as a tragic failure of the system.

A member of the Borgia family, a practitioner of falsehood, greed, and bitter rivalry, a silencer of the voices of reform, and a dedicated libertine, Alexander is likely to remain one of the most notorious popes in history for as long as the office is discussed (see Chapter 5). His open acknowledgment of his illegitimate children removes some small portion of the odor of hypocrisy from the pontificate, but this must be understood in the context of the family rivalries of the era.

He was a dedicated patron of the arts and an accomplished overseer of political and diplomatic matters. Somehow, though, these strengths seem only to emphasize his weaknesses; Alexander has come to represent the continuation of the era's increasingly disturbing emphasis of the papacy's worldly elements to the exclusion of all else.

He is known to have bought his office from a corrupt conclave. His son, Cesare Borgia, whose career he promoted with a single-minded ruthlessness, was an accomplished poisoner and one of the darkest figures of the Italian Renaissance. Alexander himself was addicted to the promotion of the political and financial interests of his family.

His distinguished career as a vice chancellor of the Holy See and his record as a seasoned administrator cannot disguise a lifestyle of rotating mistresses, a commitment to lavish favoritism toward his children, and a worldview that is as far as can be imagined from that of, say, the celibate defender of the poor, Gregory I.

Girolamo Savanarola, a critic of the excesses of the papal court and a Dominican, was executed as a false prophet during Alexander's pontificate. Europe's long wait for a vocal proponent of reform within the Church would continue.

After Alexander

Pius III (1503) was the nephew of Pius II. He died (from the gout) just 10 days after his election.

Julius II (1503–1513) had two sides. One side was the man who energetically pursued military solutions to Italy's intricate diplomatic problems, frequently donning the armor himself and leading papal armies. The other side was the benign patron of the arts whose support extended to figures such as Bramante, Raphael, and Michelangelo.

Julius's pontificate was another worldly one, and it embodied many elements that would come under heavy and open criticism during the religious upheavals that would soon follow in Europe. It is worth noting, though, that he convened the Fifth Lateran Council, which held firmly against simony in the election of popes.

On the whole, however, it is difficult to avoid the conclusion that, in Julius, the Church was led by precisely the kind of leader who made religious revolution inevitable. His pontificate must be remembered not only for the laying of the cornerstone at St. Peter's and the commission of Michelangelo to paint the ceiling of the Sistine Chapel, but also for the stark and discomforting reality that he sold indulgences at alarmingly high levels to finance such campaigns.

Julius was the last pope with the luxury of imagining that such expedients could be managed indefinitely.

A Challenge in Germany

With the pontificate of **Leo X** (1513–1521), the mutterings against abuses in the taxation and financial systems, against the sale of indulgences, and against the excesses of the Church in other areas turned into open defiance. This defiance was eventually to become open revolt and, finally, the first successful exposition of Christianity outside of the Roman Catholic Church in the history of Western Europe.

Ultimately, this momentous event challenged, strengthened, and gave a renewed sense of identity to both the Roman Church and the papacy. At the time, however, the first expression of what would come to be called the Protestant Reformation seems to have been seen as simply the latest in a series of occasional disputes with local figures. That a controversy over indulgences would somehow transform itself into a popular new expression of Christianity, one with broad appeal in various parts of Europe, appears to have taken the papacy completely by surprise. Leo was the first and most surprised of the popes whose task it was to deal with this state of affairs.

Who Was Leo?

Elevated to the Bishopric of Rome at a fateful time in the history of the Church, Leo X would seem to have been the right man to deal with a crisis.

The son of the powerful Lorenzo de Medici, one of the wealthiest and most influential men of the era, Leo had been the beneficiary of an extraordinary classical education. At the time of his election to the papacy, he had assumed de facto rulership of the city of Florence. He was a powerful, intelligent, and well-connected man of the era—but his reign would bring unique challenges, and the truth is that Leo was not able to rise to these challenges.

Bet You Didn't Know

Julius II had summoned the Fifth Lateran Council in 1512, and during Leo X's pontificate the gathering was supposed to address the implementation of a number of critical reforms. In March of 1517, Leo made the mistake of closing the council before it had accomplished any meaningful reform work. Leo and the council had planned a new crusade against the Turks. Events in Germany, however, would intervene.

Other People's Money

Somewhat naïvely, Leo believed he could ignore calls for reform, launch a new crusade, pay for the expensive work at St. Peter's, extend the sale of indulgences still further, and hike taxes—all at roughly the same time. To use the vernacular, he went to the well once too often.

The truth is sometimes painful: Leo's own shortsightedness and talent for spending other people's money helped bring about the first trembling of opposition in an earthquake that would only later be labeled the Protestant Reformation. His lavish acquisitions led to chasms of debt for which there was no fund-raising strategy that did not alienate some key sector of the Church. This financial mismanagement and disregard of the Church's key constituencies, though not without precedent, surely did not help Leo's cause in the Europe he inherited.

Would the changes have come about eventually under other circumstances? Historians continue to debate this intricate question; it is tempting to answer yes. Two things, however, are certain: The change began, and it began during Leo's extravagant and insulated reign.

Papal People
The challenge of Martin Luther was not the only difficult moment Leo X faced in 1517; several cardinals mounted an unsuccessful conspiracy to assassinate him earlier in the same year.

Beware—History and Character Ahead

Disentangling the personalities of key figures from the fateful historical events with which they are associated is a tricky business. It is certainly a stretch to hold any single pope "responsible" for the excesses that brought on the Protestant Reformation. That having been said, however, it is also difficult to assess Leo's papacy without being struck by the smallness of the man.

There is no reason to believe that he ever fully appreciated the moral dimensions of the crisis that exploded during his pontificate; he appears to have regarded it instead as a temporary interruption of his fund-raising strategy.

The crisis in question had its beginnings when a German monk, parish priest, and intellectual named Martin Luther wrote to the Archbishop Margrave Albrecht to complain that the "wanton sale of pardons" distracted his congregation and made his job as a priest far more difficult than it should have been. Luther was opposed to the dispensation of indulgences, and he had written 95 theses (arguments) in opposition to them. Would Albrecht care to comment on them?

A Family Rift

This simple query was the beginning of the biggest rift within the western European family of Christians. Like any major family argument, it was about what it was about—and also about a great deal more.

Indulgences had an ancient pedigree; they were (and are) formal acknowledgments of absolution from sin, drawing on the Treasury of Merit regarded as having been bestowed by Christ and the saints on the Church. Granted in exchange for prayers or penitential actions, they had also been used as a reward to those who joined the Crusades. By the time of Leo X, indulgences had indeed taken on a disturbing character; their sale for money had become an important source of Church revenue. This system often left the clergy bearing too close a resemblance to cheerful, pious conmen for Luther's comfort. Abuses related to indulgences were widespread, and these abuses were to be the subject of much attention.

The indulgences that first drew Luther's ire, for instance, were scraps of parchment purchased by his parishioners that had guaranteed not only their own deliverance from purgatory, but also the salvation of errant grandparents. Quite a bargain. Luther rejected the notion that believers could be, as one term of the day had it, "justified" in this manner.

But the conflict over indulgences was only a beginning.

Bet You Didn't Know

The momentous question of justification lay at the heart of the religious revolution that shook Western Christianity in the sixteenth century; the early conflicts over indulgences were precursors of the larger question in dispute. Were people justified—that is, saved and reconciled with God—solely as the result of divine grace and their own faith? Luther and his allies said yes, arguing that this state did not and could not arise from the actions or good works of human beings.

Time for a Housecleaning

The Church was ripe for reform, and had not been the beneficiary of it for more than two and a half centuries.

The moral slackness evident in the sale of indulgences had taken root in countless other ways. Clerical appointments were often disgraceful, placing unqualified men in spiritual authority over the laity for long periods. (In the middle of the sixteenth century, more than half of the clergy in one region could not recall all Ten Commandments, and a few could not say who had composed the Lord's Prayer.) Scandals involving supposedly celibate members of the clergy were distressingly common. And the popes, who had become fixated on the construction of great buildings and other campaigns, had also become fixated on raising the money necessary to pay for them. Leo was, as we have seen, a prime example.

"Semper Reformanda"

There is a saying, "semper reformanda," that captures in two words what English requires a few more to get across. The phrase means, "The Church is ever in need of reform." Because the popes in general, and Leo in particular, had neglected the responsibility for initiating reform for far too long, it fell to another man to launch the intellectual attack that would finally initiate change for the better—as well as war, schism, and political intrigue.

Cheat Sheet: Luther Under Leo X

- **1513:** A spiritual crisis in which Luther faced grave fears regarding his own salvation was resolved by deep personal study of the epistles of St. Paul, and the resulting conviction that salvation is the result of faith, not of the works of men.

- **1516:** Luther began arguing against abuses in the dispensation of indulgences.

- **1517:** Following a visit to Germany by the Dominican John Tetzel promoting the sale of indulgences, Luther dissented—thus launching and naming a movement—by posting his 95 theses (arguments) on the great door of the Wittenberg Castle Church. Luther's theses denounced the sale of indulgences and supported German control of Church affairs in his homeland. They were a direct assault on papal authority.

- **1517–1520:** Attempts at reconciling Luther to the Church's position failed.

continues

---

continued

- ◆ **1520:** Pope Leo X issued a bull of condemnation against Luther, who promptly burned it publicly and widened his attack, condemning the pope as an Antichrist and his court as "the synagogue of Satan."

- ◆ **1521:** Leo excommunicated Luther, who was later condemned at the *Diet of Worms*. According to tradition, Luther concluded his defense with these words: "Here I stand. I cannot do otherwise. God help me. Amen."

Why Did Luther Thrive?

Leo's excommunication of Luther and condemnation of him as a heretic brought support for the pope in some, but not all, quarters. The movement Luther had initiated soon had strong support, particularly in the north of Europe, and the man Leo had dismissed as "a wild boar" received the protection and support of a number of powerful political figures.

Vatican Vocabulary

The **Diet of Worms** (1521) was summoned by Charles V, the Holy Roman emperor, to address (among other matters) the turmoil initiated by Martin Luther. Luther arrived under imperial protection and steadfastly refused to compromise in his condemnation of the pope, the General Council, and the sale of indulgences.

Immediately after he was ordered seized by the Diet of Worms, Luther secured the protection of Elector Frederick III of Saxony and began work on a German translation of the Holy Scriptures.

Matters of political protection aside, Luther's protests had resonated with many believers. He was forcing issues that many clearly felt deserved to be forced, and that the papacy itself had failed to address.

Pontifical ... but Mythical

Leo X has been derided as a faithless pope, or even an atheist, based on a strange and much-circulated remark attributed to him: "What profit has not that **fable** of Christ brought us!" The quote apparently did not surface, however, until some years after Leo's death, and it is disputed by many.

The Verdict on Leo

A better, less vindictive, more farsighted leader than Leo X might have handled the crisis differently. He might have done more to ensure progress on some kind of reform at the Fifth Lateran Council, a step that could have kept Luther's initial attack from snowballing as impressively as it did. A great pope might also have been less inclined to alienate vast swaths of Europe by viewing the act of spending money as a sacred obligation.

It is impossible to separate Leo's papacy from the emergence of the revolt that became the Protestant Revolution, despite Leo's preference that his reign be remembered for its patronage of artists, its great buildings, and its surpassing (and dearly bought) splendor.

Leo is said to have once issued what may have been a tongue-in-cheek quip: "God has given us the papacy; let us enjoy it." By most accounts, there were to follow many, many times when he and his successors would not enjoy the unquestioned authority of the office in quite the same way it had been enjoyed in years past.

Until the Reformation, the popes had been able to suppress dissidents such as Luther with intimidation, whether subtle or overt. But something

> ### Papal People
>
> Desiderius Erasmus (ca. 1466–1536) was a gifted Dutch intellectual who supported reform but remained loyal to the Church, choosing to stand in opposition to the Protestant Reformation. He and Martin Luther were rivals.

had changed. A certain segment of the population would eventually determine that it was quite willing to die for the new movement that came to be known as Protestantism. Surely this was an indication of both the deep and enduring appeal of Christianity and the alienation its formal expression had managed to engender in certain sections of the continent. That both Catholics and Protestants would die in the disputes that followed Leo's reign must be reckoned one of the tragedies of the faith.

It would be years before the papacy would respond constructively to Luther's challenge. Once it did, however, a new, vital, and morally strengthened Church would emerge.

The Least You Need to Know

- ◆ At a time when Europe was ready for a strong, reform-minded, and morally firm voice, the papacy instead produced Innocent VII and Alexander VI.
- ◆ Papal accomplishments in diplomacy and in the patronage of the arts were accompanied by a continued neglect of the spiritual dimensions of the office during this period.
- ◆ Leo X closed the Fifth Lateran Council before it could address meaningful reforms.
- ◆ Abuses related to the granting of indulgences led Martin Luther to protest in Germany, launching what would later be known as the Protestant Reformation.
- ◆ Under Leo X, Luther's calls for reform resonated in a new and unexpected way in certain parts of Europe.

Chapter 15

Rift and Reformations

In This Chapter

- ◆ Luther after Leo X
- ◆ Trouble with kings and emperors
- ◆ Catholicism's long-delayed response to calls for reform
- ◆ The founding of the Society of Jesus (the Jesuits)
- ◆ Riots in Rome
- ◆ Delay—and triumph—at Trent

Two momentous reform movements affecting Christianity in Western Europe were born during the sixteenth century. The first was that of the Protestants; the second was that of the Roman Catholic Church.

The popes of this tumultuous period found themselves forced to come to grips with a new and confusing world, and their efforts to make sense of it led, ultimately, to the initiation of a forceful and long-overdue campaign of formally sanctioned reform within the Church. It had been a long time coming, but when it arrived, it changed Catholicism irrevocably … and increased the power of the papacy.

Welcome to Chaos, Your Holiness

Adrian VI (1522–1523) inherited the crisis initiated by Luther under Leo X, and his response was to issue a series of heartfelt but ultimately ineffective appeals for Luther's arrest and the suppression of his teachings. The papacy, which had only recently been a silencer of the voices of reform, had rarely looked quite so helpless in the face of doctrines it had loudly pronounced as heresies.

Adrian was the only Dutch pope—and the last non-Italian pope for 456 years. He had been the tutor of the future Holy Roman emperor, Charles V.

As pope, Adrian tried to cope with the escalating religious chaos of the period, and (to his credit) to lessen the extravagant level of papal expenditures, which had become the scandal of Europe. His reign, however, lasted only 20 months.

Adrian's successor, **Clement VII** (1523–1534), was next to preside over the troubles brewing in Germany. He was made bishop and cardinal by his cousin, Pope Leo X. Clement, who continued the papacy's historic patronage of great artists, also conducted a series of political and diplomatic intrigues that annoyed Charles V, the Holy Roman emperor.

Charles's resulting sack of Rome (1527) was a disaster Clement had not anticipated. The pope took refuge in Castel Sant'Angelo, but eventually surrendered to the emperor. After doing so, however, he managed to escape, but the invasion had been a costly one on all fronts, and Charles was to exert decisive influence in the period that followed.

During what proved to be an ominously eventful pontificate (at least in terms of conflicts with powerful heads of state), Clement at first vacillated with, and then opposed, Henry VIII of England in his divorce petitions. He had little choice, inasmuch as the powerful Charles V was the nephew of Katharine of Aragon, whom Henry wanted to divorce. Clement was thus caught between two powerful and intransigent men.

He found himself unable to prevent challenges from the English king that would have been unthinkable in previous years. Something strange and (to the Church) disconcerting was definitely afoot in Christendom. The monarchs, like a good portion of the populace, were not behaving.

Beyond Paintings and Sculptures

The complex and distracting crises with Charles and Henry consumed much of the energy of Clement's pontificate, and as a result Luther's movement continued to gain strength in Europe. The paintings and sculptures he commissioned, however, were extraordinary. Yet one senses that forces within the Church were quickly reaching the conclusion that, given the threats faced by the Church, even the sponsorship of master-pieces was not enough.

One man who reached such a conclusion was St. Ignatius of Loyola.

Papal People
Raphael and Michelangelo both created important works commissioned by Clement VII.

Papal Foot Soldiers

It was during Clement's reign that Ignatius founded the Society of Jesus, better known as the Jesuits. They would become the all-important foot soldiers in the movement to challenge heresy and reform the Church that was taking shape during this period.

The Jesuits, whose careful organization and unswerving dedication to the pope would become their distinguishing characteristics, would bring unprecedented intensity to the task of implementing constructive change within the Church. They also established Catholic educational institutions, and launched essential missionary efforts.

They were, in years to come, to become both the papacy's chief defenders and a focus of exceptional intellectual achievement within the Church.

The Man Who Knew What to Do

Paul III (1534–1549) was a far better diplomat than Clement. He was nevertheless compelled to see through to the end the now-beyond-resolution clash with Henry VIII of England.

He ordered the excommunication of the king. This was followed shortly in England by the brisk transfer of the pope's authority to the king, and a formal break with the papacy.

Bet You Didn't Know

Rome's refusal to grant an annulment of Henry VIII's marriage to Katharine of Aragon resulted in Henry's pronouncement of the Act of Supremacy, which established the king as the leader of the Church of England. Mary I (1553–1558) reigned during a brief period of communion with Rome, but an independent Church of England was restored with the rise of Elizabeth I.

Paul's legacy is not, however, to be found in the painful controversy with Henry. It was Paul who formulated the first truly constructive papal response to the Protestant movement by summoning the all-important Council of Trent.

Papal People

"(I)f we term the doctor of Wittenberg (Martin Luther) a mystic, we may sum up John Calvin as a scholastic; he gives articulate expression to the principles which Luther had stormily thrown out upon the world in his vehement pamphleteering; and the *Institutes* as they were left by their author have remained ever since the standard of orthodox Protestant belief in all the churches known as 'Reformed.'"

—*The Catholic Encyclopedia.* Herbermann and Pace, editors. (New York: Appleton, 1907–1912.)

This reform council was literally centuries overdue. It convened in 1545, but did not conclude its work during Paul's lifetime. (The first of several extended holdups in its proceedings arose following a swirl of rumors that the plague was about to sweep Trent.) Regardless of its duration, its contemporary critics, and its staggering delays, Trent was to prove a fateful and important step in the history of Catholicism. It is impossible to imagine the development of the modern Catholic Church without this council, which implemented long-overdue clerical reforms and clarified important questions concerning Scripture, the Mass, and the sacraments, as well as many other issues.

Paul presided over Church affairs competently, calmly, and intelligently during a particularly difficult period. He frankly opposed the Protestant movement, and formally recognized the new Jesuit order. He was, like his recent predecessors, a notable patron of the arts. He presided during what must have seemed interminable periods of challenge, discord, and controversy. (The

Protestant reformer John Calvin, for instance, published his *Institutes of the Christian Religion* during Paul's reign.)

Julius III (1550–1555) summoned the suspended Council of Trent back to its work in 1551, only to suspend it in 1552 when conflict over political and religious matters led to utter chaos in Europe. The high point of his pontificate was his confirmation of the Jesuit constitution in 1550.

Marcellus II (1555) had been made cardinal in 1539; he served honorably as a legate during the early years at the Council of Trent. There he did valuable work on far-seeing conciliar decrees relating to scripture, tradition, and the difficult question of justification. When he was elected pope, those who were eager for reform felt that their hour had come around at last. But after only 22 days in office, Marcellus died in his sleep.

And Then There Was Paul

When the congenitally suspicious **Paul IV** (1555–1559) died, a wave of hooliganism swept Rome. The unrest served as a measure of the loathing the citizens of the city felt against the pope and his family.

What had he done to merit such popular disfavor? In addition to the relatively common practice of promoting relatives to high office, he had stepped up the activities of the Inquisition and turned a blind eye to the overreaching and high-handed behavior of a particularly abusive nephew. This was Carlo Carafa, who quickly earned a reputation as a tyrant when Paul came to power. He was assumed, naturally enough, to be acting with the Pope's knowledge and approval, but given what followed, it seems fair to assume that Paul was kept in the dark regarding his nephew's more aggressive predations.

This, when combined with Paul's past history (he had led the Inquisition), explains the waves of rioting that accompanied Paul's death, but it does not give us a particularly clear picture of the man himself. A clearer portrait emerges when we note that Paul nursed a habitual loathing of the Spanish; one good way to secure his good faith appears to have been to plot against the Spanish monarchy. Certainly this was Carafa's pattern: He urged the pope to confront the Spaniards. He rejected the notion of *cuius regia, eius religio* (loosely translated, this means "He who rules the state may select its religion"). The concept had been a centerpiece of the carefully negotiated Peace of Augsburg (1555), and had finally brought peace to Germany—but it was rejected as inimical to papal interests.

> **Pope Watch**
>
> Carlo Carafa was a cruel and apparently avaricious nephew of Paul III's whom the pope raised (unwisely) to the rank of cardinal.

Papal People

The respected reformer Cardinal Morone was incarcerated on tenuous allegations of heresy under Paul IV. Later released, he helped to bring the long-delayed Council of Trent to a completion of its work.

This settlement, negotiated without papal approval, smarted, and it laid the groundwork for Carafa's agitation for a disastrous campaign in alliance with the French against the Spanish in 1557.

Eventually, Paul came to understand his nephew's corruption, though not, perhaps, his own tendency toward paranoia. He turned on Carafa, stripped him and his allies of their positions, and had the whole group exiled. The reversal, however, seems to have done little to improve the pope's standing in Rome.

The soap operatics involving an errant nephew, his allies, and plots against the Spanish obscure the larger historical question one is tempted to use to measure the popes of this era: How did the reform movement fare under Paul IV? The unfortunate answer is: not well at all. It was under his pontificate that the Council of Trent endured its second extended delay. He simply had no concern for its objectives of clerical reform and general renewal of the Church.

If Paul's was an era of moral and organizational reformation for the Church, it was a strange brand of reform indeed. His approach to housecleaning embraced repression of beggars, prostitutes, and Jews (who suffered particularly galling injustices under his pontificate); the imprisonment, on the flimsiest suspicions, of various members of the clergy; and the development and maintenance of a banned-book list. Indeed, the *Roman Index of Prohibited Books*, a summary document whose first promulgation forbade absurdly vast stretches of the intellectual landscape, is Paul's chief legacy. In its initial form, the *Index* deemed inappropriate virtually any writing the pope considered insufficiently Catholic.

For the most part, Paul lived in a surrealistic and almost entirely imaginary world in which enemies lurked everywhere (except where they actually did—namely, in his own family). To modern-day American observers, his pontificate resembles nothing so much as a nightmare scenario under which Joseph McCarthy somehow secured the presidency. So much energy; so little of it expended toward the common good. Paul didn't quite make the cut in Chapter 5, "Ten to Forget: Popes Who Shouldn't Have Been," but we can safely consider him the first runner-up.

The all-but-abandoned Council of Trent posted a longer period of complete inaction under Paul than under any other pope. It would be left to Paul's predecessor to reconvene it and rescue the cause of internal reform.

Pius Picks Up the Pieces

Pius IV (1559–1565) clearly saw the errors of his predecessor and set about attempting to rectify them. Cardinal Morone was set at liberty and transformed from outcast to papal ally; the list of forbidden reading materials was scaled back to manageable dimensions (thus reinstating, for instance, harmless primers on grammar); and dealings with the Spanish monarchy were set on a new and more realistic foundation. Most important of all, it was during Pius's pontificate that the final push was administered at the on-again, off-again Council of Trent. Its work was finally completed under Pius.

Vatican Vocabulary

The term **Tridentine reforms** refers to the work of the Council of Trent.

Pius's considerable diplomatic skills were necessary not only to reconvene the council, but also to nudge it persistently toward a new vision of the Church, one that put to constructive use some of the most painful attacks of the Protestants on Catholic practice. This was Pius's—and the papacy's—triumph during a period that had heretofore seen its fair share of setback and defeat (see Chapter 5).

Other popes would be remembered for enforcing and extending the holdings of Trent; Pius should be better remembered for bringing them about in the first place. He guided a quarrelsome and divided council through often-treacherous waters, and refused to take abandonment, complacency, or acceptance of the status quo as answers to the extraordinary challenges of the day.

Finally—A Reform-Minded Council

The long-delayed, seemingly forsaken Council of Trent concluded its work in 1562. It addressed both matters of outmoded doctrine and day-to-day improvement of Church policy. Its pronouncements would resonate down the centuries.

Cheat Sheet: The Council of Trent

The Council of Trent (1545–1547, 1551–1552, 1562–1563) expounded the following reforms:

◆ Clarification of formal points of doctrine related to justification, purgatory, the sacraments, transubstantiation, and other issues. (Trent erased many archaic notions from the Middle Ages and clearly addressed important questions of faith that had been raised during the turmoil unleashed by the Protestants.)

◆ Prohibition of the sale of indulgences.

continues

continued

◆ Establishment of new approaches to educating the clergy.

◆ Issuance of a clear call for the responsible fulfillment of pastoral duties, and for the clergy to live morally upright lives.

The Council of Trent served as a moral turning point for the Church and a reinvigoration of the papacy, for it was the popes who were empowered to implement its reforms. This was due in no small measure to the influence of the Jesuits during the council. Thus, the papacy, an institution that had not long before come under attack from proponents of the conciliar theory, reasserted itself briskly.

Catholic Reformation

The long period that saw the implementation of the reforms of Trent has often been referred to as the Counter-Reformation, but many Catholics reject this term.

Papal People

Pius's nephew was St. Charles Borromeo; he was pressed into the pope's service and became a key figure in the initial enforcement of the measures approved by the Council of Trent.

This is understandable, since "Counter-Reformation" suggests, vaguely but incorrectly, that no reform instinct preceded the religious movement that came to be known as the Protestant Reformation. A more appropriate label for the work initiated by the Council of Trent is Catholic Reformation.

After centuries of delay, suspicion, distraction, and neglect—maladies that had been pervasive enough to breed a permanent schism in Christendom—the Church had broken its fever. It had finally redeemed its historical role by embracing a series of measures oriented toward Christianity's "true north," measures that the greatest popes in its history would surely have welcomed with faith and enthusiasm.

This was indeed a new beginning, the initiation of a phase that would come to be identified with the modern Roman Catholic Church. And the most fateful breakthrough had occurred under Pius's leadership.

Perhaps even more important than Pius's patient insistence on progress at Trent had been his rejection of the pattern of obsessive, vindictive (and, not infrequently, violent) suspiciousness notable in his predecessor.

No rioters surged through Rome when Pius IV, who had nursed the Church through its fever, succumbed to fever himself in December 1565. This may seem a backhanded compliment, but it is in fact high praise. A very different, and possibly much more brittle, Church might well have emerged if the faithful had been asked to endure two consecutive Paul IVs.

What Now?

Reconvening and overseeing the Council of Trent had been extraordinary and essential achievements. But it had yielded only a blueprint for change. How would the building itself be constructed?

Pius's successors would inherit the difficult task of turning Trent's powerful and cleansing vision into reality. They would do so in very different ways.

The Least You Need to Know

- ◆ The first pope to make a constructive response to the challenge of the Protestant Reformation was Paul III, who summoned the Council of Trent.
- ◆ St. Ignatius of Loyola founded the Society of Jesus, or Jesuits, establishing a group that would come to be strongly identified with the papacy and with the Catholic Reformation.
- ◆ Owing to various staggering delays and the ambivalence of the fearsome and vindictive Paul IV, the Council of Trent could easily have failed.
- ◆ The blueprint for reform was completed during the pontificate of Pius IV, one of history's most underrated popes.
- ◆ Thanks to the influence of the Jesuits, responsibility for implementation of the reforms of Trent was left with the papacy, thus strengthening an institution that had not long before come under attack from proponents of the conciliar theory.

Part  4

After Trent

In this part of the book, you'll learn about the development of the Roman Catholic Church after the Council of Trent.

Here, you'll learn how the papacy responded to the task of implementing the edicts of Trent—and to growing political challenges in Europe.

Chapter 16

Building a New Church

In This Chapter

- The popes embrace reform—and consolidate their own authority within the Church
- Pius V and the triumph of piety
- Sixtus V gets things done
- Turmoil and conflict in France
- Rebellion in Bohemia

To the nine popes who followed Pius IV fell the task of reinventing a Church that had become mired in habit, excess, and complacency.

Forcefully reasserting their authority, the pontiffs of this era took differing approaches to the twin tasks of implementing the reforms of Trent and winning back influence (and believers) from Protestantism.

A Matter of Principle

An ally of St. Charles Borromeo, **St. Pius V** (1566–1572), succeeded Pius IV.

The new pope was a model of personal rectitude and piety, and a perfectly logical and appropriate choice to lead the Church after the Council of Trent. Logical and appropriate choices had not always been forthcoming from the

College of Cardinals over the past century (the elevation of the corrupt Alexander VI and the free-spending Leo X in recent years being cases in point). The election of a Dominican noted for his austerity, his dedication to both the letter and the spirit of the Tridentine reforms, and his sincere personal commitment to aid the sick and the poor was thus a welcome development.

What Happened When

- ◆ **1566:** Calvinism was strong in the Netherlands.
- ◆ **1588:** The Spanish Armada was defeated.
- ◆ **1593:** Henry IV of France became a Catholic.
- ◆ **1598:** The Edict of Nates protected the rights of French Protestants.
- ◆ **1611:** Jesuits journeyed to Peking.

Pope Watch

St. Pius V is, as of this writing, the last papal saint until St. Pius X (reigned 1903–1914). Reforms in the process of canonization have made it more difficult than in centuries past for popes (or anyone else) to be named a saint.

Pope Watch

The foreign-policy high point of Pius V's pontificate was his establishment of an alliance against the Turkish fleet at Lepanto, in Greece, which resulted in a major victory and put an end to the period of Turkish naval influence in the Mediterranean.

Here, indeed, was evidence of transformation: The Church had swiftly put the noble ideals of the recent council to good use at the very first papal conclave that followed it.

Pius V made implementing the decrees of Trent a matter of personal principle, and his vigorous work in this regard ensured that the Council's accomplishments would take the form of sustained change "on the ground." The curbing of clerical abuses and the enforcement of morally rigorous discipline at all levels of the Church would not take place quickly, but it would, this pontificate proved, be the direction mandated by the papacy as an institution, and not by a single individual.

This pope certainly made his share of errors. The choice to excommunicate Queen Elizabeth I of England, for instance, led to a wave of reprisals against English Catholics that Pius should have foreseen and avoided, and the policy toward heretical movements was at times excessively strict.

On the whole, though, Pius's pontificate was the tonic Catholicism desperately needed: equal parts moral vision, piousness, determination, and a willingness to take the initiative once again in Europe.

Pius V Endorses the Rosary (1569)

Pius explains the traditional origin of the Rosary ("as [it] is piously believed").

"The Roman Pontiffs, and the other Holy Fathers, our predecessors, when they were pressed in upon by temporal or spiritual wars, or troubled by other trials, in order that they might more easily escape from these, and having achieved tranquillity, might quietly and fervently be free to devote themselves to God, were wont to implore the divine assistance, through supplications or Litanies to call forth the support of the saints, and with David to lift up their eyes unto the mountains, trusting with firm hope that thence would they receive aid.

"Prompted by their example, and, as is piously believed, by the Holy Ghost, the inspired Blessed founder of the Order of Friars Preachers ... raised his eyes up unto heaven, unto that mountain of the Glorious Virgin Mary, loving Mother of God. For she by her seed has crushed the head of the twisted serpent, and has alone destroyed all heresies, and by the blessed fruit of her womb has saved a world condemned by the fall of our first parent ....

"And so Dominic looked to that simple way of praying and beseeching God, accessible to all and wholly pious, which is called the Rosary, or Psalter of the Blessed Virgin Mary, in which the same most Blessed Virgin is venerated by the angelic greeting repeated 150 times, that is, according to the number of the Davidic Psalter, and by the Lord's Prayer with each decade ....

"This same method St. Dominic propagated ... following the example of our predecessors, seeing that the Church militant, which God has placed in our hands, in these our times is tossed this way and that by so many heresies, and is grievously troubled, troubled and afflicted by so many wars, and by the depraved morals of men, we also raise our eyes, weeping but full of hope, unto that same mountain, whence every aid comes forth, and we encourage and admonish each member of Christ's faithful to do likewise in the Lord."

—Pope Pius V, *Apostolic Constitution on Praying the Rosary*, 1569.

The Times, They Are a-Changin'

Gregory XIII (1572–1585) is today remembered primarily for his implementation of the current calendar system, known in his honor as the Gregorian system.

Gregory continued the process of papal agitation for the reforms of the Council of Trent (he had been an important member of the council), and was deeply concerned with questions relating to education and missionary work, supporting Jesuit efforts in both Asia and the north of Europe. He made proselytizing the faith among Protestants an important priority.

Pontifical ... but Mythical

Gregory XIII's supposedly heartless reaction to news of the St. Bartholomew's Day Massacre has been misrepresented in various ways over the years. He had been informed that a Protestant rebellion had been repulsed in France.

Gregory's reputation has suffered in connection with his reaction to the Saint Bartholomew's Day Massacre; he ordered public thanksgiving and the playing of grateful hymns after receiving word that thousands of Huguenots (French Protestants) had been killed in France in 1572. This shorthand version of the event, however, does not do it full justice. Gregory was under the impression that some new Protestant rebellion had just been put down in Paris. The true nature of the violence—wanton butchery of thousands of innocent people, instigated by Catherine de Medici—was not immediately apparent.

Papal rejoicing in carnage of any kind can hardly be seen as a high point of the period, but the gesture associated with Gregory is not quite as heartless as it has sometimes been made to appear.

Bet You Didn't Know

The Saint Bartholomew's Day Massacre took place during the Wars of Religion, a bloody series of civil conflicts in France that involved the right of French Protestants to practice their religion. Controversy also swirled, as it tended to do during disputes of the period, around political issues only tangentially related to the conflict between Protestants and Catholics. The Wars of Religion raged between 1562 and 1598.

It is true, however, that the Catholic Reformation took on a more combative and militaristic air under Gregory, which may have been one of the reasons the truncated version of the story stuck.

The One They Remember

After more than 12 years in office, Gregory died at the age of 82; a few weeks later, **Sixtus V** (1585–1590) assumed the papal throne. Sixtus was to become the most renowned of the popes of the Catholic Reformation (see Chapter 4, "Ten to Remember: Popes Who Made a Difference").

Sixtus was an energetic, forbidding figure who brought to office all of the energy—and, truth be told, some of the ruthless intolerance—of the late, unlamented Paul IV. However, unlike the pope who nearly ignored the Council of Trent out of existence, Sixtus combined his aggressive managerial style with vision, a passion for efficiency, and a knack for improving systems. He was a man in love with getting things done.

Sixtus, like many of his predecessors, had no difficulty detecting enemies, and he certainly identified any quantity of them in the Protestant movement. He encouraged Catholic powers to take arms against what Rome identified as heretical insurgencies, and was an enthusiastic supporter of the Spanish Armada.

Sixtus used extreme (but effective) measures to curb crime sprees in Rome. The impossible-to-ignore strategy of posting the severed heads of offenders in public places may be distasteful to modern sensibilities, but it was definitely not without precedent, and—what mattered most to Sixtus—it worked. Focusing on what worked was to be a hallmark of his papacy; he took a similarly pragmatic, furious, and effective approach in his policy toward unruly parties who questioned his authority in the Papal States.

Vatican Vocabulary

The **Spanish Armada** was a naval campaign launched by the Spanish against the English in 1588 in the hope of overthrowing the Protestant Queen Elizabeth I and placing King Philip II of Spain on her throne. The assault failed.

Along similar lines, but more clearly connected to the reform efforts now strongly associated with the papacy, Sixtus made it clear that he meant business when it came to enforcing strictures related to clerical celibacy. It was hard not to take seriously a pontiff who instituted the death penalty against religious who had abused their vows of chastity.

Sixtus was also the first pope whose campaign to beautify Rome went out of its way to embrace—rather than distract from or paper over—the city's extraordinary history. Previous pontificates appeared to have viewed Rome's now-ancient "pagan" heritage as some kind of invitation to heresy; Sixtus, in stark contrast, moved the obelisk of the Circus of Nero into the middle of St. Peter's Square. He embarked upon a campaign of construction, renewal, and restoration the like of which had rarely been seen in Rome, which is saying something.

He appears to have viewed buildings and memorials not merely as civic improvements, but also as impressive subjects for his own public relations campaigns. Several contemporary engravings show the pope surrounded by illustrations symbolizing the achievements of his reign; most of them are exquisite buildings.

A master politician, Sixtus leaned on the College of Cardinals, setting an upper limit for its membership and delegating important business to various small subgroups within it, the better to avoid showdowns with the body as a whole.

He also brought a new efficiency and energy to the complex matter of papal finances. By the end of his pontificate, he had completely reformed financial practices, and a massive surplus resided in the treasury. If the manner by which Sixtus had accomplished this—levying new taxes, selling Church offices, plundering the resources of the Papal States—were not always clearly supported by the mantle of reform he had inherited, the methods were, as usual, too successful for most to quibble with.

Sixtus had held office for only five years. In that short time, this supremely gifted, energetic Franciscan had worked relentlessly, cut corners only when it seemed prudent to do so, and reclaimed the sense of vigorous, efficient, and more-often-than-not principled administration of authority that had been missing in the papacy for generations. He would not soon be forgotten.

> **Pope Watch**
>
> "Of all the popes of the century, (Sixtus V) came nearest to fulfilling the programme of Nicholas V, to make the external face of Rome mirror the spiritual greatness of the papacy."
>
> —Eamon Duffy, *Saints and Sinners: A History of the Popes* (New Haven: Yale University Press, 1997)

A Break in the Action

Then, as though the maelstrom of activity had been too much for the rest of the world to keep up with, there followed a series of mini-pontificates. The faithful may have suspected that it would be difficult to find someone who could follow in Sixtus's footsteps, but it seems unlikely that anyone could have predicted that an odd sequence of well-meaning but short-lived popes would follow Sixtus's remarkable reign.

Urban VII (1590) was a kind and sympathetic man whose election appeared to mark a return to the tradition of deep papal commitment to improving the lot of the poor. When Urban became pope, he asked the pastors of Rome to make him a list of the needy in their parishes. Next, he ordered bakers to keep the price of bread low, and vowed that he would make up any loss they might suffer as a result of lowering the cost. Hopes were high that he would live to conduct a great pontificate, but within three days of his election he was struck down with malaria (a not-uncommon disease in Europe during this period that was thought to result from stagnant air, but that is in fact transmitted by mosquitoes). He did not live a month after his election.

Gregory XIV (1590–1591) was a man of deep piety with little experience in political and diplomatic affairs. When he became pope his health was poor. He worked hard to further the era of discipline and vigor that had been consolidated under Sixtus V, but, like his predecessor, he simply didn't have time to accomplish much. His health soon failed him completely, and he died just over a year after his election.

The bad luck continued with **Innocent IX** (1591), who reigned for only two months before he, too, became ill and died. He had hoped to offer relief to the poor.

Leadership at Last

Finally, with the election of **Clement VIII** (1592–1605), the cardinals selected a leader willing and (physically) able to extend the work done by Sixtus V. As a contemporary observer noted, "The electors had been impelled towards that choice, not only by the esteem in which they held Cardinal Aldobrandini, but also from his being only 56 years old; for all the cardinals observed that they had had to deplore the death of three pontiffs whose united reigns had occupied only 16 months." (Source—*The Lives and Times of the Popes* by The Chevalier Artaud De Montor. New York: The Catholic Publication Society of New York, 1911.)

Clement repaired relations with the French throne following the conversion of Henry of Navarre to Catholicism. Clement also worked hard to further improve education and discipline within the clergy and to support charitable efforts in Rome. His attention to practical matters of worship was also notable. Clement ordered a revised publication of the Vulgate, the standard Latin Bible, and revised the *breviary* and the *missal*.

Clement's pontificate would be remembered for momentous diplomatic and political events, for the continuation of the pattern of internal reform, and for the pope's own personal piety. It would also, however, be remembered for the persecution of the free-thinking philosopher Giordano Bruno, who was executed as a heretic in 1600.

Pope Watch
During Clement's pontificate, the Edict of Nantes brought an end to the Wars of Religion in France and clarified the civil and religious rights of French Protestants.

Vatican Vocabulary

A **breviary** is a book of prayers, psalms, hymns, prayers, readings, and similar material to be recited daily during Mass or as part of other ceremonies. A **missal** is a book containing the prayers and other rites for a priest to deliver at the altar during Mass over the course of an entire ecclesiastical year.

Papal People
Giordano Bruno, an Italian philosopher of the sixteenth century, incorporated elements of Gnosticism within his writings and denied the existence of a single objective, knowable truth. Many of his ideas astonishingly prefigured modern scientific notions. He was executed for heresy in 1600.

A Well-Known Family, a Brief Pontificate

Leo XI (1605) was a member of the de Medici clan and a grandnephew of Leo X. He would probably have continued the famous family's traditional patronage of literature and the arts had he lived to conduct an extended pontificate. On the day of his coronation, however, he caught a cold and died within a month.

During his short reign, he managed to lower taxes and send help to Hungarian forces struggling against the Turks.

Fresh Turmoil Looms

Paul V (1605–1621) led the Church during a time of great upheaval for the Church in Europe.

Vatican Vocabulary

Gallicanism refers to the long tradition of French opposition to papal authority that preceded Paul V's pontificate and persisted through the nineteenth century. It is often contrasted with **Ultramontanism,** the belief that the pope exerts final authority over all matters arising within the Church.

The Kingdom of Naples and the Venetian Republic were, he felt, violating the rights of the clergy; Paul took energetic steps to defend the prerogatives of the papacy, but was ultimately overcome there. Disputes also arose with King James I of England and with the French Church, where a hardy strain of *Gallicanism* proved as troublesome as it had in years past.

Paul was a patron of arts and literature; he added substantially to the collection of books and manuscripts at the Vatican library. He commissioned the building of the chapel in the Basilica of Santa Maria Maggiore in Rome, and he oversaw the completion, at long last, of St. Peter's Basilica in Rome.

Paul was also keenly interested in the advancement of missionary work, which was becoming an increasingly important component of the Church's mission.

Pope Watch

Paul proved an astute internal diplomat, ironing out a dispute between the Dominicans and the Jesuits over the issue of grace. The pope held that each order was entitled to its own opinion.

A Scientist Asks the Pope for Clarification

Paul was also the recipient of a series of obsessive requests from an oddly persistent scientist who appeared to be fixated on the question of whether the earth revolved around the sun or vice versa.

As a diplomat of the day reported in a letter, "Galileo insisted on obtaining from the pope and the Holy Office a declaration that the system of Copernicus (which held that that the earth revolved around the sun) was founded on the Scriptures. He haunted the antechambers of the court and the palaces of the cardinals; he composed memorial after memorial. Galileo thought more of his own opinions than of those of his friends. After having persecuted and wearied many other cardinals, he at length won over Cardinal Orsini. The latter, with more warmth than prudence, urged His Holiness to favor the wishes of Galileo. The pope, tiring of the conversation, broke it off. Galileo carried into all these proceedings an extreme heat, which he had neither the strength nor the prudence to control. He might throw us all into great embarrassment, and I cannot see what he is likely to gain by a longer stay here." (Copernicus, it should be noted, had died in 1543.)

The conflict between the Church and Galileo Galilei would play out to its grim conclusion under another pope; Paul had no time for him.

Trouble in Bohemia

None of these remarkable happenings, however, would prove as disturbing as a strange and bitter brawl that broke out in Bohemia (present-day western Czechoslovakia) in 1618, near the end of Paul's reign.

It must have seemed at first like little more than a round of shoving and boasting: Two men were thrown from a window in the building where the Bohemian diet was being held, and shortly thereafter the Catholic King Ferdinand was declared deposed. Was this a riot? A skirmish? Something more? To Paul, the very idea of a Catholic prince being deposed must have been ludicrous, but he and the rest of Europe watched as the brawl turned into open rebellion. Before long, the Holy Roman Empire was in arms to defend the Catholic monarch's claim.

Three decades of bloody struggle between Catholics and Protestants were to follow that disturbance in Prague.

The Least You Need to Know

♦ The pontiffs after Pius IV took differing approaches to the twin tasks of implementing the reforms of Trent and winning back influence (and believers) from Protestantism.

♦ Pius V brought to his office deep personal piety and a commitment to implementing the reforms of Trent.

♦ Sixtus V conducted a vigorous and pragmatic papacy, and is considered a major figure of the Catholic Reformation.

♦ During Clement VIII's pontificate, the Edict of Nantes brought an end to the Wars of Religion in France and clarified the civil and religious rights of French Protestants.

♦ Near the end of Paul V's reign, ominous religious turmoil erupted in Bohemia.

Chapter 17

An Unfamiliar World

In This Chapter

- ◆ The Thirty Years' War
- ◆ The conflict with Galileo
- ◆ Quarrels with the French monarchy

Violent religious and political upheavals of a particularly intense variety unfolded in Europe during the seventeenth century. When this chaos finally played out, France was the power to be reckoned with.

The popes of this period, while enjoying primacy at Rome, had to contend with an unruly monarchy, a steady decline in political influence, and an increasingly complex outside world that often seemed disinclined to obey pronouncements from the Holy See. For the popes, it was a new—and doubtless unsettling—stage of development.

Ballots and Missions

To **Gregory XV** (1621–1623) belong two remarkable achievements, which are all the more striking because they were posted during a relatively brief pontificate (see Chapter 4, "Ten to Remember: Popes Who Made a Difference"). The first of these was the successful introduction of the secret ballot to papal elections, a consolidation and extension of the impulse to reform this process that had been expressed in the papacy of Gregory X.

What Happened When

- ◆ **1618:** First conflicts of the Thirty Years' War.
- ◆ **1622:** The Congregation of the Propagation of the Faith was created.
- ◆ **1640:** Publication of Cornelius Jansen's *Augustinius*.
- ◆ **1648:** The Peace of Westphalia brought the Thirty Years' War to an end.
- ◆ **1673:** The English Parliament passed the Test Act, which excluded from public office those who refused to swear loyalty to the Church of England and renounce Catholic beliefs.
- ◆ **1682:** The Gallican articles, challenging papal authority, were set out in France.
- ◆ **1685:** Louis XIV revoked the Edict of Nantes, which had brought a conclusion to the Wars of Religion by guaranteeing Protestant rights in France.

His second accomplishment was the establishment of a permanent board of control of Roman Catholic foreign missions: the *Congregation for the Propagation of the Faith*. The work conducted by this body helped the Church recover from setbacks suffered in influence following the conflicts with Protestants, and made possible the extraordinary global reach of Catholicism that followed.

Vatican Vocabulary

The **Congregation for the Propagation of the Faith** is a permanent body overseeing Catholic missionary activity worldwide. It works under the pope's authority, having evolved from earlier groups that had been headed up by cardinals.

It was during Gregory's pontificate that Catholic forces under Duke Maximilian I of Bavaria posted a series of victories against the Protestants, securing a temporary advantage in the bitter struggle that we know today as the Thirty Years' War. The ongoing carnage served as proof—as though any were needed—that the conflict between the two European versions of Christianity carried military and political implications, in addition to theological ones.

Bet You Didn't Know _____

"In addition to its international dimensions, the Thirty Years' War was a German civil war. The principalities which made up Germany took up arms for or against the Hapsburgs or, most commonly, both at different times, during the war's 30 years."
—The Thirty Years' War Homepage (www.pipeline.com/~cwa/TYWHome.htm)

Cheat Sheet: The Thirty Years' War

The military campaigns that flared in Europe between 1618 and 1648 had many dimensions. They were, however, first and foremost a succession of conflicts pitting the Holy Roman Empire (embodied in the Hapsburg Empire)—in alliance with Catholic German forces—against the Protestant monarchs of Germany. The chief events of this protracted, acrimonious, and violent struggle for supremacy in Europe are summarized here. Note that the territorial, political, and religious issues under dispute often merged into a (literally) bloody mess.

◆ **The Bohemian Phase (1618 to early 1620s):** Bohemian Protestants rebelled against the Hapsburgs; Protestant nobles deposed King Ferdinand, a Catholic, and chose Frederick the Winter King to succeed him. Imperial armies overwhelmed the Bohemians, and then established other strongholds.

◆ **The Danish Phase (1625–1629):** The forces of Christian IV of Denmark entered the conflict in support of the Protestant cause in Germany, only to be rebuffed by the Hapsburg armies.

◆ **The Swedish Phase (1630–1635):** Gustavus II of Sweden, encouraged by Cardinal Richelieu of France, entered the fray in opposition to the Hapsburgs. (Richelieu was aiming for French dominance in Europe.) The bloodshed continued at horrific levels until the Peace of Prague appeared to bring reconciliation between Protestants and Catholics.

◆ **The Swedish-French Phase (1635–1648):** Refusing to concede anything to the Hapsburgs, Richelieu saw to France's open entry into the war, which thereupon became a naked dispute over political dominance with only vestigial elements of the religious conflict that had preceded it. The Hapsburg forces were dealt significant defeats, and in 1640 an achingly slow peace process began. The conflict finally played out in 1648 with the signing of the Peace of Westphalia, which has been called "an important step toward religious toleration" in Europe (*The Columbia Encyclopedia*, fifth edition, Barbara Chernow and George Vallasi, editors. New York: Columbia University Press, 1993.)

The upshot of the conflict was that bloody clashes inspired by religious hatred eventually ceased in Europe, with Germany's Protestant movement very much alive; the slow degeneration of the Hapsburgs began, leaving the Holy Roman Empire in a seriously weakened condition. French power assumed centrality in the affairs of Europe.

Papal People

Cardinal Richelieu (Armand Jean du Plessis, Duc de Richelieu; 1585–1642) was chief minister to the French King, Louis XIII. After winning the confidence of the king's mother, Marie de Medici, he gained greater and greater degrees of power; when Marie turned against Richelieu, she found herself without the support of her son the king and was sent into exile. Richelieu then assumed effective control of the French government.

Pope Watch

"(Urban VIII) published a law compelling all bishops, the cardinals not excepted, to reside in their sees. As regarded the cardinals, the pope said to them: 'Hitherto you could excuse yourselves by saying that the pope knew and tolerated it. We, at least, will not tolerate or permit it!'"

—The Chevalier Artaud De Montor, *The Lives and Times of the Popes* (New York: Catholic Publication Society of New York, 1911)

Urban VIII (1623–1644) reigned during a period when the conflict in Europe raged mercilessly. He came, for political reasons, to distance himself from open displays of favoritism in that surrealistically complex series of campaigns, which dissolved into an undisguised struggle for political dominance during the second half of his pontificate.

Urban attempted to leave his mark in the pastoral realm by reforming liturgical practice, canonizing many saints, and instituting new religious orders. He also continued the ongoing reformation of internal practice. He was particularly emphatic in his views on where bishops settled and made their living quarters. He had no patience for bishops who presided over a region without actually living there, and he said so.

Urban was also an energetic defender of the Holy See's territorial claims. In 1626, the pope reiterated the initiatives of Pius V and others, forbidding the transmission of lands that belonged to, or were to revert to, the papacy.

None of this, however, is what people tend to remember about Urban. For it was under this pope that the conflict between the Church and the great Italian scientist Galileo Galilei unfolded.

A Showdown with Galileo

The persistent Galileo had published, in 1632, a volume entitled *Dialogue Concerning the Two Chief World Systems*. The book is a landmark in scientific and philosophical inquiry ... and it is also the chief relic of the papacy's effort to manage the intellectual analysis of the world in which it (and humanity as a whole) operated.

The Church Urban headed held to the comforting metaphorical certainties of the Ptolemaic theory of the universe. In other words, it assumed an earth around which the sun revolved. This idea may seem awkward to modern observers, but it was nevertheless a staple of orthodoxy in seventeenth-century Catholicism.

In publishing a rigorous rejection of that theory that masqueraded as a "dialogue" between proponents of the Ptolemaic and Copernican (sun-centered) systems, Galileo, who had by this point already been summoned to Rome once before on the matter, knew that he was testing the limits of the era. His conviction that whatever risks he encountered were worth courting because he was demonstrably right has inspired science and inquiry down the centuries.

The conflict between the two men, which seemed to have far more to do with the maintenance of papal authority than with the accurate observance of the movements of heavenly bodies, is not one of the high points of Urban's career, of the papacy, or of Church history. And it is what most people remember first about this pontificate.

Urban Sends a Message

Urban's point was that there were limits to what would be tolerated from agitators who set out to challenge fundamental Church doctrines loudly and prominently—a description that certainly fit Galileo. With the advantage of historical hindsight, this seems an unfortunate line to draw—but draw it, and hold to it, Urban did. He did so in response to a new and utterly unfamiliar way of looking at the natural world that he could only compare to heresy.

Galileo was summoned before the Inquisition in Rome and put on trial; he was shown the instruments of torture in a successful effort to persuade him to renounce his beliefs. Centuries later, the Church would formally acknowledge its error. At the time, however, the authorities compelled strict obedience and, under Urban, forced Galileo to renounce formally all he had so carefully and painstakingly established regarding the movement of the planets.

The great scientist probably didn't glance down at the earth and mutter, *"Eppur si muove"* ("And still it moves"), after pronouncing the recantation he had agreed to recite, but the image of him doing so has nevertheless lodged in the communal memory of Western civilization. Galileo has, over the centuries, become a kind of secular saint for the cause of intellectual and scientific inquiry—surely the last thing Urban had in mind for him.

It is not always remembered that, having won his showdown, Urban later set the quarrelsome scientist free.

The Unconsulted Pope

Innocent X (1644–1655) condemned the Peace of Westphalia—the settlements of 1648 that brought an end to decades of bloody religious conflict—because he had not been a party to it. It was Innocent's fate, however, to rule at the period when the political leaders of Europe had concluded that popes need no longer be consulted about such matters as the declaration of war or the conclusion of peace, and so his condemnation gained little attention.

The snub was a precursor of episodes of political irrelevancy to come.

Bloody Strife Between Catholics and Protestants Draws to a Close

"In the name of the most holy and individual Trinity: Be it known to all, and every one whom it may concern, or to whom in any manner it may belong, That for many Years past, Discords and Civil Divisions being stir'd up in the Roman Empire, which increas'd to such a degree, that not only all Germany, but also the neighbouring Kingdoms, and France particularly, have been involv'd in the Disorders of a long and cruel War ... from whence ensu'd great Effusion of Christian Blood, and the Desolation of several Provinces. It has at last happen'd, by the effect of Divine Goodness, seconded by the Endeavours of the most Serene Republick of Venice, who in this sad time, when all Christendom is imbroil'd, has not ceas'd to contribute its Counsels for the publick Welfare and Tranquillity; so that on the side, and the other, they have form'd Thoughts of an universal Peace .... (I)n the presence and with the consent of the Electors of the Sacred Roman Empire, the other Princes and States, to the Glory of God, and the Benefit of the Christian World, the following Articles have been agreed on and consented to, and the same run thus ... That there shall be a Christian and Universal Peace, and a perpetual, true, and sincere Amity, between his Sacred Imperial Majesty, and his most Christian Majesty .... That they shall not act, or permit to be acted, any wrong or injury to any whatsoever; but that all that has pass'd on the one side, and the other, as well before as during the War, in Words, Writings, and Outrageous Actions, in Violences, Hostilitys, Damages and Expences, without any respect to Persons or Things, shall be entirely abolish'd in such a manner that all that might be demanded of, or pretended to, by each other on that behalf, shall be bury'd in eternal Oblivion."

—Excerpt from a contemporary translation of the treaty concluding the Peace of Westphalia, 1648. Note the avoidance of any reference to a papal role in the conclusion of the 30-year-old war, which had by this point evolved into a secular conflict.

Troubles with the French King

Alexander VII (1655–1667) reigned during a period of troublesome relations with France. As pope, he experienced great difficulties with the French King Louis XIV, who nearly marched on Rome before peace was established at a meeting in Pisa.

In 1655, Alexander received the era's most renowned convert, Queen Christina of Sweden, who chose to give up the throne in order to become a Catholic.

A Pope for the World Stage

Before assuming the papacy, **Clement IX** (1667–1669) had been the author of the 1639 opera *Chi Soffre Speri*. His work in the theater may well have helped him to prepare for the considerable (and often overlooked) improvisational and role-playing demands of the diplomat and the statesman; as pope, he used these gifts to help put an end to war between France and Spain.

Clement's personal devotion to his pastoral duties can be glimpsed in the habit he made of personally hearing confessions at St. Peter's. One wonders at the state of mind of the penitent who settled into the confession box and then recognized the familiar voice of the Holy Father at the beginning of the rite of reconciliation.

The heretical movement of Jansenism, despite having been condemned in earlier years, was now active, and Clement was one of many popes forced to deal with the group. Despite papal opposition, the Jansenists, ardent rivals of the Jesuit order, would not exit Catholicism's stage until the early eighteenth century.

Bet You Didn't Know

The dour movement known as Jansenism (from the Dutch theologian Cornelius Otto Jansen) was the target of vigorous resistance from the Jesuits. Jansen felt mainstream Catholic theologians rejected Luther's doctrines of grace in a way that put too much weight on human responsibility and thus discounted God's role. Jansen and his adherents emphasized extraordinary individual piety and holiness and embraced the notion of predestination. The movement, which had no influence outside of Catholicism but inspired fierce debate within, was condemned as heretical in 1653 but persisted for decades after that. It was especially influential in France.

Clement X (1670–1676), a compromise candidate, was elected after a long and bitter conclave; he was almost 80 at the time of his elevation. When named a cardinal by Clement IX the year before, he had been told by the pope himself: "You will be our successor." At the time, it had seemed like an unlikely prediction, leading one to wonder about the previous Clement's prophetic abilities.

Clement had been an accomplished attorney before entering the clergy. Charity was a hallmark of his papacy; he also attempted to improve agriculture and to promote industry throughout the Papal States. He was particularly insistent about the regulation of Church practice with regard to removing the relics of saints from their burial grounds, and pronounced a threat of excommunication against those who sought to sell such items for profit.

Some cardinals may have voted for him in the hope that his would be a brief and comparatively inconsequential "interim" pontificate. If so, they were doubtless surprised at the enlightened, open, and surprisingly energetic reign that unfolded over the next six years.

More Trouble with the French

Innocent XI (1676–1689) was elected as a result of his personal piety and his deep commitment to reform. His reign, however, would be remembered primarily for disputes with France.

Innocent denounced King Louis XIV's claims of authority over the French Church, and had even harsher words for the Four Gallican Articles, which held kings to be immune from the authority of the pope and demanded that Rome bow to the customs of local churches in France. In essence, Louis sought to bring the French church under his own control. Conflict with Louis continued when the king revoked the Edict of Nantes, which had brought an end to the Wars of Religion by guaranteeing the rights of French Protestants. To his credit, Innocent denounced this move.

All in all, the picture is one of a French church, and a French king, eager to pick a fight, and a pope forced to stand his ground. The dispute with the French crown would drag on endlessly, a reminder that the papacy's days of clear and undisputed dominance over secular powers were long past.

And as though all that weren't enough, the Jansenists kept making waves.

Alexander VIII (1689–1691) continued the papal opposition to the Jansenists and to the Gallican articles of 1682. He attempted to maintain neutrality in the War of the League of Augsburg between the Catholic states of Austria and France.

The last act of his pontificate—which lasted little over a year—was to declare the Gallican articles null and void, and to beg Louis XIV to follow the dictates of his faith in the conduct of his foreign policy.

The Old Century Wanes

The last four consecutive popes had been 65 years of age or older; **Innocent XII** (1691–1700), who was 76 at the time of his election, continued the string. He had diplomatic experience, having been a papal nuncio. It came in handy.

Through Innocent's negotiations, Louis XIV of France at last renounced the Four Gallican Articles that had so troubled the previous two popes. In exchange for this renunciation, however, Louis won the right to direct vacant sees.

Innocent also condemned a work of the French archbishop Fenelon of Cambrai called the *Maximes des Saints*. This was a work associated with the doctrine of Quietism, a mystic approach to Christianity that invoked passivity and argued that its practitioners, in obliterating the self, also obliterated its capacity for sin.

Most important of all, Innocent proved that the moral rectitude expressed at Trent would continue to be a guiding light for the successors of St. Peter. Over a century after the council, this pope who took the strongest stance yet against nepotism in his own office, forbidding popes from bestowing property or income to family members. It was a fit conclusion to the old century.

A New Era

As the eighteenth century dawned, daunting new challenges on the political and intellectual fronts awaited the papacy ... and in particular, its staunchest defenders, the Jesuits, who would come under sustained attack.

The Least You Need to Know

♦ When the Thirty Years' War—a bitter and bloody series of struggles in Europe—finally concluded, it had taken on a political nature; all the same, it established zones of dominance for Protestants and Catholics.

♦ Various difficult challenges from France met the papacy following the Thirty Years' War.

♦ The Jansenists set off a long debate within Catholicism that survived papal condemnation of their movement.

♦ Urban VIII faced down Galileo in 1633.

♦ Innocent XII decreed the formal abolition of papal nepotism.

Chapter 18

Showdown with the Monarchs

In This Chapter

- ◆ A strong papal stand against nepotism
- ◆ Increasingly intense challenges from European heads of state
- ◆ The persistence of the Jansenist movement
- ◆ The Jesuits under attack

In the first half of the eighteenth century, unique intellectual and political challenges beset the papacy, and the popes often looked like men painted into a corner.

Their territories and prerogatives increasingly came under dispute, and even their brilliant and methodically organized missionary, educational, and diplomatic corps—the Society of Jesus, also known as the Jesuits—came to be reviled by the ruling powers of Europe. In an earlier era, open assaults on movements closely identified with the pope would have been unthinkable. But times had changed.

What Happened When

- ◆ **1723–1726:** Christian missionaries in China were persecuted.
- ◆ **1749:** Jansenist dispute intensified in France.
- ◆ **1759:** Jesuits forced out of Portugal.
- ◆ **1762:** Jean-Jacques Rousseau published *Emile*, a seminal work of Deism. Deism was a philosophical movement of the Enlightenment (or Age of Reason) that rejected traditional religious and theological conceptions and saw natural processes as proof of God's existence. The Deists denied supernatural phenomena.
- ◆ **1769:** Movement to disband the Society of Jesus gains momentum among Catholic heads of state.

"Sufficient Qualifications"

The talented scholar, academic, and diplomat **Clement XI** (1700–1721) was among the most reluctant popes in history. He had to be persuaded by no fewer than four eminent theologians that he would be guilty of a clear moral fault if he refused the call of the College of Cardinals. Relenting at last, he assumed the throne of St. Peter only after having said of his own candidacy, "All the same, it would be preferable if I had sufficient qualifications for the ministry in question."

His own misgivings aside, Clement served competently and with remarkable calm during a phase when the Holy See encountered fragmentation and near schism within the clergy, a rising incidence of intellectual challenge to its teachings that might well be considered "Galileo's revenge," and repeated insult from the great powers of Europe.

One of his first official acts was to order a number of bishops enamored of life in the big city away from Rome and back to their dioceses; the new pope gave the bishops 12 days to conclude their business, pack their belongings, and return to their flocks. It was a sign of sure-footed authority and reverence for discipline that left no doubt as to the kind of man who had been elevated. The same order was given to lesser ecclesiastics who were bound to particular geographic regions, but who had come up with various reasons for remaining in the city.

Pope Watch

During a boyhood visit to Rome, Clement noticed a massive swarm of bees that had, for some reason, picked out the window of the room in which he was staying as the one on which to settle. The incident marked the second time that bees had alighted in their numbers near his quarters, and it came to be regarded by the faithful, in later years, as a fateful and auspicious portent.

Another early sign of far-sighted concern was Clement's clampdown on the bustling traffic in Roman antiquities, now being unearthed thanks to recent excavation campaigns. He forbade the quiet looting of the city's priceless statuary, inscriptions, mosaics, and other works of art, punished the thieves in question, and thus ensured that countless relics and works of art would remain within Rome and subject to civic control and regulation.

Clement was a notable patron not only of the arts, but also of the sciences. Three quarters of a century or so after the persecution of the problematic Galileo, the papacy became the source of ample funding for one Bianchini, a mathematician and astronomer whose supreme achievement was the Clementine Meridian at the Carthusian Church of St. Mary of the Angels. This 200-foot-long structure accurately predicted the appearance of heavenly bodies from an earth whose motion, once apparently heretical, was now both a mathematical certainty and an important dating and navigational principle.

It would be a grave mistake, however, to view Clement's embrace of carefully chosen scientific advances as a victory for open and unrestrained intellectual inquiry in Europe. In 1707, a work by Anthony Collins entitled *A Discourse on Freethinking* was condemned in Rome; Collins had dared to contrast the energetic application of human reason with the complacent acceptance of religious authority. For this pope, and for many to follow during the *Enlightenment*, such arguments were to remain objects of contempt and attempted suppression.

Vatican Vocabulary

The eighteenth-century **Enlightenment,** or Age of Reason, grew out of the remarkable advances in science and inquiry of the seventeenth century. The Enlightenment embraced rationalism, progressive thought, and advancement of human knowledge and freedom. The movement is closely identified with such figures as Jean-Jacques Rousseau, Francois Marie Arouet de Voltaire, and Thomas Jefferson.

The Family Problem

Clement was the first pope elected after Innocent XII's bull forbidding papal nepotism, and was therefore the center of much curious observation, not least from his own family. Would he abide by, or attempt to undermine, Innocent's pronouncement?

The new pope wasted little time establishing his position. He made it known to both relatives and allies that there would be no turning back from the position of Innocent XII regarding the dispensation of property or offices to those close to the pope. Papal initiatives often depend more on the outlook of the pontiff who succeeds than on the inclination of the pontiff who pronounces; this reform, Clement made clear, would endure during his reign. He was as good as his word.

Bet You Didn't Know

Much of Clement's pontificate was spent coping with the diplomatic and military consequences of the dispute between Spain and France known as the War of Spanish Succession (1701–1714), which he attempted without success to prevent. The Treaty of Utrecht, which ended this conflict, demonstrated the decline of papal influence in European political affairs, doling out as it did papal lands with casual disrespect for the interests of the Holy See.

In the political realm, Clement had to contend again and again with monarchs who cared little about his wishes or conception of his own authority. His furious letter to Joseph, the Holy Roman emperor, illustrates the uphill journey he was compelled on more than one occasion to travel in his dealings with the rulers of the day.

Trouble with the Emperor

"Moreover, if you are not ashamed to fight against the Church and God himself, if you deviate from the ancient Austrian piety, and especially from that of your father Leopold, who was always so reverent to the Church, and who was so magnificently helped by the Church during the Hungarian war, as the house of Austria always has been by the pontiffs, remember that the same God who giveth kingdoms can also destroy them."

—Letter from Pope Clement XI to Joseph I, Holy Roman emperor

The Debate over Jansenism

Responsive to urgings from King Louis XIV of France, Clement renewed papal denunciation of the divisive Jansenist movement. This time, the vehicle of condemnation was an authoritative one that was impossible for Catholics in Europe to ignore: a papal bull, *Unigenitus Dei Filius*. Issued in 1713, it was the second papal bull issued against the movement.

Clement eventually excommunicated a number of prominent Jansenists. French bishops declared their support for *Unigenitus*, and describing it as "a dogmatic judgment of the universal church, every appeal from which (is) null, frivolous, illusory, rash, scandalous, insulting to the Holy See and to the episcopal body, contrary to the authority of the Church, schismatic, and tending to renew and foment condemned errors." Indeed, Clement's bull won open and explicit support from bishops throughout Europe, though the Jansenist controversy would continue in France.

A Difficult Question in China

Catholic missionaries in China had begun to make inroads in that ancient civilization by accommodating themselves to the customs of the people there. These accommodations, however, proved controversial, and questions for the pope arose: "Is it permissible to prostrate oneself before the idol Chachinchiam? Is it permissible to sacrifice to Confucius?"

Clement reviewed the matter closely and answered in the negative. The result, as the missionaries no doubt could have predicted, was twofold: rejection of the missionary campaign by the Chinese people, and a wave of abuse against missionaries there. These thorny questions would remain a matter of heated discussion (conducted at great distances) well into the next pontificate, but Clement's policy was to remain in place. There were, even in important missions, some concessions that were not worth making to local custom.

All in all, Clement's long reign had been notable for its intelligence, its pragmatism, its integrity, and its poise, which was often severely tested. He was regarded at the time as man of rare qualities and an exceptional leader of the faithful at a time when the Church experienced challenge after challenge. The record offers no reason to dispute this assessment of his pontificate.

"No Longer of This World"

Shortly after his election, **Innocent XIII** (1721–1724) ordered a random survey of the loaves produced by Roman bakers; the new pope, vigilant on behalf of the underprivileged citizens of Rome, was eager to ferret out any inadequate or fraudulently sold bread.

During his short pontificate, he proclaimed Charles VI, Holy Roman emperor, the sovereign of the kingdom of Naples. Innocent also stood firm against the Jansenists, and continued Clement XII's prohibition against performing certain "Chinese rites" to win support in that country. He also continued the papal tradition of urging almsgiving on behalf of Christians in the Holy Land.

Two years and 10 months after his election, Innocent's health began to deteriorate. As his condition worsened, he was urged to name new cardinals to fill four vacancies that had occurred. He declined these entreaties, informing his entourage that such acts were inappropriate now: "We are no longer of this world."

He died of a fever resulting from a ruptured hernia at the age of 69. His reign had not been long enough for him to initiate any grand plan or notable undertaking of his own. In his work *Memoirs upon Italy*, Count d'Albon praised Innocent's "great virtues" and mastery of "the science of government."

Reform in the Abstract

Outraged by extravagance as an abstract idea, Innocent's successor, **Benedict XIII** (1724–1730), spoke out against an obsessive concern with material things by the cardinals, whether it be excessive spending or shameful accumulation of wealth. However, he had difficulty implementing this principle as a matter of policy; his own choice to oversee papal affairs, Niccolo Coscia, was one of the worst of the spendthrifts and money hoarders.

> **Bet You Didn't Know**
>
> In 1724, a coalition of orthodox clergy broke with the Eastern Church and renewed ties with Rome. The movement, known as the Greek Catholic Church (or Melkites), was initiated by orthodox Christians educated in Europe, and has been led by a series of patriarchs. Currently the church has approximately 1 million followers.

Benedict was a deeply pious man who may well have been out of his depth in the world of administration and political influence that he inherited. A Dominican, he was persuaded to accept the papacy only when commanded to do so by a superior within the order. It turned out that he had made a private vow to God not to accept the office; apparently, he made this vow out of concern that doing so would be a sign of pride and worldliness on his part. His first concern upon acceding to the command he had been given was to request absolution for the breach of his oath. He had bewildered his entourage by spending the first three days of his reign in private prayer; during this same period, he had requested the use of his convent bed, complete with wool sheets and rough-textured blankets.

Benedict's was a reign of continuity and good intention, without vigorous new initiatives. He continued the opposition to Jansenism and the adoption of "Chinese rites" that his predecessors had pronounced. He was a quiet man who refused to put on airs and strove to take a practical approach to the problems put before him. At one point, he happened to hear a peasant complaining of the injustice of a certain tax. The pope took it upon himself to look into the matter, concluded the Church's tax was in fact unfair, and personally saw to its abolition.

The Pope Who Refused Confession

It fell to **Clement XII** (1730–1740) to put into practice what Benedict had preached. He fined and jailed Cardinal Coscia, his predecessor's chief administrator, for abusing his office to amass wealth.

Clement came under criticism, however, for his use of a lottery to raise funds for the Church. He continued the papal stand against Jansenism and issued a bull condemning freemasonry (the doctrines associated with the secret fraternal order of the Masons, which had strong anticlerical tendencies). When Cardinal Alberoni attacked and then annexed

San Marino, a 24-square mile nation in southwest Italy whose independence had been recognized for a century, Clement restored liberty to the minute republic.

Not too much should be read into the San Marino episode. The office Clement held was continuing its steady decline in European political influence. When he offered himself as a mediator in a conflict between the Corsicans and the Genoan republic, he suffered the indignity of flat rejection from the Genoan senate. A stern and officious man, Clement conducted an efficient pontificate that endured for a longer period than may have been expected at the time of his election. (He was 78 when elevated.) By the time of his final struggle with gout at the age of 88, his severe demeanor had apparently become a habit that overwhelmed even his own perceived need for confession.

After receiving a polite reminder that he might wish to consider acts undertaken during his pontificate for which he had need of forgiveness, he curtly responded that there had been no such acts. His shocked would-be confessor managed to stammer that the pope might perhaps wish to consider the act of contrition for something *overlooked* over the past 10 years. "No," Clement answered, "neither on that point do we feel any remorse of conscience."

The Brilliant Benedict

Upon his election by the College of Cardinals, **Benedict XIV** (1740–1758) responded intelligently and to the point: "I accept for three reasons. The first is, I am unwilling to disdain your kindness; the second, I will not resist the will of God, which I know this to be, because I have never desired such a dignity; and the third is my desire to put an end to our conclave, which has already lasted so long as to cause general scandal."

Benedict was a brilliant leader of the Church renowned for his learning. He wrote a classic treatise on canonization; scholars and artists were welcomed to his court. His status as a man of letters did not prevent him, however, from condemning a number of works of contemporary philosophy, including Mary Huber's *Letters on the Religion Essential to Man.*

This pope, like many of his predecessors, did much to beautify Rome. He repeated and reinforced the position against Jansenism. Benedict also spoke out forcefully against abuses suffered by the native peoples of Paraguay during a period of controversy connected to the disbanding of Jesuit *reductions* there.

Benedict also saw to it that Eastern Catholic rites were not Latinized, thus retaining support in a new flock who had recently pronounced their acceptance of the authority of the pope.

Vatican Vocabulary

Reductions were Church-conducted communities of native peoples in colonial South America, initiated in the early seventeenth century and strongly associated with the Jesuits. (Civil rulers occasionally founded and led reductions, as well.) The aim of the reductions was to mobilize indigenous labor and to spread Spanish culture in the New World. The Jesuits who led reductions were firm in their pronouncements but generally compassionate; one priest assumed responsibility for spiritual matters, while another handled administrative responsibilities. Reductions were, on the whole, successful social and economic groupings that substantially increased the store of European knowledge regarding South America.

Clement XIII (1758–1769) had been educated by Jesuits at Bologna, and was a strong supporter of the group. It was a severe shock to him when the Jesuits to whom he owed his intellectual growth came under extraordinary attack, mainly at the hands of secular Catholic rulers who saw the Jesuits' obedience to the pope as undermining their powers. (The king of Portugal, for instance, came to believe that the Jesuits had been conspiring to assassinate him.)

Papal People

During Clement XIII's reign, King Charles II of Spain concluded that the Jesuits were behind a campaign to depose him, and deported thousands of them to Italy.

Portugal suppressed the Jesuits, as did Spain, France, Naples, and the papal state of Parma. Clement XIII declared Parma's actions null and void, which caused France to seize the papal territory of Avignon, and Naples to take over Benevento. The dominoes continued their fall when the courts of Bourbon and Portugal ordered that Clement disband the Jesuits. The order had been opposed by the leaders of the influential Jansenist movement for years; the Jesuits' pervasiveness and unshakable loyalty to the initiatives of the pope were, in the current political climate, beginning to inspire deep antagonism.

The attacks on the Jesuits, though sometimes ludicrously overblown, were nevertheless effective, and soon Catholic Europe was in revolt against the "army" indomitably in league with the Holy Father. An influential publication of the period attacking supposed Jesuit perfidy in Paraguay bore a lengthy and rabble-rousing title: *Abridged Relation of the Republic which the Religious of the Society of Jesus of the Province of Portugal and Spain Have Established in the Domains of the Two Monarchies, and of the War which They Have Declared and Sustained against the Spanish and Portuguese Armies.* The title, like the publication to which it was attached, was a masterstroke of propaganda; the Spanish and Portuguese had no armies in Paraguay.

The Jesuits Under Attack

"We beg Your Majesty, with the most ardent expression of desire, not to banish the Jesuits. Their cause is essentially connected with that of the Catholic religion; most sacred rights of religion are at stake. If lay magistrates violate them, religion itself will perish. The rules of a holy institute approved and confirmed by the Holy See are concerned; they cannot in any manner be abandoned (to) the decisions of magistrates. The pontiff, after addressing fervent prayers to God, recurs now with confidence to the royal authority. He conjures the King to remedy such imminent evils, to avoid scandal which must arise, to extend his protecting arm to a tottering society, and at the same time to religion itself."

—Clement XIII's breathless (and unsuccessful) letter appealing to the French King Louis XV

Clement's health failed as the crisis unfolded; one gets the distinct impression that the severity of the attacks on the Society of Jesus had a good deal to do with his physical decline. He died of pulmonary failure while the Catholic powers of Europe were clamoring more loudly than ever for the destruction of the order most strongly associated with the defense of the papacy. It would be left to his predecessor, surrounded, like Clement, by baying monarchs, to decide what to do next.

Pope Watch

"The faithful should obey the apostolic advice not to know more than is necessary, but to know in moderation."

—Clement's XIII "need-to-know" approach to lay education offers believers an alternative to the information overload proposed by the philosophers and theorists of the Age of Reason

The Least You Need to Know

- The popes resisted the Enlightenment, or Age of Reason.
- Disputes over Catholic missionary work in Paraguay and China accompanied the Church's extension of its influence into the New World.
- *Unigenitus Dei Filius*, issued in 1713, was an important papal bull issued against the Jansenist movement.
- During Clement XIII's reign, the Jesuits came under bitter attack from the Catholic heads of state.

Chapter 19

Victory by Defeat

In This Chapter

- ◆ The suppression of the Jesuits
- ◆ A decline in papal influence under Clement XIV and Pius VI
- ◆ The conflict with Napoleon—and the trials and triumphs of Pius VII
- ◆ The restoration of the Jesuits

Disputes between the Church and various political powers continued in the late eighteenth and early nineteenth centuries. The most momentous of these featured the ignominious defeat and abuse of a remarkable pope ... a man who outlasted his tormentor and helped to define the modern papacy.

What Happened When

- ◆ **1773:** The Jesuits were suppressed by papal order.
- ◆ **1789:** Political upheaval in France led to revolution.
- ◆ **1799:** Rise of Napoleon as first consul.
- ◆ **1801:** Concordat between Napoleon and the Roman Catholic Church.
- ◆ **1814:** Jesuits were restored.
- ◆ **1815:** Napoleon was defeated at Waterloo.
- ◆ **1829:** Parliament repeals anti-Catholic statutes.

Clement Under Fire

With **Clement XIV** (1769–1774), a Franciscan, the bubble burst. Under pressure from each and every one of the rulers of Catholic Europe, he was forced to suppress the Jesuits, whose aggressive pursuit of an activist Catholic agenda with deep allegiances to Rome was ruffling feathers. There had been three years of procrastination on the fateful issue of how to respond to the clamor raised against the Jesuits. The question of whether the pope could be bent to the combined will of secular powers, however, was finally settled. He could.

The Jesuits had brought unique energy and vigor to the Catholic Reformation. Their missionary work in South America, Canada, and the Far East had been nothing short of extraordinary; they had made superior educational institutions a priority; and they had, first and foremost, demonstrated unswerving allegiance to the pope. Now they had been curbed by the papacy itself, under pressure from the very institutions they were attempting to transcend.

A letter purportedly from Clement to his successor, supposedly rescinding the abolition of the Jesuits, was published in 1789, but its authenticity is questionable. What happened during this period was all too clear: The Catholic heads of state in Europe had kept up the assault initiated under Clement XII, and the next Clement had yielded.

Pope Watch

"(I)t is hardly, if at all, possible to restore a true and lasting peace to the Church as long as (the Society of Jesus) remains in existence."

—Pope Clement XIV, in the papal bull *Dominus ac Redemptor noster,* 1773

His reign saw yet another decline in papal influence on the affairs of Europe, and Clement's deference to those in political power on the issue of the Jesuits stands as the chief feature of his papacy. It should not be forgotten, though, that this pope was deeply concerned with fulfilling the legacy of the Council of Trent. His patience for financial and administrative mischief on the part of the clergy was short indeed; in the very first year of his pontificate, he issued a bull condemning abuses in taxes and benefices.

Clement Speaks His Mind on "Abuses in the Exercise of Spiritual Power"

"It is altogether befitting for the ministers of the Church and the dispensers of divine mysteries to be exempt from any suspicion, however light, of avarice; then they can be free to exercise their sacred ministry in such a way that they can justly glory that their hands have acted free of any reward ...."

"(W)ith sorrow We have learned that many abuses in the exercise of spiritual power (which not only totally destroy ecclesiastical discipline, but also enfeeble and bring the greatest shame upon your dignity and power) still exist in your ecclesiastical curias. To be sure your piety, your holy mode of life, your solicitude for your churches is more than sufficiently known to Us. We also know that these abuses have been introduced in the past, first from some secondary ministry or other, and have been gradually spread from diocese to diocese, perhaps without the knowledge of bishops ...."

"Accordingly, you can in no way be blamed; rather you are worthy of commendation because, as We have learned, you are grieved by these abuses and wish to extirpate them. We, however, perceiving how much you will be detested for this and how great the obstacles will be unless the Apostolic Authority assists you in this enterprise, accordingly make this intervention ...."

"(I)t is difficult to reconcile with the decrees of the Council of Trent the following rather corrupt customs of bishops and their officials: receiving during the visitation a remuneration for inspecting certain wills or for reviewing the accounts required from administrators of churches and pious places; receiving transportation on horseback or at least their provisions for the entire time of the visitation; or claiming as their own lamps or candles placed on the main and other altars of the church. Being contrary to the sacred canons, these and similar practices are to be completely eliminated."

—Pope Clement XIV, *Decet Quam Maxime* (On Abuses in Taxes and Benifices), 1769

Pius VI Struggles for His Footing

Pius VI (1775–1779) inherited an extremely chaotic period in Europe, and was not equal to it.

He spent a good deal of his long reign being battered about by, or railing ineffectively against, forces beyond his control. His pontificate may well represent rock bottom in the papacy's political and moral influence on affairs of state and intellect in Europe and the Americas.

He set the tone for his reign with an early assault on the Enlightenment.

"These Accursed Philosophers"

"You yourselves, established as scouts in the house of Israel, see clearly the many victories claimed by a philosophy full of deceit. You see the ease with which it attracts to itself a great host of peoples, concealing its impiety with the honorable name of philosophy. Who could express in words or call to mind the wickedness of the tenets and evil madness which it imparts? ... (S)uch men ... have come to such a height of impiety that they make out that God does not exist, or if He does that He is idle and uncaring, making no revelation to men. Consequently it is not surprising that they assert that everything holy and divine is the product of the minds of inexperienced men smitten with empty fear of the future and seduced by a vain hope of immortality ....

"When they have spread this darkness abroad and torn religion out of men's hearts, these accursed philosophers proceed to destroy the bonds of union among men, both those which unite them to their rulers, and those which urge them to their duty. They keep proclaiming that man is born free and subject to no one, that society accordingly is a crowd of foolish men who stupidly yield to priests who deceive them and to kings who oppress them, so that the harmony of priest and ruler is only a monstrous conspiracy against the innate liberty of man.

"Everyone must understand that such ravings and others like them, concealed in many deceitful guises, cause greater ruin to public calm the longer their impious originators are unrestrained. They cause a serious loss of souls redeemed by Christ's blood wherever their teaching spreads, like a cancer; it forces its way into public academies, into the houses of the great, into the palaces of kings, and even enters the sanctuary, shocking as it is to say so."

—*Inscrutabile* (Encyclical of Pope Pius VI on the Problems of the Pontificate), December 25, 1775

But philosophers, in and of themselves, were not Pius's most immediate problem. Political isolation was. During his pontificate, Emperor Joseph II embraced the notion of Febronianism, which held that the pope's role in affairs of government had no basis in law, scripture, or history, and that all bishops stood equal to the bishop of Rome. Joseph's attraction to this idea led to major challenges to the pope's authority in parts of Europe.

Already convoluted matters got still more complex with the initial phase of the French Revolution in 1789. Rome greeted the new government's decision to reorganize the

French church with a passive policy that could have reflected either strategic wariness or confusion. In 1791, however, when the French clergy were forced to swear allegiance to the state, the pope denounced the whole situation, and relations with the revolutionary government soured.

If Pius held any consolation that things at least couldn't be expected to get much worse, he was sadly mistaken. In 1796, Napoleon Bonaparte mounted an assault on the Papal States on behalf of the revolutionary government in France; this was followed by a costly armistice and, in 1797, further predations supposedly in consequence of the death of a French general in Rome. A Roman republic was proclaimed, and the pope was pronounced deposed as secular ruler. A year and a half of shameful flight and imprisonment in all but name followed for Pius, who died at Valence in August 1799.

The papacy was in a free fall, and the general who had set about to conquer it was soon to assume unchallenged control of the levers of military and political power in France.

Pius VII: Humiliation and Triumph

With **Pius VII** (1800–1823), we encounter one of those extraordinary popes who captured the popular imagination and memorably inspired the faithful (see Chapter 4, "Ten to Remember: Popes Who Made a Difference").

That he did this without actually setting out to is perhaps beside the point; he remains a touchstone of papal virtue and compassion, thanks to the challenges and hardships he faced during a period in European history unlike any other. He emerged from the chaos of the Napoleonic period as the first pope whose utter lack of political or military power proved a powerful public relations asset. As such, he can be seen as a precursor to popes such as John Paul II and John XXIII.

A Benedictine, Pius was a compromise candidate, and there were clear rifts within the Church at the time of his elevation. Factions representing Naples and Austria jockeyed for position and advantage. Within three months of his election, many of the intricate political calculations that had produced an impasse within the conclave (and the compromise selection of a comparatively inoffensive monk) became irrelevant.

This was because Napoleon Bonaparte had triumphed over the Austrians at Marengo, named himself first consul, and proposed a reconciliation with the Catholic Church, whose possessions and holdings he had plundered.

Napoleon Loots the Church

"Regarding the Church's property, wealth which has been vowed, holy money, the substance of the saints—the business of God, as Fathers, councils, and scripture state—shall We give you any instructions about this now that the Church has been wretchedly stripped of them? Only this: to devote your efforts so that everyone will realize the truth of the short statement of the synod of Aachen long ago: 'Whoever takes away or intends to take away what other faithful have given from the heritage of their possessions for the care of their souls, the honor of God, the beauty of His Church and the use of its ministers, assuredly turns the gifts of others into danger for his own soul.'"

—*Diu Satis* (Encyclical of Pope Pius VII on a Return to Gospel Principles), 1800

Napoleon needed the support of the pope to settle a restless France. He offered return of portions of the Papal States, and a recognition of the pope's religious role in France. In return, the new pope was to acknowledge the legality of the new government. "Tell the pope," Napoleon had said, "that I want to make him a present of 30 million Frenchmen." He could also have offered to make a present of the Church property he had recently stolen, but he opted not to do so.

Bet You Didn't Know

The Concordat of 1801 served as the basis for the reestablishment of Roman Catholicism and papal authority in France. It outlined a system whereby the French government would nominate candidates to fill vacant bishoprics, with the pope actually bestowing the offices. The reorganization of the French diocesan system, on papally approved terms, followed the agreement. The concordat served as an essential model for papal relations with the states of the nineteenth century.

Negotiations ensued, and the Concordat of 1801, which addressed (among other things) the question of the selection of bishops in France, was signed on July 15 of that year.

Trouble set in, however, soon after the signing of the concordat. Napoleon delayed its publication; when he finally allowed it to be circulated, he appended extensive and (to the pope) disturbing passages. These were the 77 so-called Organic Articles, which undercut much of what had just been so painstakingly negotiated. The articles demonstrated both the first consul's arrogance and his continued willingness to take unilateral action against the interests of the Church. Both traits would resurface in the years to follow.

It must have seemed as though Napoleon were daring the pope to walk away from the concordat. In the end, Pius chose not to do so, desiring (as Napoleon surely knew) to reestablish papal authority in France. Calculating the political, ecclesiastical, and military realities, Pius chose to protest, but not to challenge Napoleon directly.

Napoleon on the Ascent

In 1804, the French Senate proclaimed Napoleon emperor; the same year, Napoleon forced the pope to come to Paris to consecrate his (Napoleon's) coronation. If Pius held hopes that relations with the French government would improve after such a step, they were to be dashed. The years that followed brought only upheaval, assault, and betrayal for the pope.

Napoleon's armies stormed Rome in 1808, surrounded Pius's residence with cannons, and held him under what amounted to house arrest. The emperor assumed full control of the Papal States in 1809 and demanded that the pope formally abdicate all claims as secular ruler. When Pius not only refused, but also excommunicated those who had risen against the Holy See, he was arrested, isolated from his advisers, and held under guard on the Italian Riviera. Shortly thereafter, Napoleon annexed Rome.

Europe was again under assault from one of history's most skilled and resilient conquerors.

A Napoleonic Tantrum

From captivity in Italy, Pius refused to endorse the emperor's choices to fill bishoprics. In 1812, he was ordered transferred to France; his health was deteriorating, and the last rites were administered to him during the journey. In physical and emotional decline, Pius was held in strict isolation at Fontainebleau; when the emperor reappeared in 1813, he had just been defeated in Russia.

Napoleon's recent setbacks had not diminished his capacity to bully or threaten. He was still quite capable of verbally and physically abusing a 77-year-old man, and so proceeded during a meeting with Pius to throw crockery about the room, grab Pius by the cassock, and attempt to shake him into submission. (So, at least, goes the legend.) The old man agreed to sign a new concordat entirely of the emperor's devising.

Pius later renounced the agreement.

Pius's Triumph: The Jesuits Return

The conflict with Napoleon set the stage for some of Pius's greatest moments—indeed, some of the greatest moments of the papacy.

With Napoleon's ouster and exile to Elba, the pope's return to Rome was triumphant. Esteem for Pius was widespread, and this high regard survived the emperor's escape from exile and final military campaign. Suddenly everything was possible again. The pope secured what had once seemed outlandish diplomatic and political victories: the restoration of the Papal States and—what was just as remarkable—the restoration of the Jesuits in 1814. This was made considerably easier due to the refusal, years earlier, of Russia and Prussia to obey the reluctant bull of Pius VI suppressing the Society of Jesus. In these countries, the Jesuits had endured.

Pius saw to the reinvigoration of Roman Catholicism in post-Napoleonic Europe. His most important contribution to the history of the papacy had to do, however, not with territorial or diplomatic accomplishments—or even with the establishment of the Church's influence in Europe or abroad—but with Pius's continuing relationship to Napoleon and the former emperor's family.

> **Bet You Didn't Know**
>
> Having escaped from the island of Elba to march on France and secure a brief reestablishment of authority in Paris (known as the Hundred Days), Napoleon was defeated at the Battle of Waterloo in 1815. He was exiled to the secluded British island of Saint Helena.

Pius's Modern Legacy

Amazingly, the most extraordinary part of the story was yet to come. In the years following Napoleon's defeat at Waterloo and exile to Saint Helena, Pius served as protector of the family of the man who had betrayed and tormented him, and personally appealed for improvements in Napoleon's treatment in exile.

Pius's ongoing compassion for Napoleon has inspired countless people of all faiths. There may well be a pope before Pius who more diligently and assiduously fulfilled the biblical command to pray for and do well to one's enemies, and applied the noble principles explicitly to a political adversary, but he does not spring readily to mind. John Paul II's meeting with his would-be assassin is the only later parallel.

It would be wrong to view Pius VII's pontificate as the turning point in the papacy's attitude toward the Church's maintenance of political power; for most of the nineteenth century, the popes would cling stubbornly to their prerogatives as secular leaders. They were often intransigent when presented with challenges or slights to their political authority in Rome or the Papal States, which they tended to identify closely with their spiritual and pastoral roles.

> **Pope Watch**
>
> "Pius VII's stolidity in the face of humiliation began a revival of personal popularity for the pope that has since characterized Catholicism."
>
> —*The Columbia Encyclopedia*, fifth edition, Barbara A. Chernow and George A. Vallasi, editors. (New York: Columbia University Press, 1993)

In Pius's pontificate, the universal Church would find an extraordinary example of moral courage in the face of secular assault. This example reinforced the papacy's role as exemplar of the commandment of Jesus to bear wrongs patiently, live out the dictates of the faith, and incorporate an element of personal dignity and morality to the completion of duties. Pius may be regarded as the first modern pope.

"Will You Elect a Skeleton?"

Leo XII (1823–1829) was 63 years old, and already in failing health, when he was elected. He is said to have asked the conclave, "Will you elect a skeleton?"

He was a forceful supporter of the campaign to repeal anti-Catholic laws in England, but the tolerance and open-mindedness he sought for English Catholics was not always in evidence in his own policies. His was a reactionary and largely blinkered pontificate whose prominent features were a period of arrogant and divisive rule in the Papal States, rigid segregation of Jews there, and a deep suspicion of the modern notion that Christians might advance spiritually by reading vernacular translations of the Holy Scriptures.

"Those Deadly Pastures"

"You have noticed a society, commonly called the Bible society, boldly spreading throughout the whole world …. (I)t works by every means to have the holy Bible translated, or rather mistranslated, into the ordinary languages of every nation. There are good reasons for fear that (as has already happened in some of their commentaries and in other respects by a distorted interpretation of Christ's gospel) they will produce a gospel of men, or what is worse, a gospel of the devil! … (We) exhort you to try every means of keeping your flock from those deadly pastures. Do everything possible to see that the faithful observe strictly the rules of our Congregation of the Index. Convince them that to allow holy Bibles in the ordinary language, wholesale and without distinction, would on account of human rashness cause more harm than good."

—Leo XII, *Ubi Primum* (Encyclical on Assuming the Pontificate), 1824

Pius VIII (1829–1830) is best known for his knowledge of canon law and for his firm line against nepotism. He was worried by the revolutions of 1830, but reluctantly recognized the revolutionary government of King Louis-Philippe of France. He viewed the rising trend of mixed marriages between Protestants and Catholics with alarm, and was even more concerned about the continued tendency of philosophers to launch open attacks on the Church.

"No Longer Secretly and Clandestinely"

"Although God may console Us with you, We are nonetheless sad. This is due to the numberless errors and the teachings of perverse doctrines which, no longer secretly and clandestinely but openly and vigorously, attack the Catholic faith. You know how evil men have raised the standard of revolt against religion through philosophy (of which they proclaim themselves doctors) and through empty fallacies devised according to natural reason. In the first place, the Roman See is assailed and the bonds of unity are, every day, being severed. The authority of the Church is weakened and the protectors of things sacred are snatched away and held in contempt. The holy precepts are despised, the celebration of divine offices is ridiculed, and the worship of God is cursed by the sinner. All things which concern religion are relegated to the fables of old women and the superstitions of priests ...."

"Among these heresies belongs that foul contrivance of the sophists of this age, who do not admit any difference among the different professions of faith and who think that the portal of eternal salvation opens for all from any religion .... This is certainly a monstrous impiety which assigns the same praise and the mark of the just and upright man to truth and to error, to virtue and to vice, to goodness and to turpitude. Indeed this deadly idea concerning the lack of difference among religions is refuted even by the light of natural reason. We are assured of this because the various religions do not often agree among themselves. If one is true, the other must be false; there can be no society of darkness with light."

—Pope Pius VIII, *Traditi Humilitati* (Encyclical on His Program for the Pontificate), 1829

It was during Pius VIII's brief pontificate that the English finally passed the Catholic Emancipation Act of 1829.

The Traditionalist

Gregory XVI (1831–1846) came to office at a time when there was a popular revolt in the Papal States. He suppressed this movement with the aid of the Austrians.

Gregory was a staunch conservative. He aligned the papacy with the conservative European monarchies and opposed democracy, liberalism, republicanism, and the notion of separation of church and state. He also opposed Italian nationalism.

This pope's insistence on tradition and on the temporal authority of the pope contributed to an overall image of rigidity, yet this rigid traditionalist managed to restore a new sense of global vision to the Church on two important fronts. He strengthened and sustained the missionary movement, which had fallen into a period of indolence, and he spoke out vigorously against the practice of slavery.

"Shamefully Blinded by the Desire of Sordid Gain"

"We have judged that it belonged to Our pastoral solicitude to exert Ourselves to turn away the Faithful from the inhuman slave trade in Negroes and all other men. … In the process of time, the fog of pagan superstition being more completely dissipated and the manners of barbarous people having been softened, thanks to Faith operating by Charity, it at last comes about that, since several centuries, there are no more slaves in the greater number of Christian nations. But—We say with profound sorrow—there were to be found afterwards among the Faithful men who, shamefully blinded by the desire of sordid gain, in lonely and distant countries, did not hesitate to reduce to slavery Indians, Negroes, and other wretched peoples, or else, by instituting or developing the trade in those who had been made slaves by others, to favour their unworthy practice …. We warn and adjure earnestly in the Lord faithful Christians of every condition that no one in the future dare to vex anyone, despoil him of his possessions, reduce to servitude, or lend aid and favour to those who give themselves up to these practices, or exercise that inhuman traffic by which the Blacks, as if they were not men but rather animals, having been brought into servitude, in no matter what way, are, without any distinction, in contempt of the rights of justice and humanity, bought, sold, and devoted sometimes to the hardest labor. Further, in the hope of gain, propositions of purchase being made to the first owners of the Blacks, dissensions and almost perpetual conflicts are aroused in these regions. We reprove, then, by virtue of Our Apostolic Authority, all the practices above mentioned as absolutely unworthy of the Christian name. By the same Authority We prohibit and strictly forbid any Ecclesiastic or lay person from presuming to defend as permissible this traffic in Blacks under no matter what pretext or excuse, or from publishing or teaching in any manner whatsoever, in public or privately, opinions contrary to what We have set forth in this Apostolic Letter."

—Pope Gregory XVI, *In Supremo Apostolatus* (Apostolic Letter Condemning the Slave Trade), 1839

Recovering from the reactive, seemingly unrecoverable confusion of Pius VI's pontificate, the papacy had only slowly begun to come to terms with the new world in which it found itself, and it remained especially suspicious of democracy, egalitarianism, and popular political movements.

As a result, the next pope would contend with chaos on the political front that rivaled even that which had unfolded thus far in the nineteenth century. He would be remembered primarily, however, not for that chaos, but for two inspiring and distinctive doctrines of modern Catholicism—and for a wave of popular reverence for the Virgin Mary that showed the true nature of the papacy's authority in the nineteenth and twentieth centuries.

The Least You Need to Know

◆ Clement XIV yielded to pressures to suppress the Jesuit movement.

◆ Pius VI was overwhelmed by political and military upheavals in Europe.

◆ Pius VII conducted the first great modern pontificate, largely because of his personal dignity, courage, and compassion in the face of great trials during and after the Napoleonic Wars.

◆ One highlight of that extraordinary pontificate was the Concardat of 1801, which reestablished papal authority in France and served as a model for future agreements with secular powers.

◆ In addition, Pius VII restored the Jesuit order.

◆ Gregory XVI, a staunch traditionalist, had a global vision; he reinvigorated the Catholic missionary movement and issued a stinging condemnation of slavery.

Part  5

From Potentate to Pastor

Here, you'll learn how the popes have responded to the tests of the modern world.

These chapters include profiles on the popes who are most memorable to contemporary Catholics, including St. Pius X, Pius XI, John XXIII (who summoned the momentous Second Vatican Council), Paul VI, and John Paul II.

Chapter 20

Three Men and the Modern World

In This Chapter

- ◆ Pius IX
- ◆ Leo XIII
- ◆ Pius X

Three lengthy and distinctive pontificates struggled, in very different ways, to lead the Church and interact with contemporary society in the late nineteenth and early twentieth centuries. Each offered a fascinating character study; each man found different ways of coping with momentous changes in the nature of the office—and in the world at large.

In for the Long Term

Pius IX (1846–1878), who conducted the longest pontificate on record, is remembered primarily for the declaration of the dogma of the Immaculate Conception (1854) and for convoking the First Vatican Council (1870), which issued a decree of papal infallibility. These two momentous events helped to define the Roman Catholic faith in the modern world. But there was a great deal more to his pontificate.

What Happened When

- ◆ **1848:** Revolution in Rome.

- ◆ **1854:** Establishment of the doctrine of the Immaculate Conception.

- ◆ **1870:** The First Vatican Council issues a decree of papal infallibility; French troops withdraw from Rome with the outbreak of the Franco-Prussian War, and Italian republican troops quickly take over the city.

- ◆ **1872:** German Catholics founded a political party, and the resulting conflict with political authorities led to a period of harassment and oppression known as the *Kulturkampf* (struggle between civilizations).

- ◆ **1891:** The encyclical *Rerum Novarum* directly addressed the social issues related to the rise of socialism.

- ◆ **1914:** Outbreak of World War I.

Pope Watch

Pius IX was officially pronounced "Blessed" by John Paul II on September 3, 2000—the first step toward canonization (sainthood). In September of 2001, there was a flurry of reports that anti-Semitic remarks attributed to Pius IX had surfaced. As the debate about this pope continues, efforts to have him declared a saint may lose momentum.

Under Pius, the papacy was dragged unwillingly into accommodation with the political realities of the nineteenth century. Formal acknowledgment of those realities, which precluded secular rule over Rome and the Papal States by the Roman pontiff, would not come about until much later. But it was during this pontificate that the exercise of political power became a memory, rather than a duty, of the papacy.

Pius's Dual Role

Pius began by attempting to initiate a series of much-needed reforms in the Papal States. He also saw to the institution of a democratically elected municipal authority in Rome. His refusal to take a role in leading an Italian war against Austria, however, made it clear that he wanted no part in ruling over a federalized Italy.

The price of such leadership—the prospect of which had captured popular imagination in Rome—would have been steep indeed: a narrow focus on Italian nationalism that simply could not be sustained by the leader of a global religion. The notion of the Church leading a war against a Catholic nation (which Austria was) could only have been deeply offensive to Pius, and he explicitly refused to accept it. His popularity plummeted.

Where before he had been seen as a figure of independence and liberation, Pius now was regarded as one who had betrayed the very same causes. In 1848—a year in which revolutionary fervor swept Europe in general and Rome in particular—the painful contradictions of the pope's dual role as secular ruler and pastor to the universal Church became impossible to ignore. Pius joined the unhappy fraternity of popes to have been driven from the holy city.

He came back in 1850, supported by French troops, thereby joining the happier fraternity of popes to have reestablished his former position with the aid of a foreign power. He had bought time, but not much else, by appealing to Catholic nations for support. This was to be the last time (to date, at any rate) such a sequence events was to play out.

> **Pope Watch**
>
> In 1848, following the assassination of his prime minister, the layman Pelegrino Rossi, Pius escaped from Rome disguised as a humble priest. Revolt was underway in the city.

There had been many uprisings in the holy city over the centuries. There was something different, however, about this particular period of violence, crusade, and confusion in Rome. It was rooted in an emerging sense of Italian nationalism, and it would eventually succeed in securing Rome as the capital of a united Italy.

Before that came to pass, however, Pius presided over the adoption of a doctrine now inextricably associated with Roman Catholicism. It overshadowed, for a time, the extraordinary political developments with which he coped only when convinced he could not pronounce or ignore them out of existence.

The Immaculate Conception

In 1854, Pius resolved with authority the question of the Virgin Mary's sinlessness by approving the doctrine of the Immaculate Conception. The doctrine was quickly promulgated around the world—and with customary vigor—by the Jesuits.

> **Pontifical ... but Mythical**
>
> A matter of occasional confusion among non-Catholics, the Immaculate Conception holds not that Jesus was conceived sinlessly (a position that had already stood for centuries), but that Mary herself was conceived and born free from original sin.

"Free from All Taint of Original Sin"

"From the very beginning, and before time began, the eternal Father chose and prepared for his only-begotten Son a Mother in whom the Son of God would become incarnate and from whom, in the blessed fullness of time, he would be born into this world. Above all creatures did God so love her that truly in her was the Father well pleased with singular delight. Therefore, far above all the angels and all the saints so wondrously did God endow her with the abundance of all heavenly gifts poured from the treasury of his divinity that this mother, ever absolutely free of all stain of sin, all fair and perfect, would possess that fullness of holy innocence and sanctity than which, under God, one cannot even imagine anything greater, and which, outside of God, no mind can succeed in comprehending fully. And indeed it was wholly fitting that so wonderful a mother should be ever resplendent with the glory of most sublime holiness and so completely free from all taint of original sin that she would triumph utterly over the ancient serpent."

—Pope Piux IX, *Ineffabilis Deus* (Apostolic Constitution of Pope Pius IX: The Immaculate Conception), 1854

That Pius took this step on his own, without conciliar endorsement, was seen by many as a welcome expression of papal authority. Of this doctrine, the papal chamberlain, Monsignor Talbot, said, "The most important thing is not the new dogma itself, but the way in which it was proclaimed." That may have been overstating the matter, but the move nevertheless marked an important new chapter in the way the Church saw itself and its pope.

Pius's devotion to the Virgin was extraordinary—he regarded his recuperation from epilepsy as an example of her benevolent intercession in human affairs—and during his pontificate an extraordinary flowering of Marian observance began within the Church. Reverence for Mary had an ancient history, of course, but shortly after Pius's formal embrace of the doctrine of the Immaculate Conception, it took on a staggering new popularity among the faithful. This fierce embrace of piety and reverence was fueled in part by accounts the Virgin herself appearing at Lourdes, France, in 1858, and by a torrent of reports of miracles from pilgrims who later journeyed there.

Pius had—with the apparent help of the Virgin to whom he made frequent public acknowledgment—brought about an extraordinary spiritual renewal within the Church. The pope's claim to primacy as pastor of the universal Church had rarely been stronger.

Closer to home, though, matters would soon become more troublesome in the political arena.

More Political Problems for Pius

Pius was irrevocably opposed to the idea of unifying Italy under a single flag, and his popularity in Rome suffered once again when it became clear that he would refuse to budge on this point. He clung stubbornly to old prerogatives, and dealt with the changes sweeping through Italy (and the rest of Europe, and North America, for that matter) by assuming that social transformation itself could be managed somehow by decree.

Pius chose not to dignify the increasingly vocal antipapal movement with much attention, and turned his attentions instead to overseeing a general Church council, the first in more than 300 years.

The First Vatican Council

The First Vatican Council (1869–1870), conducted during a time of momentous political change, pronounced, among other things, the notion of papal infallibility so strongly associated with the Roman Church today. (Many non-Catholics believe, mistakenly, that the formal pronouncement of this doctrine is of considerably older vintage.) It is true, of course, that the infallibility of the Church in general and the pope in particular had been a matter of long-standing tradition and observance, but the nature and source of the infallibility had never been specifically set out. (Indeed, many within the Church were quite nervous about attempting to define it at all.)

When the Council had finished its work on this controversial matter, it had elucidated a distinctive (and frequently misinterpreted) principle of Church practice: the establishment of a specific realm of pronouncements not to be challenged by Catholics.

The council emphasized that it is only the pope's pronouncements *ex cathedra* (from the throne) concerning faith and morals that are infallible. The language carefully limits itself to the infallibility of the pope's *speech* (regarding specific areas of doctrine), rather than the general infallibility of an *individual* (when, say, he makes a casual remark). In other words, if the pope says it's going to snow tomorrow and it doesn't snow, no one is under any obligation to regard snow as having fallen in some mystical or theological manner.

The council also denounced contemporary godlessness and materialism, and clarified matters of canon law.

"Supreme Apostolic Authority"

"Therefore, faithfully adhering to the tradition received from the beginning of the Christian faith ... we teach and define as a divinely revealed dogma that when the Roman Pontiff speaks ex cathedra, that is, when, in the exercise of his office as shepherd and teacher of all Christians, in virtue of his supreme apostolic authority, he defines a doctrine concerning faith or morals to be held by the whole Church, he possesses, by the divine assistance promised to him in blessed Peter, that infallibility which the divine Redeemer willed his Church to enjoy in defining doctrine concerning faith or morals. Therefore, such definitions of the Roman Pontiff are of themselves, and not by the consent of the Church, irreformable."

—Vatican Council I, 1870

The month of June 1870 was eventful; the outbreak of the Franco-Prussian War coincided almost exactly with the sessions of the Vatican Council, and the French withdrew their troops from Rome. Republican troops seized Rome shortly after the vote on infallibility passed the council, which promptly scattered. The First Vatican Council would not officially adjourn until 92 years later, with the commencement of the equally momentous Second Vatican Council in 1962.

Pontifical ... but Mythical

The doctrine of papal infallibility, which centers on formal pronouncements regarding matters of faith and morals, does *not* require Catholics to believe that every word spoken by the pope is infallibly correct. Nor does it permit the pope to reconstruct the Church verbally whenever the mood strikes him. The pope may not alter fundamental tenets of belief (for instance, the triune nature of God).

The Prisoner of the Vatican

Thus political changes continued to present themselves at a pace not entirely to the pope's liking.

The period of the pope's actual role as a temporal ruler over the lands known as the Papal States, which began in 756, had come to an end in 1860 with the annexation by Italy of most of the lands in question. With the hasty and (unanticipated) termination of the First Vatican Council, another unwelcome transformation took place. Pius was forced to negotiate a settlement with the republican forces of Giuseppe Garibaldi. Before the year 1870 was out, Rome had been annexed as the capital of the kingdom of Italy. The passage of a Law of Guarantees to deal with the question of the pope's special standing took place in November 1870.

Pius rejected it, and, from 1871 forward, remained in the Vatican, having declared himself a prisoner of what he considered to be an anticlerical regime.

The papacy's secular authority now encompassed a tiny sliver of land. Its pastoral authority, on the other hand, extended across the world.

Pastor of the Global Church

The final resolution of the various unresolved and knotty questions regarding the pope's official status would not come until the Lateran Treaty of 1929. For now, the undeniable reality was that Pius was no longer a political ruler in any realistic sense of the term. He, like all the popes who have followed him, would have to be content with limiting himself to the duties of pastor of the global Church.

Pius had been born in 1792; when he died in 1878 at the age of 86, the world had been transformed many times over. Under his lengthy and frequently chaotic pontificate, two extraordinary certainties had emerged. They had to do with the Virgin Mary and the nature of the pope's teaching, respectively, and they each have the air of doctrines that somehow persisted for centuries before they actually came into formal existence.

After Pius IX

Leo XIII (1878–1903) attempted to help in the formation of Roman Catholic attitudes appropriate to life in the modern world. He tried, for instance, to make sure the church was not instinctively opposed to each new instance of scientific progress; his *Aeterni Patris* insisted there need be no conflict between science and faith. He founded the institute of Thomistic philosophy (after the philosophy of St. Thomas Aquinas) at the University of Louvain, and opened the Vatican's library to all scholars.

His was a pontificate forced to address new ideas, systems of living, and governments; it is to his credit that he did not build his reign around the (ineffective) strategy of refusing to acknowledge the existence or impact of modern social and political movements. To the contrary, in 1885, Leo issued an encyclical, *Immortale Dei*, which incorporated a vision of Catholic belief in the context of secular democracy.

> **Pope Watch**
>
> Leo XIII encouraged Bible study and founded a permanent Biblical Commission.

Leo also set himself against the haughty movement of royalists in France, who viewed the Gallic expression of Catholicism as something separate and apart from the rest of the Church. His support for Catholics in democratic systems was a valuable and essential step forward for a church that had for centuries adopted a monarchistic world outlook. Even this, however, paled in importance when compared with his decision, in 1891, to issue an encyclical letter, *Rerum Novarum*, which examined the social and political abuses that had led to the rise of the socialist movement in Europe.

"A Yoke Almost of Slavery"

"After the old trade guilds had been destroyed in the last century, and no protection was substituted in their place, and when public institutions and legislation had cast off traditional religious teaching, it gradually came about that the present age handed over the workers, each alone and defenseless, to the inhumanity of employers and the unbridled greed of competitors. A devouring usury, although often condemned by the Church, but practiced nevertheless under another form by avaricious and grasping men, has increased the evil; and in addition the whole process of production as well as trade in every kind of goods has been brought almost entirely under the power of a few, so that a very few rich and exceedingly rich men have laid a yoke almost of slavery on the unnumbered masses of non-owning workers."

—Leo XIII, *Rerum Novarum* (Encyclical Letter on the Condition of the Working Classes), 1891

The success generally accorded to Leo's pontificate is primarily the result of his willingness, in *Rerum Novarum*, to discuss frankly the social realities of the period, and to examine without flinching the predations of the wealthy classes of his time. Such honesty existed side by side with a deep sense of spiritual obligation and a concern for the Church's future mission.

It is said that, one day in 1884 after saying a Mass, Leo heard a deep, growling voice boast that it needed only 75 to 100 years, and greater power over the people under its control, to destroy the Catholic Church. Supposedly, this is what prompted him to add the following prayer to the conclusion of each Mass:

"Saint Michael the Archangel, defend us in battle, be our safeguard against the wickedness and snares of the devil. May God rebuke him, we humbly pray, and do thou, O Prince of the Heavenly Host, by the power of God, cast into Hell Satan and the other evil spirits who prowl about the world for the ruin of souls, Amen."

The prayer was said at the conclusion of Mass until 1964.

The Pope Takes a Stand Against Modernism

St. Pius X (1903–1914) was a political and religious conservative who spoke out against theological modernism and revolutionary movements. He was deeply committed to the support of pious religious observance among the laity.

On September 8, 1907, he issued the now-famous encyclical *Pascendi*, a lucid and detailed rejection of modernism. This document, according to the *Catholic Encyclopedia*, addresses the dangers of the modernist systems "in relation to philosophy, apologetics, exegesis, history, liturgy, and discipline, and shows the contradiction between that innovation and the ancient faith; and, finally, it establishes rules by which to combat efficiently the pernicious doctrines in question." To deal with the threat, Pius saw to the creation of an official corps of censors and the establishment of a committee of vigilance. Pius considered *modernism* "the summation of all heresies."

Vatican Vocabulary

Modernism, as the term was applied in the late nineteenth and early twentieth century, refers to a movement within Catholicism emphasizing the role of human reason, affirming the separation of church and state, and opposing the pope's claims to temporal power.

The Oath

"I entirely reject the heretical misrepresentation that dogmas evolve and change from one meaning to another different from the one which the Church held previously. I also condemn every error according to which, in place of the divine deposit which has been given to the spouse of Christ to be carefully guarded by her, there is put a philosophical figment or product of a human conscience that has gradually been developed by human effort and will continue to develop indefinitely .... I also condemn and reject the opinion of those who say that a well-educated Christian assumes a dual personality—that of a believer and at the same time of a historian, as if it were permissible for a historian to hold things that contradict the faith of the believer, or to establish premises which, provided there be no direct denial of dogmas, would lead to the conclusion that dogmas are either false or doubtful."

—Pius X, *Oath Against Modernism*, 1910, "to be sworn to by all clergy, pastors, confessors, preachers, religious superiors, and professors in philosophical-theological seminaries"

Pius was responsible for such important liturgical reforms as the revival of plainsong (also known as plainchant), revision of the catechism, and a number of important eucharistic decrees. He set up a commission to adapt and systematize canon law; this resulted in publication of the new code in 1917 (effective in 1918) under his successor.

Pius is remembered particularly for his decision to lower the age at which children may receive First Communion to seven (previously it had been 12 or 14) and for his promotion of the practice of taking communion frequently. The latter initiative was more than a simple matter of agitating for piety among the faithful; Jansenism had counseled against excessive communion, whatever that was. By successfully promoting regular (and, in the ideal circumstance, daily) communion, Pius was striking the final blow against that remarkably hardy dissident movement within Catholicism.

The author of a vigorous campaign to encourage all of the faithful to read the Holy Scriptures, Pius was a profoundly committed traditionalist whose deep personal spirituality was centered on (as he put it) "the renewal of all things in Christ." He died shortly after the outbreak of World War I.

Pius was canonized in 1954, and his pontificate is today a signpost for many Catholics who share his commitment to celebrating the Catholic tradition and its role in addressing the challenges of contemporary secular society.

His last will and testament contained the following celebrated declaration: "I was born poor, I have lived in poverty, and I wish to die poor."

Storms on the Horizon

Deprived of secular power, the papacy would attempt to forge a new role for itself, one that maintained and supported the ancient traditions of the Church and set moral guidelines for an increasingly complex and diverse modern society. Two bloody world wars would soon demonstrate the difficulty of the job, as well as the intricate and occasionally intractable nature of the challenges awaiting those who would lead the Church through its next phase.

The Least You Need to Know

- Under Pius IX's frequently chaotic pontificate, two doctrinal certainties emerged: that of the Immaculate Conception and the First Vatican Council's pronouncement regarding papal infallibility.

- Pius IX also presided over the loss of papal secular authority in Rome and the Papal States.

- Leo XIII attacked the social abuses that gave rise to the socialist movement in *Rerum Novarum*.

- Pius X rejected modernism; canonized in 1954, he was a profoundly committed traditionalist whose deep personal spirituality was centered on "the renewal of all things in Christ."

Chapter 21

The World in Flames

In This Chapter

- ◆ The failed papal peace plan for World War I
- ◆ Condemnations of the Nazi and Fascist movements
- ◆ The truth about Pius XII

Over nearly 19 centuries, the Catholic Church had survived state-sponsored persecution, rampaging marauders, aggressive monarchs, hostile empires, and bloodthirsty opportunists of countless types. It had never, however, seen anything like the grim episodes of war that ravaged the globe in the first half of the twentieth century. Nor had humanity.

In centuries past, the papacy had often jockeyed for advantage during periods of military turmoil in Europe. Now, stripped of its political and military authority, it tried to master the role of peacemaker and comforter of the afflicted.

What Happened When

◆ **1914–1918:** The Great War (or First World War).

◆ **1917:** Revolution in Russia.

◆ **1929:** The Lateran Treaty was signed, marking the resolution of the Roman Question.

◆ **1939–1945:** The Second World War.

◆ **1950:** Doctrine of the Assumption of the Virgin Mary.

◆ **1956:** Vatican condemns Soviet suppression of anti-Communist movement in Hungary.

The Church and the Great War

In the face of shocking casualties, **Benedict XV** (1914–1922) maintained a policy of strict neutrality during the fearful conflict now known as World War I (1914–1918). (At the time, it was referred to as the Great War.)

Benedict had hoped to use his carefully sustained neutrality to help bring about an end to the conflict. His role as mediator was rejected, however, and he had to content himself with ongoing Vatican support for prisoners of war and displaced civilians. The conflict had been so bitter that it is likely that no third party could have played the role Benedict wanted to play. Several powers, in fact, saw him as secretly supporting their enemies—in part because, in his ardent desire not to take sides, he had declined to speak out against various well-publicized atrocities. (Another factor was that Italy suspected him of wishing to raise papal claims to Italian territories during negotiations.)

Benedict XV's Failed Peace Plan

"Benedict XV, on August 1, 1917, issued a specific peace plan which came to be known as the Papal peace note …. This formal plan for peace stated that (1) 'the moral force of right … be substituted for the material force of arms,' (2) there must be 'simultaneous and reciprocal diminution of armaments,' (3) a mechanism for 'international arbitration' must be established, (4) 'true liberty and common rights over the sea' should exist, (5) there should be a 'renunciation of war indemnities,' (6) occupied territories should be evacuated, and (7) there should be 'an examination … of rival claims.'

"With the Allies looking disfavorably the Pope's note, the Central Powers also sent replies. Bulgaria and Austria-Hungary were the most favorable, while Germany sent an inconclusive answer which cited the refusal of the Allies to halt the war and the preference that there be no third party involvement in negotiations ..."

—John R. Smestad Jr., *Europe: 1914–1915: Attempts at Peace* (New Orleans: Loyola University Department of History)

(Benedict made no further attempt to bring about a peace agreement.)

Benedict was, like his predecessor, an energetic promoter of Catholic missionary work. He supported the dawning effort to promote local (rather than European) clergy in faraway lands. He also made an attempt to reunite the Eastern and Western Churches; this effort was, however, like all such attempts since 1054, doomed to failure. He even canonized Joan of Arc, the French national heroine who had claimed divine guidance during the Hundred Years' War, and who had been executed for heresy in 1431. (This was a particularly effective piece of ecclesiastical diplomacy on Benedict's part, one that successfully signaled a desire for reconciliation and concord with the French church.)

Despite his best efforts, Benedict's pontificate was overshadowed by the war, suffering, deprivation, and diplomatic double-dealing that engulfed all of Europe at the time. This was a shame, because he was passionately devoted to the cause of peace, and would have welcomed any opportunity to help bring it about.

> ### Pope Watch
>
> In 1917, Benedict officially introduced the new Code of Canon Law (*Codex iuris canonici*).

Benedict Tries to Open the Door

"(T)his Apostolic See has never wearied of teaching during the war such pardon of offenses and the fraternal reconciliation of the peoples, in conformity with the most holy law of Jesus Christ, and in agreement with the needs of civil life and human intercourse; nor did it allow that amid dissension and hate these moral principles should be forgotten. With all the more reason then, now that the Treaties of Peace are signed, does it proclaim these principles .... (C)oncord between civilized nations is maintained and fostered by the modern custom of visits and meetings at which the Heads of States and Princes are accustomed to treat of matters of special importance. So then, considering the changed circumstances of the times and the dangerous trend of events, and in order to encourage this concord, We would not be unwilling to relax in some measure the severity of the conditions justly laid down by

continues

continued

> Our Predecessors, when the civil power of the Apostolic See was overthrown, against the official visits of the Heads of Catholic states to Rome."
>
> —Benedict XV, *Pacem, Dei Munus Pulcherrimum* (Encyclical on Peace and Christian Reconciliation), 1920

"The Peace of Christ"

The energetic **Pius XI** (1922–1939) took as his motto "the peace of Christ in the Kingdom of Christ." His goal was nothing less than the construction of a new Christendom based on the principle of world peace, and he was willing to agitate feverishly in the world's diplomatic circles in an attempt to bring his vision about.

Pope Watch

Pius XI negotiated the Lateran Treaty of 1929, which resolved the legal and diplomatic impasse that had existed for years between the papacy and the Italian state. The solution to the long-unresolved "Roman question" lay in the creation of a new nation—the Vatican City—and the recognition of Roman Catholicism as the sole state religion of Italy.

Pius's "Kingdom of Christ" was an inspiring goal, but events on the ground were ultimately to prove uncooperative to the attainment of Pius's vision. His pontificate encompassed not only the period following World War I, but also the more terrifying phase that saw economic devastation, the rise of Hitler in Germany, and the gathering of new war clouds in Europe.

Rifts with Mussolini and Hitler

Pius had no patience for the efforts of Fascist officials to indoctrinate Italian youth; he eventually attacked Fascism openly in a papal letter in 1931, a move that led to a worsening of relations with Mussolini.

A similar but even more impassioned drama played out with Hitler, who in 1933 negotiated a concordat with the Church and subsequently ignored the agreement. After enduring a long period in which the Nazis had victimized the clergy, interfered with Church affairs, and launched a vigorous campaign to get German Catholics to put Nazism above their religious faith, Pius decided he had had enough.

He issued one of the great papal encyclicals; its German (rather than Latin) title, *Mit Brennender Sorge* ("With Burning Anxiety") left no doubt as to the message's point of view—or its audience.

"Our God Cannot Tolerate a Rival"

"Take care, Venerable Brethren, that above all, faith in God, the first and irreplaceable foundation of all religion, be preserved in Germany pure and unstained. The believer in God is not he who utters the name in his speech, but he for whom this sacred word stands for a true and worthy concept of the Divinity. Whoever identifies, by pantheistic confusion, God and the universe, by either lowering God to the dimensions of the world, or raising the world to the dimensions of God, is not a believer in God. Whoever follows that so-called pre-Christian Germanic conception of substituting a dark and impersonal destiny for the personal God, denies thereby the Wisdom and Providence of God who "Reacheth from end to end mightily, and ordereth all things sweetly" (Wisdom 8:1). Neither is he a believer in God. Whoever exalts race, or the people, or the State, or a particular form of State, or the depositories of power, or any other fundamental value of the human community—however necessary and honorable be their function in worldly things—whoever raises these notions above their standard value and divinizes them to an idolatrous level, distorts and perverts an order of the world planned and created by God; he is far from the true faith in God and from the concept of life which that faith upholds. Beware, Venerable Brethren, of that growing abuse, in speech as in writing, of the name of God as though it were a meaningless label, to be affixed to any creation, more or less arbitrary, of human speculation. Use your influence on the Faithful, that they refuse to yield to this aberration. Our God is the Personal God, supernatural, omnipotent, infinitely perfect, one in the Trinity of Persons, tri-personal in the unity of divine essence, the Creator of all existence. Lord, King and ultimate Consummator of the history of the world, who will not, and cannot, tolerate a rival God by His side."

—Pope Pius XI, *Mit Brennender Sorge* (Encyclical on the Church and the German Reich), 1937

A Stand Against Communism

Pius was equally concerned about the global effects of Communism. He denounced the Communist movement in terms just as harsh and explicit as those he had turned on Hitler's regime.

"Rivers of Blood"

"(T)he struggle between good and evil remained in the world as a sad legacy of the original fall. Nor has the ancient tempter ever ceased to deceive mankind with false promises. It is on this account that one convulsion following upon another has marked the passage of the centuries, down to the revolution of our own days. This modern revolution, it may be said, has actually broken out or threatens everywhere, and it exceeds in amplitude and violence anything yet experienced in the preceding persecutions launched against the Church. Entire peoples find themselves in danger of falling back into a barbarism worse than that which oppressed the greater part of the world at the coming of the Redeemer. This all too imminent danger, Venerable Brethren, as you have already surmised, is bolshevistic and atheistic Communism, which aims at upsetting the social order and at undermining the very foundations of Christian civilization ....

"In the beginning Communism showed itself for what it was in all its perversity; but very soon it realized that it was thus alienating the people. It has therefore changed its tactics, and strives to entice the multitudes by trickery of various forms, hiding its real designs behind ideas that in themselves are good and attractive. Thus, aware of the universal desire for peace, the leaders of Communism pretend to be the most zealous promoters and propagandists in the movement for world amity. Yet at the same time they stir up a class warfare which causes rivers of blood to flow, and, real-izing that their system offers no internal guarantee of peace, they have recourse to unlimited armaments ....

"See to it, Venerable Brethren, that the Faithful do not allow themselves to be deceived! Communism is intrinsically wrong, and no one who would save Christian civilization may collaborate with it in any undertaking whatsoever ...."

—Pope Pius XI, *Divini Redemptoris* (Encyclical on Atheistic Communism), 1937

Principled Opposition, Constructive New Initiatives

This pope was also a vigorous opponent of nationalism, racism, and anti-Semitism. He had deep misgivings about the potentially destructive effects of laissez-faire capitalism, and emphasized the importance of social reform efforts. In addition, he promoted lay involvement in Church affairs, emphasized the importance of new communications tech-nologies in perpetuating the Church's message, and worked to preserve the distinctive practices of Eastern rite Catholics.

Pius's "burning anxiety" regarding the excesses of the Reich turned out to be completely justified. His death in February 1939 meant that he did not live to see the cataclysm that erupted in Europe later that year when Hitler invaded Poland. Suddenly, the world was engulfed in another round of bloody conflict, and the "peace of Christ in the Kingdom of Christ" seemed very far away indeed.

Pius and World War II

Having served as the previous pope's secretary of state, **Pius XII** (1939–1958) was an experienced diplomat by the time of his election, and was in fact the motivating force behind many of Pius XI's agreements and pronouncements, having produced, for instance, the initial draft of *Mit Brennender Sorge*.

Pius XII was pope during the most horrific war in human history, and for over a decade after its conclusion. His press has been spotty in recent years, to say the least. In fact, he has emerged as the most controversial of the twentieth-century popes. Why is this so? Does this pontificate deserve the criticism it has received since 1963, when a German play entitled *The Deputy* by Rolf Hochhuth painted him as a money-obsessed Nazi sympathizer?

Any responsible discussion of this pontificate must address not only what Pius supposedly failed to accomplish, but also what he actually did accomplish. Let's look at both sides of this story.

> **Pope Watch**
>
> Pius XII was the first secretary of state to be elected pope since Clement IX in 1667.

A Voice of Principle

After centuries of involvement as an interested party in the seemingly endless political and military disputes of Europe, the papacy was now to serve, even more directly than during World War I, primarily as a sanctuary for the afflicted, injured, and pursued. Under Pius XII, it was a voice of principle and an example of humanitarian service in the face of Nazi aggression.

No one familiar with the record can seriously dispute Pius's work in service of refugees and victims of persecution during the Second World War. He was manifestly not an ally, silent or otherwise, of the Third Reich; he was not "Hitler's pope." Those who suggest otherwise defame the memory of a good man.

The popular opinion that Pius XII was either a closet Nazi or a contented, passive observer of their policy of genocide against the Jews simply does not withstand scrutiny. Those who wish to argue casually that Pius "did nothing" to assist persecuted Jews during World War II overlook the following documented facts:

♦ When Hitler occupied the city of Rome following the collapse of the Italian government (1943), Pius made Vatican City a haven for Jewish refugees.

♦ During the course of the war, Pius granted Vatican citizenship to approximately a million and a half refugees, many of them Jews.

♦ Through the Pontifical Aid Commission, Pius coordinated an immense relief effort for victims of the bloody upheavals of World War II, both Jewish and Gentile.

♦ With Pius's knowledge and support, there arose in Italy during the war a massive underground network of priests, religious, and lay people who helped to shelter victims of Nazi oppression. Many of those who benefited from this underground network were Jews; once the war ended, the head of the Jewish community in Rome praised Pius's work in this area, and himself became a Roman Catholic.

♦ Shortly after his death in 1958, Pius XII's efforts on behalf of Jews during World War II were praised by the World Jewish Congress, the Antidefamation League, the Synagogue Council of America, the Rabbinical Council of America, the American Jewish Congress, the New York Board of Rabbis, the American Jewish Committee, the Central Conference of American Rabbis, the National Conference of Christians and Jews, and the National Council of Jewish Women (source: www.catholicleague. org, "Frequently Asked Questions about Pius XII and the Holocaust," 2001).

If this was a man who hated Jews, he had a strange and misdirected way of expressing his hatred.

Pius and the Holocaust

What, then, is all the fuss about?

Pius's (responsible) detractors take issue with his words, not his deeds. It was, of course, on this pope's watch that one of the greatest crimes in human experience was perpetrated: the Holocaust. The pope had the opportunity—and, many now argue, a duty—to issue a clear and unmistakable denunciation of the Nazi campaign of genocide *specifically as it applied to the Jewish people.*

He did not do so, choosing instead, in his Christmas message of 1942, to draw attention to "the hundreds of thousands who, through no fault of their own, and solely because of their nation or race, have been condemned to death or progressive extinction."

Had he inserted a sentence making specific reference to the sufferings of the Jews, the controversy of later years would never have arisen. Yet there was no such sentence. It was clear enough to the Germans, however, what he was getting at. After the release of the 1942 Christmas message, the Gestapo countered with what would today be considered a defensive sound bite: "(The pope) is virtually accusing the German people of injustice toward the Jews, and makes himself the mouthpiece of the Jewish war criminal" (source:

www.catholicleague.com, "Frequently Asked Questions about Pius XII and the Holocaust," 2001).

The Controversy Unfolds

Pius's omission, in 1942 and the years following, of any direct reference to the genocidal campaign against the Jews is certainly unfortunate. It is fair to ask, however, what such a denunciation would have actually accomplished during World War II ... and why the furor over its absence in the years after the war only arose after Pius's death.

One answer to the latter question—provided, it must be noted, by Pius's defenders—runs as follows: Beginning in the 1960s, certain left-leaning historians sought to sully the pope's memory by suggesting that, during the war, he had consented to the Holocaust and/or argued on Germany's behalf in order to forward an anti-Communist agenda.

> **Pope Watch**
>
> In 2001, David I. Kertzer's carefully researched *The Popes Against the Jews* (New York: Alfred A Knopf) attracted worldwide attention. Kertzer argued that the controversy over Pius XII's policy toward the Nazi regime was ultimately less important than questions regarding papal support for, or tolerance of, anti-Semitism through the centuries.

> **Pope Watch**
>
> Pius's strident anti-Communism occasionally raised hackles. In 1949, he excommunicated Catholics in Italy who joined the Communist Party.

> **Bet You Didn't Know** _____
>
> "It may surprise the contemporary generation to learn that the local Jewish communities and the world Jewish bodies did not, for the most part, urge the pope to 'speak out.' Their objective was far more concrete and down-to-earth .... The crying need in those years was for effective pressure on persecuting governments, pressure that often enough could only be exercised by discreet and roundabout methods."
>
> —Robert A. Graham, S.J., "How to Manufacture a Legend: The Controversy over the Alleged Silence of Pope Pius XII in World War II," article on *nbci.com*, 2001

That later generations would prefer that Pius had spoken out openly against the Holocaust is beyond debate. That he should have is equally clear. That he cooperated in any way, shape, or form with the Nazis, however, is utterly unsupported by the evidence. Equally implausible is the idea that the Vatican withheld secret documents on his Nazi sympathies.

The Last Word

The debate over Pius XII's actions during World War II has unfortunately obscured the other events of his pontificate (such as the definition of the doctrine of the *Assumption of the Virgin Mary*, or the liturgical and other reforms that paved the way for the Second Vatican Council). The controversy has, however, refused to go away, and for that reason alone it merits close attention. Those who are still uncertain on this matter are referred to the words of Israel's minister of foreign affairs in 1958 (and later, its prime minister):

Vatican Vocabulary

Pius XII expressed the "divinely revealed dogma" of the **Assumption of the Virgin Mary** in 1950. It held that the "immaculate mother of God, when the course of her earthly life was run, was assumed in body and soul to heavenly glory." (*Munificentissimus Deus*, Encyclical on the Dogma of the Assumption of the Blessed Virgin)

"During the 10 years of Nazi terror, when our people went through the horrors of martyrdom, the pope raised his voice to condemn the persecutors and commiserate with the victims." Golda Meir spoke these words upon the death of Pius XII in 1958 in remarks delivered on the floor of the United Nations General Assembly.

The Least You Need to Know

◆ Benedict XV tried, and failed, to play peacemaker at the end of World War I.

◆ Pius XI's vision of the "Peace of Christ in the Kingdom of Christ" went unrealized during his lifetime; war clouds gathered near the end of his pontificate.

◆ His successor, Pius XII, has been unjustly accused of harboring Nazi sympathies during World War II.

◆ Pius XII was a fervent anti-Communist, as was his predecessor.

Chapter 22

A New Wind Blows

In This Chapter

- ◆ John XXIII stirs things up
- ◆ The Second Vatican Council
- ◆ Paul VI oversees a revolution … and, subsequently, doesn't

Two remarkable men presided over the greatest period of change in Catholicism since the Council of Trent. One is remembered as joyous, the other as, occasionally, rather dour. Together, they made possible an "open window" that few observers had thought possible in previous years.

Opening a Window: John XXIII

If Pius IX had been dragged into the political world of the nineteenth century kicking and screaming, **John XXIII** (1958–1962) showed that the papacy was itself capable of dragging the Church into the twentieth.

At the time of his election, anyone hoping to wager money that this pope would emerge as the most aggressive reformer-pope since Pius IV, who had reconvened the Council of Trent, could have gotten steep odds against the proposition. John XXIII had been a compromise choice meant to buy time; the conclave that followed Pius XII's death was grievously divided between supporters of the previous pope's administration and a new generation of cardinals who wished to make a clean and energetic break with the past.

What Happened When

- ◆ **1960:** John F. Kennedy was elected president of the United States; he was the first Catholic to hold the office.
- ◆ **1962–1965:** The Second Vatican Council outlined a "new opening" to contemporary society.
- ◆ **1964:** First papal visit to a foreign country in 150 years.
- ◆ **1966:** During the period of Cultural Revolution in China, the Red Guard closed all Christian houses of worship.
- ◆ **1967:** Revocation of ancient pronouncements of excommunication between Roman Catholic Church and Eastern Orthodox Church.
- ◆ **1968:** Catholic prohibitions on artificial birth control were upheld in *Humanae Vitae*, leading to worldwide controversy and dissent.
- ◆ **1978:** Murder of kidnapped Italian Christian Democrat politician Aldo Moro.

In settling on the patriarch of Venice, the conclave promoted to the throne of St. Peter an innocuous man of 77 whose apparent mandate was simply to serve as an interim figure for two or three years while the Church sorted out its internal differences. Perhaps, the cardinals reasoned, the next conclave would provide a younger leader with the vision and energy some of the cardinals were clamoring for—then again, perhaps not. The pontiff they had designated to succeed Pius XII could presumably be counted on to maintain the status quo. As historian Eamon Duffy observes, "Human calculation has seldom been more spectacularly mistaken."

Beyond Black and White

In John XXIII, the Catholic Church found a leader of fascinating contradictions.

He was, as advertised, orthodox in his own conception of theological matters, yet his vision of the Church was one profoundly influenced by notions of renewal and reform. (He had written a five-volume biography of St. Charles Borromeo, who played a crucial role at the Council of Trent.) He was a veteran of the papal diplomatic service, and thus a confirmed "insider"—yet his experiences in Turkey and Bulgaria had exposed him firsthand to the religious lives of Eastern Orthodox Christians and Muslims, and these experiences had left an indelible impression. Finally, and perhaps most importantly, he was an unusual kind of traditionalist, one whose respect for tradition demanded elements of openness, experimentation, and a love of what he called *aggiornamento*. The older rank of cardinals who voted for him got a good deal more than they bargained for.

He had managed to make no enemies whatsoever in the course of his career in the diplomatic corps; this fact was considerably more significant than most people realized at the time of his election. For the new pope was, as his many biographers and chroniclers have noted, simply in love with people. As pope, John XXIII would time and again refuse to see the world in terms of black and white, enemy and ally, faithful and heretic. He would embrace the human experience in its totality, and he was determined to enjoy himself in the process.

Vatican Vocabulary

Aggiornamento, a word strongly associated with the pontificate of John XXIII, translates as "bringing up to date."

His joy in humanity never faded, but his days of enemy-making began shortly after his election.

A Council That Transformed the Church

Shortly after assuming the papal throne, John announced that there would a general council, the first since Pius IX's First Vatican Council eight decades earlier.

It was soon clear that this gathering would not be a stuffy recapitulation of old certainties or a condemnation of troublesome modern philosophical movements—options that had been explored during the final years of the previous pontificate. John intended the Second Vatican Council to be an opportunity of the Church's 3,000 bishops to gather in Rome to confer openly and creatively about the challenges of the future … and the changes that would be necessary to meet them. This would be a council of *aggiornamento*.

The old guard was horrified, and recent research has made clear that it did its best to drag its feet. John was, however, determined to have a council that was capable of taking down barriers and opening up the Church to a world it had so long seemed to barricade itself against. And this is precisely what he did.

Three years elapsed between John's initial announcement and the first session of the Second Vatican Council, now known popularly as Vatican II. During that period, John overcame numerous internal obstacles and successfully defended his vision of the council. It would not be overstating the case to say that he and the bishops he aimed to empower mounted—and won—a running battle with Vatican bureaucrats, who were eager to promote a council of a very different kind. John's victory ensured that Vatican II would, like the Council of Trent more than four centuries earlier, stand as one of the defining gatherings of the faith.

"To the Future Without Fear"

"In calling this vast assembly of bishops, the latest and humble successor to the Prince of the Apostles who is addressing you intended to assert once again the magisterium (teaching authority), which is unfailing and endures until the end of time, in order that this magisterium, taking into account the errors, the requirements, and the opportunities of our time, might be presented in exceptional form to all men throughout the world.

"It is but natural that in opening this Universal Council we should like to look to the past and to listen to its voices whose echo we like to hear in the memories and the merits of the more recent and ancient pontiffs, our predecessors. These are solemn and venerable voices, throughout the East and the West, from the fourth century to the Middle Ages, and from there to modern times, which have handed down their witness to those Councils. They are voices which proclaim in perennial fervor the triumph of that divine and human institution, the Church of Christ, which from Jesus takes its name, its grace, and its meaning …. Illuminated by the light of this Council, the Church—we confidently trust—will become greater in spiritual riches and gaining the strength of new energies therefrom, she will (also) look to the future without fear."

—Pope John XXIII, Opening Speech to the Vatican II Council, 1962

Five Amazing Years

John died before the council could conclude its work; his reign was only five years long. His pontificate, which had been notable for its human touch and its openness, had been brief but earth-shattering. In addition to convening the council, he had promoted social reform; taken stands for workers, the underprivileged, orphans, outcasts, and prisoners; reached out to leaders of other branches of Christianity (and even to Shinto leaders); spoken out against nuclear brinksmanship; and continued the Church's opposition to Communism.

Pope Watch

A memorable event of John's pontificate was his meeting with John F. Kennedy, the first Catholic to be elected president of the United States.

This last initiative was accomplished by explicitly forbidding Catholics to vote for Communists; interestingly, however, he also developed a friendship with Nikita Khrushchev during his pontificate.

His infectious enthusiasm, combined with his evident affection for humanity, led to great popularity. He was, in fact, the most beloved pope of the century.

Paul Guides the Council

John's successor, **Paul VI** (1963–1978), was the perfect man to see the Second Vatican Council through to completion. A careful balancer of constituencies, he was nevertheless just as deeply convinced as John that the time had come for change in the Church, and he brought a political savvy to the papacy that the earnest John had sometimes lacked. In short, he knew his way around the Vatican.

In 1965, the Second Vatican Council completed its labors. It had, by then, utterly changed the face of Catholicism.

The Second Vatican Council

Among the changes in outlook and practice associated with the Second Vatican Council (1962–1965) were these:

♦ Liturgical vernacularization (use of local language in the Mass) and reform.

♦ Greater participation by the laity in Church affairs.

♦ Initiatives of Christian unity, and encouragement of outreach efforts to other Christian denominations. (John XXIII had established a Secretariat for Christian Unity in 1960; the Second Vatican Council offered one of its most dramatic expressions of support for the growing ecumenical movement when it invited observers from Protestant and Eastern Orthodox denominations to its deliberations.)

♦ Specific emphasis on the importance of observing universal human rights.

♦ Historic reversal of the Church's position on the religious rights of non-Catholics. (The council held that "the human person has a right to religious liberty," thus overturning centuries of precedent for the suppression of heresy and the imposition of Catholic orthodoxy, often seen as duties of the Church.)

♦ Denunciation of the notion that the Jews bore moral responsibility for the death of Christ. (This was a clear rejection of one of the prime justifications for anti-Semitism.)

♦ Promotion of an optimistic regard for the worth of the human voyage through history—a stark departure from the grim condemnations of all things "modern" that had been so common in earlier years.

Beyond a Compulsion to Belief

"First, the council professes its belief that God Himself has made known to mankind the way in which men are to serve Him, and thus be saved in Christ and come to blessedness. We believe that this one true religion subsists in the Catholic and Apostolic Church, to which the Lord Jesus committed the duty of spreading it abroad among all men. Thus He spoke to the Apostles: 'Go, therefore, and make disciples of all nations, baptizing them in the name of the Father and of the Son and of the Holy Spirit, teaching them to observe all things whatsoever I have enjoined upon you' (Matt. 28: 19–20). On their part, all men are bound to seek the truth, especially in what concerns God and His Church, and to embrace the truth they come to know, and to hold fast to it.

"This Vatican Council likewise professes its belief that it is upon the human conscience that these obligations fall and exert their binding force. The truth cannot impose itself except by virtue of its own truth, as it makes its entrance into the mind at once quietly and with power.

"Religious freedom, in turn, which men demand as necessary to fulfill their duty to worship God, has to do with immunity from coercion in civil society. Therefore it leaves untouched traditional Catholic doctrine on the moral duty of men and societies toward the true religion and toward the one Church of Christ …. This Vatican Council declares that the human person has a right to religious freedom. This freedom means that all men are to be immune from coercion on the part of individuals or of social groups and of any human power, in such wise that no one is to be forced to act in a manner contrary to his own beliefs, whether privately or publicly, whether alone or in association with others within due limits."

—*Declaration on Religious Freedom*, Second Vatican Council, 1965.

It was left to Paul to implement the reforms of Vatican II, and he did so both energetically and cautiously. This may seem to be a contradiction in terms, but it is an accurate description of his working style.

Paul was careful not to administer too much shock to the system of the Church at a time, and he had a habit of balancing important reforms with initiatives that offered evidence of his regard for the interests of conservative forces within the Church. To some, it seemed like irresolution. Those who take the trouble to compare what was actually taking place in Catholic practice in 1963, when he assumed office, and in 1978, when he died, will find it difficult to believe that this pontificate was conducted by a man who lacked resolution.

Suddenly the Mass was being conducted in the language of the people, rather than the dignified but incomprehensible Latin of specially educated celebrants. Catholics were being urged to reach out to join prayer and study groups with Protestants. Rules relating to fasting and abstinence were loosened. The pattern of increased communication with other Christian denominations that had begun under John XXIII continued. Even the ancient excommunication of the Eastern Church became a thing of the past when, in 1967, Paul met with the Orthodox Patriarch Athenagoras in Rome and the two formally revoked the mutual condemnation of nine centuries earlier. It wasn't a reunion with the Orthodox faith, of course, but the gesture was clear evidence that old obstructions were being cast away.

> **Pope Watch**
>
> Paul traveled to a number of foreign nations during his pontificate, a break with modern practice. When he visited the Holy Land in 1964, no pope had journeyed beyond Italy in a century and a half.

Ideals and Reality

To the list of Paul's initiatives may be added the transfer of certain powers from the Curia to the bishops; the internationalization of the College of Cardinals; and the continuation of a campaign to revise canon law, initiated under John. There was even a less caustic approach to leaders of Communist nations, some of whom visited the Vatican.

Pausing occasionally to build alliances with conservatives by holding the line in areas where he genuinely agreed with them (such as the question of clerical celibacy), Paul managed to turn into practical reality the reform ideals outlined during Vatican II.

Yet, he is remembered by many as an intransigent man, and primarily for one encyclical. He issued it in 1968; it had to do with the controversial issue of artificial birth control.

A Polarized Church

After referring the issue of the Church's formal position on contraception to a committee for study—and thus encouraging hope that he would consider a change of position in the Church's long-standing prohibition of contraceptive measures—Paul rejected the committee's recommendations, followed his own instincts, and affirmed the Church's existing teaching in this area.

He may have hoped that by celebrating human sexuality within the context of marriage, which the encyclical did, he would win a measure of approval for (or at least a fair appraisal of the merits of) a long-held position. It was not to be.

In fact, the encyclical polarized the Church (particularly in America), led to bitter criticism in the media, obscured the many accomplishments of his pontificate, and brought about a sharp drop in his popularity. This was doubtless not what the pontiff expected from the announcement of a decision to continue a teaching of long standing.

"Repugnant to the Nature of Man and of Woman"

"The fact is, as experience shows, that new life is not the result of each and every act of sexual intercourse. God has wisely ordered laws of nature and the incidence of fertility in such a way that successive births are already naturally spaced through the inherent operation of these laws. The Church, nevertheless, in urging men to the observance of the precepts of the natural law, which it interprets by its constant doctrine, teaches that each and every marital act must of necessity retain its intrinsic relationship to the procreation of human life …. Men rightly observe that a conjugal act imposed on one's partner without regard to his or her condition or personal and reasonable wishes in the matter, is no true act of love, and therefore offends the moral order in its particular application to the intimate relationship of husband and wife. If they further reflect, they must also recognize that an act of mutual love which impairs the capacity to transmit life which God the Creator, through specific laws, has built into it, frustrates His design which constitutes the norm of marriage, and contradicts the will of the Author of life. Hence to use this divine gift while depriving it, even if only partially, of its meaning and purpose, is equally repugnant to the nature of man and of woman, and is consequently in opposition to the plan of God and His holy will."

—Pope Paul VI, *Humanae Vitae* (Encyclical on the Regulation of Birth), 1968

Pope Watch

A low point of Paul's pontificate was the assassination of the Italian politician Aldo Moro, who had been a close friend of the pope's. (Paul had been the target of an unsuccessful assassination attempt in 1970.) In 1978, the pope made his final public appearance when he presided at Moro's funeral.

Humanae Vitae was a deeply divisive document. The furor it aroused appeared to take the pope completely by surprise, and the pronouncement on contraception was to be his last encyclical.

The years after *Humanae Vitae* were not always easy, and the dispute was indicative of deeper problems. The Church's alignment with an empowered and often recalcitrant laity and clergy proved more difficult than the lofty and optimistic pronouncements that Vatican II suggested.

For Paul, the divisions within Catholicism that followed the historic council were difficult trials. He bore them with the air of a man who knows he has done his best and acted in accordance with what he believes to be right. Despite all he had worked so hard to achieve, the actual initiation of the anticipated era of unity, progress, respect, and tolerance within the Church was sometimes hard to discern.

To the increasingly loud choruses of dissent in areas where he held traditional views—such as contraception, divorce, abortion, and priestly celibacy—Paul turned a deaf ear. One revolution per papacy would be sufficient.

Shortly before he died, he expressed deep misgivings at the discord and controversy that had unfolded within the Church after the great council. He was approaching his 81st birthday when he suffered a heart attack as Mass was being said at his bedside.

The Least You Need to Know

- John XXIII, imagined to be an innocuous selection by the College of Cardinals, stunned the old guard by conducting a vigorous reform-minded pontificate that energetically promoted the notion of *aggiornamento* ("bringing up to date").

- Often working against his own bureaucracy, John convened the Second Vatican Council (or Vatican II), but died before it finished its work.

- Deep affection for humanity and a fresh approach to ecclesiastical issues made John among the most beloved popes of all time.

- Paul VI saw Vatican II through to its conclusion; its staggering list of reforms and new pronouncements included the vernacularization of the Mass, a call for greater involvement in Church affairs from the laity, and a new approach to other Christian traditions.

- Deep divisions within Catholicism beset Paul in later years; his encyclical on birth control was particularly controversial.

A Global Stage, an Enduring Mission: The Papacy in Our Time

In This Chapter

- ♦ John Paul I
- ♦ John Paul II
- ♦ The papacy, old and new

Two men concluded the papacy's work in the twentieth century. This was a century that embraced both unprecedented change in the papacy's strategy of propagating the faith—and reaffirmation of the continuity of the ancient doctrines of Catholicism.

What Happened When

- ◆ **1979:** Extremes of Liberation Theology were condemned; Mother Teresa won the Nobel Peace Prize for her five decades of work with the impoverished in Calcutta.

- ◆ **1981:** Assassination attempt on the pope.

- ◆ **1980s:** Political upheavals in Poland and the Philippines draw support from Catholic opposition to repressive regimes in both countries.

- ◆ **1991:** Final collapse of Communist governments in Europe.

- ◆ **1998:** The Vatican issued a message directly addressing the Holocaust.

- ◆ **2001:** Pattern of high-profile papal journeys abroad continued; total number of countries visited by John Paul II reached 116.

John Paul I (1978) had been vice president of the Italian conference of bishops before becoming patriarch of Venice; his election as pontiff was greeted with great enthusiasm. He was also the first pope to choose a double name. His selection of John Paul as his papal name was intended as a signal that he sought to consolidate the work of his two remarkable predecessors—and, by implication, uphold the legacy of the Second Vatican Council, with which both John XXIII and Paul VI would be forever linked. Shortly after his inauguration, he assured the faithful that his intent was to follow in Paul's footsteps, putting into practice the decrees of Vatican II while reinforcing traditional guidelines.

Pope Watch

A huge conclave of 138 cardinals elected John Paul I.

And there it ended. Questions about the precise manner in which he would succeed the two remarkable men who had preceded him were to be left unanswered; he died of a coronary embolism just over a month after his election. Evidence in support of the melodramatic rumor that he was the victim of poisoning has never surfaced.

It had been the shortest reign of any pope since Leo XI in 1605; it was notable, however, for something other than its brevity. In an interesting initial display of symbolism, John Paul had opted against coronation, choosing instead to receive the woolen ceremonial garment known as a pallium. It was as though he wanted to be sure the world saw that he understood both the power and the limitations of ceremony, and that he intended to use it to convey positive messages wherever possible. The emphasis on optimism and personal humility was carried through in his installation homily, leaving Catholics to wonder how the contrast with the occasionally morose and aloof Paul VI might continue to play out. It would remain one of history's unanswered questions.

"A Special Mission"

"Jesus changes Simon's name to Peter, thus signifying the conferring of a special mission. He promises to build on him his church, which will not be overthrown by the forces of evil or death. He grants him the keys of the kingdom of God, thus appointing him the highest official of his church, and gives him the power to interpret authentically the law of God. In view of these privileges, or rather these superhuman tasks entrusted to Peter, St. Augustine points out to us: 'Peter was by nature simply a man, by grace a Christian, by still more abundant grace one of the apostles, and at the same time the first of the apostles.' .... Our mind re-echoes spontaneously the emotion-filled words that our great saintly predecessor, St. Leo the Great, addressed to the faithful of Rome: 'Blessed Peter does not cease to preside over his See. He is bound to the eternal priest in an unbroken unity .... Recognize therefore that all the demonstrations of affection that you have given me because of fraternal amiability or filial devotion have with greater devotedness and truth been given by you and me to him whose See we rejoice to serve, rather than preside over it.'"

—Pope John Paul I, Installation Homily, 1978

The Superstar Pontificate

John Paul I's brief reign was followed by a rather lengthier one that held the lines Paul VI had drawn regarding human sexuality, divorce, clerical celibacy, contraception, and a host of other contested issues. The last pope of the twentieth century—and the first of the twenty-first—has managed, however, to inspire a personal respect (and even awe) that always seems to transcend the disputes of the day. He has done this, at least in part, through the shrewd use of modern communication methods. This approach to propagating the faith has given the world its first superstar pope. **John Paul II** (1978 to present) is the first Polish pope in history, and the first non-Italian pope in more than 450 years. He has inspired, mesmerized, energized, and frustrated contemporary Catholics, and he has never been far from their notice (or indeed, the notice of the entire world).

Progressive members of the Church, particularly those in America, have lamented his conservatism on any number of social issues, but to focus narrowly on such matters is to miss the global nature of his achievement. John Paul—the first pope to embrace the modern media age with arms wide open—has conducted a restless, globe-trotting, and profoundly camera-friendly pontificate in a manner hardly conceivable before 1978. His travels have fueled media coverage unprecedented in the office. In pursuing his media-savvy mission, John Paul has, in large degree, fulfilled the vision of contact with the outside world outlined by Cardinal Montini in a letter to priests in his diocese composed just six months before he was elevated to the papacy as Paul VI:

"(T)he Church is ... looking for the world, and trying to come into contact with society ... by engaging in dialogue with the world, interpreting the needs of the society in which it is working, and observing the defects, the necessities, the sufferings, and the hopes and aspirations that exist in human hearts."

The words were written in the context of the Second Vatican Council, but they resonate equally effectively with the impossible-to-ignore reign of John Paul II. Paul VI, of course, was no stranger to travel and news coverage, having shattered tradition by traveling to the Holy Land in 1964. But no pope has come close to logging the miles, or attracting the headlines, that John Paul has.

> ### Pope Watch
>
> In 1981, the pope was seriously wounded during an assassination attempt. The pope eventually met with (and forgave) his assailant, a Turkish national named Mehmet Ali Agca. Both the shooting and the reconciliation received global press coverage.

There have been great popes, and there have been popes who occasionally made international news. There has never before, however, been a great pope who was consistently newsworthy—a pope, that is to say, who played the global media machinery to perfection in promulgating the Gospel message.

During the first 10 years alone of his pontificate, he attracted extraordinary attention as he visited 50 countries. In 1998, his journey to Cuba was covered worldwide; in 2000, he made a prominent trip to the Holy Land; in 2001, at the age of 81, he journeyed to the Ukraine in an attempt to heal ancient divisions with the Orthodox Church. In its coverage of this trip, *The New York Times* observed what was, by this point, obvious to all: "All (of John Paul II's) papal trips receive intense news media coverage and carry resounding political messages."

Television, radio, airplanes, and photographs existed for many years before this pope's election, but no pope in history has used these inventions as his primary tools for the fulfillment of his pastoral mission. For this, as much as for his continuing implementation of the reforms of the Second Vatican Council and his vigorous anti-Communist outlook, John Paul will be remembered.

The Papacy in the Age of Computers and Mass Media

"With the advent of computer telecommunications and what are known as computer participation systems, the Church is offered further means for fulfilling her mission. Methods of facilitating communication and dialogue among her own members can strengthen the bonds of unity between them. Immediate access to information makes it possible for her to deepen her dialogue with the contemporary world."

—Pope John Paul II, *The Church Must Learn to Cope with Computer Culture* (Statement for World Communications Day), 1989

"I have chosen as the theme for this year's World Communications Day 'Mass media: a friendly companion for those in search of the Father.' The theme implies two questions: How might the media work with God rather than against him? And how might the media be a friendly companion to those searching for God's loving presence in their lives? It also implies a statement of fact and a reason for thanks: that the media do at times make it possible for those who are searching for God to read in new ways both the book of nature, which is the realm of reason, and the book of revelation, the Bible, which is the realm of faith. Finally the theme implies an invitation and a hope: that those responsible for the world of social communications will be ever more committed to help rather than hinder the search for meaning which is at the very heart of human life."

—Pope John Paul II, *Proclaiming Christ in the Media at the Dawn of the New Millennium* (Message for World Media Day, 2000)

John Paul II's Remarkable Reign

Supported by his masterful use of the media, John Paul II's extraordinary pontificate has been notable for the following undertakings:

♦ *An unapologetic embrace of the notion of papal teaching authority.* His energetic and orthodox approach to a host of issues lacking mainstream popular support has led many conservative Catholics to view his pontificate as a welcome alternative to the often-chaotic "openness" that followed Vatican II. The reforms that he helped to bring about as a bishop during that council, however, have remained in place.

♦ *Support for Catholics facing oppression from Communist authorities.* Personal experience had left John Paul II irrevocably opposed to the Communist movement. His election galvanized his overwhelmingly Catholic Polish homeland, as did his visit there the following year. The fall of the Communist regimes in Europe in later years was a notable highlight for the papacy as an institution, which had pronounced against the movement for over a century, and for John Paul personally.

> **Pope Watch**
>
> John Paul II has laid special emphasis on devotion to the Virgin Mary during his pontificate. He attributed his survival of the 1981 attempt on his life to her intercession.

♦ *An emphasis on Christ's role in the elucidation of both divine nature and human nature.* An early encyclical in this area was 1979's *Redemptor Hominis*; it followed through ideas outlined in *Gaudium et Spes*, an important document of the Second Vatican Council which had been drafted, in large part, by the future pope.

♦ *Stricter establishment of papal direction in theological matters.*

♦ *Ongoing efforts to heal divisions between Christians and Jews.* In 1998, the Vatican issued an extraordinary statement observing that the Holocaust had left an "indelible stain on the 20th century" and urging Catholics to "examine themselves for the responsibility which they, too, have for the evils of our time." Two years later, he visited the Yad Veshem Holocaust Museum in Jerusalem, having said that his aim was "to pay homage to the millions of Jewish people who—stripped of everything, especially of human dignity—were murdered in the Holocaust." His silent homage there to the suffering of the victims of Hitler's campaign of genocide was the subject of international attention.

Vatican Vocabulary

The **Liberation Theology movement** was a theological understanding of the Gospel emphasizing notions of political emancipation and the rejection of economic oppression. To John Paul, it appears to have smelled suspiciously like a hybrid of Catholic progressivism and Marxism.

Papal People

Hans Kung, a Swiss theologian and author, became, in 1971, the first major Roman Catholic academic to publicly challenge the notion of papal infallibility. His right to teach Roman Catholic theology was revoked during John Paul II's reign (1979).

♦ *Continuation of traditional teachings regarding contraception and human sexuality.*

♦ *Explicit condemnation of abortion and rejection of the "culture of death" supporting it.*

♦ *Rejection of the* Liberation Theology *movement, and of political office-holding by the clergy.*

♦ *Reassertion of conservative theological principles, and imposition of measures restricting a number of liberal teachings.*

♦ *Continuation of Paul VI's willingness to promote interfaith dialogue, and to meet with prominent religious leaders of other faiths.*

♦ *Dismissal of the effort to ordain women as priests.*

♦ *Ongoing commitment to the difficult (some would say impossible) goal of reconciling Roman Catholicism with Eastern Orthodox Christianity.*

♦ *Stark criticism of the excesses of modern capitalism.* In *Dives et Misericordia* (1980), he attacked a "fundamental defect, or rather a series of defects, indeed a defective machinery … at the root of contemporary economics and material civilization."

♦ *Continued emphasis on the themes of peace, human dignity, and tolerance in the international arena, and those of forgiveness and grace among Christians.*

Peace and Forgiveness

"Without a willingness to respect the freedom of every people, nation, and culture, and without a worldwide consensus on this subject, it will be difficult to create the conditions for peace .... This presupposes a conscious public commitment on the part of each nation and its government to renounce claims and designs injurious to other nations. In other words, it presupposes a refusal to accept any doctrine of national or cultural supremacy."

—Pope John Paul II, *Message for the 1981 World Day for Peace*

"Throughout his life Jesus proclaimed God's forgiveness, but he also taught the need for mutual forgiveness as the condition for obtaining it. In the Lord's Prayer he makes us pray: 'Forgive us our trespasses, as we forgive those who trespass against us' (Matt. 6:12). With that 'as,' he places in our hands the measure with which we shall be judged by God."

—Pope John Paul II, *Offer Forgiveness and Receive Peace* (Message for World Day of Peace, 1997)

The Papacy After John Paul II

Even when faced with serious declines in his health, the pope has continued his remarkable and determined mission, a mission like that of no other pope in recent memory. He has inspired the world—not merely the Catholic world, and not merely the Christian world—and has, in the process, redefined his office.

Modern observers are inclined to emphasize the pope's significant accomplishments rather than the opposition he has sometimes encountered. Three recent assessments of his pontificate follow.

"The energies released by the Second Vatican Council seem to point the Church in the direction of greater cultural and theological pluralism, more lay participation, less hierarchy, more dialogue. The abilities and inclination of the last pope of the twentieth century seem to point elsewhere, to a more exalted, lonely, and hierarchic vision of the Church it serves—or rules."

—Eamon Duffy, *Saints and Sinners*, Yale University Press, 1997

"When (John Paul II) stood silent in Yad Vashem—whose plain and stark memorialization of the horrors that befell the Jewish people at the hands of the Nazis positively begs for silence—he left a drop of the kind of healing balm on the hearts of Jews that the Church had never before found the means (assuming the desire) to do."

—Midge Decter, at *The Future of the Papacy: A Symposium*, 2001

"In the Epilogue of his monumental biography of John Paul II, George Weigel lists eight areas in which that pope has made significant impact. Prominent on the list are fidelity to Vatican II, religious freedom, the priority of culture, ecumenism, interreligious dialogue, and worldwide evangelization. In areas such as these John Paul II has built on the achievements of Paul VI, who likewise followed his recent predecessors. The continuities between these papacies, while they do not erase the differences, are at least equally important. That past must inform our thinking about the future of the papacy as well."

—Cardinal Avery Dulles, at *The Future of the Papacy: A Symposium*, 2001

Much speculation about John Paul II's successor has circulated in recent years, as his infirmities have become more evident. Whoever emerges as the next pope, he will certainly have a hard act to follow.

The Papacy, Old and New

John Paul II has led the Church without the monarchic authority and political power of most of his predecessors, without the ability or inclination to conduct troops or set military strategy, without alliances to empires or potentates, and without condemning competing religious traditions. He has been, I think, most inspiring in his later years, when his devotion to his cause has persisted and even intensified despite the stripping away of his physical abilities—and recently the measure of the man has become clearer. In addressing the stripping away of its historic political and diplomatic powers, the papacy itself has also, somehow, come closer to its true self. Its path has become clearer, its mission more focused, and its commitment to fulfill it more concentrated. The measure of the office itself has become clearer as the centuries have passed and the many trials faded.

The current pope has shown the power of an ancient and enduring idea, one that has outlasted even the aspirations of the office that grew around it: "Anyone who wishes to be a follower of mine must leave self behind. Whoever cares for his own safety is lost, but if a man will let himself be lost for my sake and for the Gospel, that man is safe" (Mark 8:34–35).

John Paul II's true legacy to the Church will take years to determine, but it is hard to see how it will not encompass this ancient inheritance of Peter's. And if it were only that, it would be more than enough.

The Least You Need to Know

◆ John Paul I's pontificate was the shortest since Leo XI in 1605.

◆ John Paul II has conducted the first superstar pontificate; he has inspired, mesmerized, energized, and frustrated contemporary Catholics, and he has never been far from their notice (or indeed, the notice of the entire world).

◆ The current pope is a great one who has played the global media machinery to perfection in promulgating the Gospel message, expressing a commitment to bring the papacy to the people, and holding the line on many orthodox points of doctrine.

◆ Whoever emerges as the next pope, he will certainly have a hard act to follow.

Chapter 24

Epilogue: In Their Own Words

In This Chapter

- ◆ Papal observations on faith
- ◆ Papal observations on tradition
- ◆ Papal observations on religious practice

Objects of veneration, obedience, rebellion, love, fear, and, above all, rapt attention from untold millions of people for nearly two millennia, the popes have maintained what may well be the oldest continuously functioning institution in human history. They have seldom, if ever, left those who encountered them feeling lukewarm about the papacy or its inheritors.

The diversity of opinion, expression, and personality within the office over the years has truly been remarkable. The popes, it seems, have always had something to say that just can't be ignored, and they have always found a way to say it that distinctively reflects the current occupant of the throne of St. Peter.

It seems fitting, in recognition of both their multiplicity of voice and their shared heritage down the centuries, to let them close this book themselves. They have, as a general but reliable rule, been their own most fascinating representatives for twenty centuries or so.

The trend is likely to continue.

The Ever-Quotable Popes

Here, then, is a brief sampling, from a wide variety of sources, of intriguing papal observations on many subjects.

On Assuming and Holding the Papal Office

"Blessed Peter does not cease to preside over his See. He is bound to the eternal priest in an unbroken unity .... Recognize therefore that all the demonstrations of affection that you have given me because of fraternal amiability or filial devotion have with greater devotedness and truth been given by you and me to him whose See we rejoice to serve, rather than preside over it."

—St. Leo I

"Anybody can be Pope; the proof of this is that I have become one."

—John XXIII's response to a boy who wrote him a letter asking if he should be a pope or a policeman

"Others are called to the role of caring, but only Peter is raised to the fullness of power. Now therefore you see who is the servant who is set over the household, truly the vicar of Jesus Christ, the successor of Peter, the Christ of the Lord, the God of Pharoah."

—Innocent III

"God has given us the papacy—let us enjoy it."

—Leo X

"The popes, like Jesus, are conceived by their mothers through the overshadowing of the Holy Ghost. All popes are a certain species of man-gods, for the purpose of being the better able to conduct the functions of mediator between God and mankind. All powers in Heaven, as well as on earth, are given to them."

—Stephanus V

"My predecessors did not know how to be popes."

—Clement VI (who had a reputation for extravagant spending)

"Witnesses to tradition? *I am* the tradition!"

—Pius IX, to a cardinal who had emphasized the role of bishops as witnesses to Church tradition during the First Vatican Council

"The pope is becoming a missionary, you will say. Yes, the pope is becoming a missionary, which means a witness, a shepherd, an apostle on the move."

—Pope Paul VI, announcing his plans to visit India in 1964

On Communism

"(T)he unspeakable doctrine of Communism, as it is called, (is) a doctrine most opposed to the very natural law. For if this doctrine were accepted, the complete destruction of everyone's laws, government, property, and even of human society itself would follow."

—Pius IX

"(There is a) sect of men who, under various and almost barbarous names, are called socialists, Communists, or nihilists, and who, spread over all the world, and bound together by the closest ties in a wicked confederacy, no longer seek the shelter of secret meetings, but, openly and boldly marching forth in the light of day, strive to bring to a head what they have long been planning—the overthrow of all civil society whatsoever."

—Leo XIII

"(A)nd when they have attained to power, it is unbelievable, indeed it seems portentous, how cruel and inhuman they show themselves to be. Evidence for this is the ghastly destruction and ruin with which they have laid waste immense tracts of Eastern Europe and Asia, while their antagonism and open hostility to Holy Church and to God Himself are, alas! but too well-known and proved by their deeds."

—Pius XI

"Communism in fact is materialistic and anti-Christian; communist leaders, even if now and then in word they agree not to fight against religion, nevertheless in reality, both in doctrine and in action, they show themselves to be opposed to God, to the true religion, and to the Church of Christ."

—Pius XII

"(B)oth workers and employers should regulate their mutual relations in accordance with the principle of human solidarity and Christian brotherhood. Unrestricted competition in the liberal sense, and the Marxist creed of class warfare, are clearly contrary to Christian teaching and the nature of man."

—John XXIII

"These are the reasons which compel us, as they compelled our predecessors and, with them, everyone who has religious values at heart, to condemn the ideological systems that deny God and oppress the Church, systems which are often identified with economic, social, and political regimes, amongst which atheistic Communism is the chief."

—Paul VI

On Connecting with the Faithful

"A mighty thing is eloquence … nothing so much rules the world."

—**Pius II**

"If I cannot explain myself too well in your language—I mean our language—you will correct me if I make a mistake."

—**John Paul II**, greeting the crowd in Saint Peter's Square in Italian, shortly after his election. The grammatical mistake may have been an accident, or could have been made intentionally to create a theatrical touch. Regardless of the reason for the slip, the Italian crowd was thrilled and gave the new pope a warm welcome.

"You can't come to me, so I have come to you."

—**John XXIII**, to inmates at the Regina Coeli prison in Rome

On Correction

"I didn't say see what you can do, I said fire him."

—**Benedict XV**, on receiving a less-than-ringing response from an elderly seminarian to a papal order about a controversial rector; the clarification was accompanied by a brisk tug of the seminarian's beard

"See everything, overlook a great deal, correct a little."

—**John XXIII**

On Dealings with Other Religious Traditions

"If any man sets out to free the Church of God at Jerusalem out of pure devotion and not out of love for glory or gain, the journey shall be accounted a complete penance on his part."

—**Urban II**, preaching the First Crusade

"Use against heretics the spiritual sword of excommunication—and if this does not prove effective, use the material sword."

—**Innocent III**

"It is altogether necessary for salvation for every human creature to be subject to the Roman pontiff."

—**Boniface VIII**

"The equal toleration of all religions … is the same thing as atheism."

—Leo XIII

"Spiritually, we are all Semites."

—Pius IX

"The pope—and we know this well—is without doubt the most serious obstacle on the ecumenical road."

—Paul VI

"(We hope to) accomplish a service of love recognized by all concerned."

—John Paul II, to non-Catholic religious leaders and theologians

On Dealings with Secular Authorities

"(To) Charles, most pious Augustus, crowned by God, great and peace-loving emperor, life and victory."

—Leo III, praising Charlemagne

"Who does not know that kings and rulers sprang from men who were ignorant of God, who assumed because of blind greed and intolerable presumption to make themselves masters of other men, their equals, by means of pride, violence, bad faith, murder, and almost every other kind of crime? Surely the devil drove them on."

—Gregory VII, on the right of the pope to excommunicate the king of Germany and Holy Roman Emperor Henry IV

"The state has not the right to leave every man free to profess and embrace whatever religion he may desire."

—Pius IX, whose pontificate featured many conflicts with the emerging Italian state

"(T)he privileges of this see existed before your empire and will remain when it has long gone."

—Nicholas I, to Emperor Michael

On Divine Power

"My hope is in Christ, who strengthens the weakest by His Divine help. I can do all in Him who strengthens me. His Power is infinite, and if I lean on him, it will be mine. His Wisdom is infinite, and if I look to Him for counsel, I shall not be deceived. His Goodness is infinite, and if my trust is stayed in Him, I shall not be abandoned."

—St. Pius X

On Effort

"He rests well who works well and, in his turn, he who works well must rest well."

—John Paul II

"Consult not your fears but your hopes and your dreams. Think not about your frustrations, but about your unfulfilled potential. Concern yourself not with what you tried and failed in, but with what it is still possible for you to do."

—John XXIII

On Encounters with Modern Trends and Discoveries

"(We reject the view that) the Roman pontiff can and should reconcile himself with progress, liberalism, and recent civilization."

—Pius IX

"Inequality of rights and power proceeds from the very author of nature, from whom all paternity in heaven and earth is named."

—Leo XIII

"One Galileo in 2,000 years is enough."

—Pius XII

"God has no intention of setting a limit to the efforts of man to conquer space."

—Paul VI, on interplanetary exploration

"It can therefore be said that, from the viewpoint of the doctrine of the faith, there are no difficulties in explaining the origin of man, in regard to the body, by means of the theory of evolution."

—John Paul II

On Excuses

"An excuse is worse and more terrible than a lie, for an excuse is a lie guarded."

—John Paul II

On Faith

"If the authority of the Holy See were visibly displayed in majestic buildings, imperishable memorials, and witnesses seemingly planted by the hand of God himself, belief would grow and strengthen like a tradition from one generation to another, and all the world would accept and revere it."

—**Nicholas V**

"Let the storm rage and the sky darken—not for that shall we be dismayed. If we trust as we should in Mary, we shall recognize in her, the Virgin Most Powerful 'who with virginal foot did crush the head of the serpent.'"

—**St. Pius X**

"Of all human activities, man's listening to God is the supreme act of his reasoning and will."

—**Paul VI**

On the Family

"The family [is] the first essential cell of human society."

—**John XXIII**

"Every mother is like Moses. She does not enter the promised land. She prepares a world she will not see."

—**Paul VI**

"To maintain a joyful family requires much from both the parents and the children. Each member of the family has to become, in a special way, the servant of the others."

—**John Paul II**

"Italians come to ruin most generally in three ways: women, gambling, and farming. My family chose the slowest one."

—**John XXIII**, who came from a poor family; his father had to rent the land they used for farming. Thirteen children, as well as aunts, uncles, and cousins, were crowded into their farmhouse.

On the Human Condition

"Bodily pain affects man as a whole down to the deepest layers of his moral being. It forces him to face again the fundamental questions of his fate, of his attitude toward God and fellow man, of his individual and collective responsibility, and of the sense of his pilgrimage on earth."

—**Pope Pius XII**, in an address to a group of international heart specialists

"(A) woeful system …"

—**Paul VI,** on capitalism that produces economic inequalities

"People cannot live without love."

—**John Paul II,** to the young people of Camaguey, Cuba

On the Human Side of the Pontiff

"I am made to tremble and I fear!"

—**John XXIII,** on being told of his election to succeed Pius XII

"If someone had told me I would be pope one day, I would have studied harder."

—**John I**

"I have a sweet tooth for song and music. This is my Polish sin."

—**John Paul II**

"As books vary from one to the other, so too do bishops. Some bishops, in fact, resemble eagles, who sail loftily with solemn documents. Others are nightingales who marvelously sing the praise of the Lord. Others, instead, are poor wrens, who only twitter as profound subjects. I belong to the [last] category."

—**John Paul I**

"Miracles they want now! As if I didn't have enough to do already."

—**St. Pius X**

On Marriage

"The fear of making permanent commitments can change the mutual love of husband and wife into two loves of self—two loves existing side by side—until they end in separation."

—**John Paul II**

On the Mission of the Pope

"I recall with sadness what I was not long ago in the monastery, how I grew in contemplation to rise over all that changes and decomposes, my only thoughts those of the enduring gifts of heaven …. Now, however, as the result of my pastoral duties … (I am) befouled with the dust of the world …. I heave a sigh, and am as a man who stares with longing at the shore he has departed."

—St. Gregory I

"(This Church I lead) is everywhere battered by stormy waves and through ill fortune and negligence has come near to being shipwrecked and submerged."

—Gregory VII

"Here I am, at the end of the road and at the top of the heap."

—John XXIII

"The post is unique. It brings great solitude. I was solitary before, but now my solitariness becomes complete and awesome."

—Paul VI

"I shall be able to rest one minute after I die."

—Pius XII, to physicians who asked him to curtail his work

"The pope must suffer."

—John Paul II

On Peace

"The true and solid peace of nations consists not in equality of arms, but in mutual trust alone."

—John XXIII

"If you wish to be brothers, let the arms fall from your hands. One cannot love while holding offensive arms."

—Paul VI

"True courage lies in working for peace."

—John Paul II, during a visit to Ireland

On Religious Practice and Observance

"Holy Communion is the shortest and safest way to Heaven."

—St. Pius X

"Man is great only when he is kneeling."

—Pius XII

"Anything done for another is done for oneself."

—Boniface VIII

"God could have given us the Redeemer of the human race, and the Founder of the Faiths in another way than through the Virgin, but since Divine Providence has been pleased that we should have the Man-God through Mary, who conceived Him by the Holy Spirit and bore Him in her womb, it only remains for us to receive Christ from the hands of Mary."

—St. Pius X

On Repentance

"Who could fail to be roused to the same emotions by the prayers of thanksgiving to God for blessings received by the petitions, so humble and confident, for blessings still awaited, (or) by the cries of a soul in sorrow for sin committed?"

—St. Pius X

"What we talked about will have to remain a secret between him and me. I spoke to him as a brother whom I have pardoned and who has my complete trust."

—John Paul II after hearing the confession of his would-be assassin, the imprisoned Mehmet Ali Agca

On Scripture

"(C)omposed as it was under divine inspiration, (it) has, from the very beginnings of the Church, shown a wonderful power of fostering devotion among Christians as they offer 'to God a continuous sacrifice of praise, the harvest of lips blessing his name.'"

—St. Pius X

On Violence and War

"Social justice cannot be attained by violence. Violence kills what it intends to create."

—John Paul II, to workers in São Paulo, Brazil

"No more war—war never again."

—Paul VI, at the United Nations in 1965

And Finally ...

"It often happens that I wake at night and begin to think about a serious problem and decide I must tell the Pope about it. Then I wake up completely and remember that I am the Pope."

—John XXIII

The Least You Need to Know

- ◆ The popes have, over nearly two millennia, maintained what may well be the oldest continuously functioning institution in human history.
- ◆ They have seldom, if ever, left those who encountered them feeling lukewarm about the papacy or its inheritors.
- ◆ The popes are extraordinarily quotable; they have been their own most fascinating representatives for twenty centuries or so.

The Popes in Sequence

Note: Dates and sequences for most of the leaders of the Roman Church from St. Peter to St. Callistus I are extremely uncertain.

St. Peter
Reigned: First century

St. Linus
Reigned: First century

St. Anacletus (Cletus)
Reigned: First century

St. Clement I
Reigned: ca. 96

St. Evaristus
Reigned: First century

St. Alexander I
Reigned: Second century

St. Sixtus I
Reigned: Second century

St. Telesphorus
Reigned: Second century

St. Hyginus
Reigned: Second century

St. Pius I
Reigned: Second century

St. Anicetus
Reigned: Second century

St. Soter
Reigned: Second century

St. Eleutherius
Reigned: Second century

St. Victor I
Reigned: Second century

St. Zephyrinus
Reigned: Late second and early third century

St. Callistus I
Reigned: Third century

St. Urban I
Reigned: ca. 222–ca. 230

St. Pontain
Reigned: 230–235

St. Anterus
Reigned: 235–236

St. Fabian
Reigned: 236–250

St. Cornelius
Reigned: 251–253

St. Lucius I
Reigned: 253–254

St. Stephen I
Reigned: 254–257

St. Sixtus II
Reigned: 257–258

St. Dionysius
Reigned: 260–268

St. Felix I
Reigned: 269–274

St. Eutychian
Reigned: 275–283

St. Caius (Gaius)
Reigned: 283–296

St. Marcellinus
Reigned: 296–304

St. Marcellus I
Reigned: 308–309

St. Eusebius
Reigned: 309 or 310

St. Miltiades
Reigned: 311–314

St. Sylvester I
Reigned: 314–335

St. Mark
Reigned: 336

St. Julius I
Reigned: 337–352

Liberius
Reigned: 352–366

St. Damasus I
Reigned: 366–383

St. Siricius
Reigned: 384–399

St. Anastasius I
Reigned: 399–401

St. Innocent I
Reigned: 401–417

St. Zosimus
Reigned: 417–418

St. Boniface I
Reigned: 418–422

St. Celestine I
Reigned: 422–432

St. Sixtus III
Reigned: 432–440

St. Leo I (the Great)
Reigned: 440–461

St. Hilarius
Reigned: 461–468

St. Simplicius
Reigned: 468–483

St. Felix III (II)
Reigned: 483–492

St. Gelasius I
Reigned: 492–496

Anastasius II
Reigned: 496–498

St. Symmachus
Reigned: 498–514

St. Hormisdas
Reigned: 514–523

St. John I
Reigned: 523–526

St. Felix IV (III)
Reigned: 526–530

Boniface II
Reigned: 530–532

John II
Reigned: 533–535

St. Agapetus I
Reigned: 535–536

St. Silverius
Reigned: 536–537

Vigilius
Reigned: 537–555

Pelagius I
Reigned: 556–561

John III
Reigned: 561–574

Benedict I
Reigned: 575–579

Pelagius II
Reigned: 579–590

St. Gregory I (Gregory the Great)
Reigned: 590–604

Sabinian
Reigned: 604–606

Boniface III
Reigned: 607

St. Boniface IV
Reigned: 608–615

St. Deusdedit (Adeodatus I)
Reigned: 615–618

Boniface V
Reigned: 619–625

Honorius I
Reigned: 625–638

Severinus
Reigned: 640

John IV
Reigned: 640–642

Theodore I
Reigned: 642–649

St. Martin I
Reigned: 649–655

St. Eugene I
Reigned: 655–657

St. Vitalian
Reigned: 657–672

Adeodatus (II)
Reigned: 672–676

Donus
Reigned: 676–678

St. Agatho
Reigned: 678–681

St. Leo II
Reigned: 682–683

St. Benedict II
Reigned: 684–685

John V
Reigned: 685–686

Conon
Reigned: 686–687

St. Sergius I
Reigned: 687–701

John VI
Reigned: 701–705

John VII
Reigned: 705–707

Sisinius
Reigned: 708

Constantine
Reigned: 708–715

St. Gregory II
Reigned: 715–731

St. Gregory III
Reigned: 731–741

St. Zachary
Reigned: 741–752

Stephen II
Reigned: 752

Stephen III
Reigned: 752–757

St. Paul I
Reigned: 757–767

Stephen IV
Reigned: 767–772

Adrian I
Reigned: 772–795

St. Leo III
Reigned: 795–816

Stephen V
Reigned: 816–817

St. Paschal I
Reigned: 817–824

Eugene II
Reigned: 824–827

Valentine
Reigned: 827

Gregory IV
Reigned: 827–844

Sergius II
Reigned: 844–847

St. Leo IV
Reigned: 847–855

Benedict III
Reigned: 855–858

St. Nicholas I
Reigned: 858–867

Adrian II
Reigned: 867–872

John VIII
Reigned: 872–882

Marinus I
Reigned: 882–884

St. Adrian III
Reigned: 884–885

Stephen VI
Reigned: 885–891

Formosus
Reigned: 891–896

Boniface VI
Reigned: 896

Stephen VII
Reigned: 896–897

Romanus
Reigned: 897

Theodore II
Reigned: 897

John IX
Reigned: 898–900

Benedict IV
Reigned: 900–903

Leo V
Reigned: 903

Sergius III
Reigned: 904–911

Anastasius III
Reigned: 911–913

Lando
Reigned: 913–914

John X
Reigned: 914–928

Leo VI
Reigned: 928

Stephen VIII
Reigned: 929–931

John XI
Reigned: 931–935

Leo VII
Reigned: 936–939

Stephen IX
Reigned: 939–942

Marinus II
Reigned: 942–946

Agapetus II
Reigned: 946–955

John XII
Reigned: 955–963

Leo VIII
Reigned: 963–964

Benedict V
Reigned: 964

John XIII
Reigned: 965–972

Benedict VI
Reigned: 973–974

Benedict VII
Reigned: 974–983

John XIV
Reigned: 983–984
Given name: Peter Caneponava

John XV
Reigned: 985–996
Given Name: John Crescentius

Gregory V
Reigned: 996–999
Given Name: Bruno of Carinthia

Sylvester II
Reigned: 999–1003
Given Name: Gerbert of Aurillac

John XVII
Reigned: 1003
Given Name: John Sico

John XVIII
Reigned: 1003–1009
Given Name: John Fasanus

Sergius IV
Reigned: 1009–1012
Given Name: Pietro Buccaporca

Benedict VIII
Reigned: 1012–1024
Given Name: Theophylact III of
Tusculum

John XIX
Reigned: 1024–1032
Given Name: Romanus of Tusculum

Benedict IX
Reigned: 1032–1044
Given Name: Theophylact III of
Tusculum

Sylvester III
Reigned: 1045
Given Name: John of Sabina

Benedict IX
Reigned: 1045
Given Name: Theophylact III of
Tusculum

Gregory VI
Reigned: 1045–1046
Given Name: John Gratian

Benedict IX
Reigned: 1047–1048
Given Name: Theophylact III of
Tusculum

Clement II
Reigned: 1046–1047
Given Name: Suidger of Bamberg

Damasus II
Reigned: 1048
Given Name: Poppo of Brixen

St. Leo IX
Reigned: 1049–1054
Given Name: Bruno of Egisheim

Victor II
Reigned: 1055–1057
Given Name: Gebhard of
Dollnstein–Hirschberg

Stephen X
Reigned: 1057–1058
Given Name: Frederick of Lorraine

Nicholas II
Reigned: 1058–1061
Given Name: Gerard of Lorraine

Alexander II
Reigned: 1061–1073
Given Name: Anselm of Baggio

St. Gregory VII
Reigned: 1073–1085
Given Name: Hildebrand

Blessed Victor III
Reigned: 1086–1087
Given Name: Desiderius of Monte
Cassino

Blessed Urban II
Reigned: 1088–1099
Given Name: Odo of Lagery

Paschal II
Reigned: 1099–1118
Given Name: Rainerius of Bieda

Gelasius II
Reigned: 1118–1119
Given Name: John of Gaeta

Callistus II
Reigned: 1119–1124
Given Name: Guido of Burgundy

Honorius II
Reigned: 1124–1130
Given Name: Lambert of Scannabecchi

Innocent II
Reigned: 1130–1143
Given Name: Gregorio Papareschi

Celestine II
Reigned: 1143–1144
Given Name: Guido di Castello

Lucius II
Reigned: 1144–1145
Given Name: Gherardo Caccianemici

Blessed Eugene III
Reigned: 1145–1153
Given Name: Bernardo Pignatelli

Anastasius IV
Reigned: 1153–1154
Given Name: Conrad of Rome

Adrian IV
Reigned: 1154–1159
Given Name: Nicholas Breakspear

Alexander III
Reigned: 1159–1181
Given Name: Orlando Bandinelli

Lucius III
Reigned: 1181–1185
Given Name: Ubaldo Allucingoli

Urban III
Reigned: 1185–1187
Given Name: Uberto Crivelli

Gregory VIII
Reigned: 1187
Given Name: Alberto di Morra

Clement III
Reigned: 1187–1191
Given Name: Paulo Scolari

Celestine III
Reigned: 1191–1198
Given Name: Giacinto Boboni

Innocent III
Reigned: 1198–1216
Given Name: Lothar of Segni

Honorius III
Reigned: 1216–1227
Given Name: Cencio Savelli

Gregory IX
Reigned: 1227–1241
Given Name: Ugolino dei Conti di Segni

Celestine IV
Reigned: 1241
Given Name: Goffredo da Castiglione

Innocent IV
Reigned: 1243–1254
Given Name: Sinibaldo Fieschi

Alexander IV
Reigned: 1254–1261
Given Name: Rainaldo dei Conti di Segni

Urban IV
Reigned: 1261–1264
Given Name: Jacques Pantaleon

Clement IV
Reigned: 1265–1268
Given Name: Guy Foulques

Blessed Gregory X
Reigned: 1271–1276
Given Name: Tedaldo Visconti

Blessed Innocent V
Reigned: 1276
Given Name: Pierre of Tarantaise

Adrian V
Reigned: 1276
Given Name: Ottobono Fieshchi

John XXI
Reigned: 1276–1277
Given Name: Pedro Juliano

Nicholas III
Reigned: 1277–1280
Given Name: Giovanni Gaetano Orsini

Martin IV
Reigned: 1281–1285
Given Name: Simon de Brie

Honorius IV
Reigned: 1285–1287
Given Name: Giacomo Savelli

Nicholas IV
Reigned: 1288–1292
Given Name: Girolamo Masci

St. Celestine V
Reigned: 1294
Given Name: Pietro del Morrone

Boniface VIII
Reigned: 1294–1303
Given Name: Benedetto Caetani

Blessed Benedict XI
Reigned: 1303–1304
Given Name: Niccolo Boccasino

Clement V
Reigned: 1305–1314
Given Name: Bertrand de Gof

John XXII
Reigned: 1316–1334
Given Name: Jacques Duese

Benedict XII
Reigned: 1334–1342
Given Name: Jacques Fouriner

Clement VI
Reigned: 1342–1352
Given Name: Pierre Roger

Innocent VI
Reigned: 1352–1362
Given Name: Etienne Aubert

Blessed Urban V
Reigned: 1362–1370
Given Name: Guilliaume de Grimoard

Gregory XI
Reigned: 1370–1378
Given Name: Pierre Roger

Urban VI
Reigned: 1378–1389
Given Name: Bartolommeo Prignano

Boniface IX
Reigned: 1389–1404
Given Name: Pietro Tomacelli

Innocent VII
Reigned: 1404–1406
Given Name: Cosimo Gentile dei Migliorati

Gregory XII
Reigned: 1406–1415
Given Name: Angelo Correr

Martin V
Reigned: 1417–1431
Given Name: Odo Colonna

Eugene IV
Reigned: 1431–1447
Given Name: Gabriele Condulmaro

Nicholas V
Reigned: 1447–1455
Given Name: Tommaso Parentucelli

Callistus III
Reigned: 1455–1458
Given Name: Alfonso Borgia

Pius II
Reigned: 1458–1464
Given Name: Aeneas Silvio Piccolomini

Paul II
Reigned: 1464–1471
Given Name: Peitro Barbo

Sixtus IV
Reigned: 1471–1484
Given Name: Francesco della Rovere

Innocent VIII
Reigned: 1484–1492
Given Name: Giovanni Battista Cibo

Alexander VI
Reigned: 1492–1503
Given Name: Roderigo de Borgia

Pius III
Reigned: 1503
Given Name: Francesco Todeschini

Julius II
Reigned: 1503–1513
Given Name: Giuliano della Rovere

Leo X
Reigned: 1513–1521
Given Name: Giovanni de Medici

Adrian VI
Reigned: 1522–1523
Given Name: Adrian Dedel

Clement VII
Reigned: 1523–1534
Given Name: Giulio de' Monte

Paul III
Reigned: 1534–1549
Given Name: Alessandro Farnese

Julius III
Reigned: 1550–1555
Given Name: Giovanni del Monte

Marcellus II
Reigned: 1555
Given Name: Marcello Cervini

Paul IV
Reigned: 1555–1559
Given Name: Giovanni Pietro Caraffa

Pius IV
Reigned: 1559–1565
Given Name: Giovanni Angelo Medici

St. Pius V
Reigned: 1566–1572
Given Name: Michele Ghislieri

Gregory XIII
Reigned: 1572–1585
Given Name: Ugo Buoncompagni

Sixtus V
Reigned: 1585–1590
Given Name: Felice Peretti

Urban VII
Reigned: 1590
Given Name: Giambattista Castagna

Gregory XIV
Reigned: 1590–1591
Given Name: Nicolo Sfondrati

Innocent IX
Reigned: 1591
Given Name: Giovanni Antonio Fachinetti

Clement VIII
Reigned: 1592–1605
Given Name: Ippolito Aldobrandini

Leo XI
Reigned: 1605
Given Name: Alessandro de Medici

Paul V
Reigned: 1605–1621
Given Name: Camillo Borghese

Gregory XV
Reigned: 1621–1623
Given Name: Alessandro Ludovisi

Urban VIII
Reigned: 1623–1644
Given Name: Maffeo Barberini

Innocent X
Reigned: 1644–1655
Given Name: Giambattista Pamfili

Alexander VII
Reigned: 1655–1667
Given Name: Fabio Chigi

Clement IX
Reigned: 1667–1669
Given Name: Giulio Rospigliosi

Clement X
Reigned: 1670–1676
Given Name: Emilio Altieri

Blessed Innocent XI
Reigned: 1676–1689
Given Name: Benedetto Odescalchi

Alexander VIII
Reigned: 1689–1691
Given Name: Pietro Ottoboni

Innocent XII
Reigned: 1691–1700
Given Name: Antonio Pignatelli

Clement XI
Reigned: 1700–1721
Given Name: Gianfrancesco Albani

Innocent XIII
Reigned: 1721–1724
Given Name: Michelangelo de Conti

Benedict XIII
Reigned: 1724–1730
Given Name: Pietro Francesco Orsini-Gravina

Clement XII
Reigned: 1730–1740
Given Name: Lorenzo Corsini

Benedict XIV
Reigned: 1740–1758
Given Name: Prospero Lorenzo Lambertini

Clement XIII
Reigned: 1758–1769
Given Name: Carlo della Torre Rezzoncio

Clement XIV
Reigned: 1769–1774
Given Name: Lorenzo Ganganelli

Pius VI
Reigned: 1775–1799
Given Name: Giovanni Angelo Braschi

Pius VII
Reigned: 1800–1823
Given Name: Barnaba Chiaramonte

Leo XII
Reigned: 1823–1829
Given Name: Annibale della Genga

Pius VIII
Reigned: 1829–1830
Given Name: Franceso Saverio Castiglione

Gregory XVI
Reigned: 1831–1846
Given Name: Bartolommeo Capellari

Blessed Pius IX
Reigned: 1846–1878
Given Name: Giovanni Maria Mastai-Ferretti

Leo XIII
Reigned: 1878–1903
Given Name: Gioacchino Vincenzo Pecci

St. Pius X
Reigned: 1903–1914
Given Name: Giuseppe Melchior Sarto

Benedict XV
Reigned: 1914–1922
Given Name: Giacomo della Chiesa

Pius XI
Reigned: 1922–1939
Given Name: Achille Ratti

Pius XII
Reigned: 1939–1958
Given Name: Eugenio Pacelli

Blessed John XXIII
Reigned: 1958–1963
Given Name: Angelo Giuseppe Roncalli

Paul VI
Reigned: 1963–1978
Given Name: Giovanni Battista Montini

John Paul I
Reigned: 1978
Given Name: Albino Luciani

John Paul II
Reigned: 1978 to present
Given Name: Karol Jozef Wojtyla

Appendix B

The Antipopes in Sequence

St. Hippolytus
Claimed the Papacy: 217–ca. 235

Novatian
Claimed the Papacy: 251–258

St. Felix II
Claimed the Papacy: 355–365

Eulalius
Claimed the Papacy: 418

Laurence
Claimed the Papacy: 498–499,
501–506

Dioscorus
Claimed the Papacy: 530

Theodore
Claimed the Papacy: 686–687

Paschal
Claimed the Papacy: 687

Constantine
Claimed the Papacy: 767–768

Philip
Claimed the Papacy: 768

John
Claimed the Papacy: 827–844

Anastius Bibliothecarius
Claimed the Papacy: 855

Christopher
Claimed the Papacy: 903–904

Boniface VII
Claimed the Papacy: 974

Benedict X
Claimed the Papacy: 1058–1059
Given Name: John Mincius

Honorius (II)
Claimed the Papacy: 1061–1064
Given Name: Peter Cadalus

Clement III
Claimed the Papacy: 1080,
1084–1100
Given Name: Guibert of Ravenna

Theodoric
Claimed the Papacy: 1100–1101

Albert
Claimed the Papacy: 1101–1102

Sylvester IV
Claimed the Papacy: 1105–1111
Given Name: Maginulf

Gregory (IX)
Claimed the Papacy: 1118–1121
Given Name: Maurice Burdanus

Celestine II
Claimed the Papacy: 1124
Given Name: Teobaldo

Anacletus II
Claimed the Papacy: 1130–1138
Given Name: Pietro Pierleoni

Victor IV
Claimed the Papacy: 1138
Given Name: Gregorio Conti

Victor IV
Claimed the Papacy: 1159–1164
Given Name: Ottaviano of Monticello

Paschal III
Claimed the Papacy: 1164–1168
Given Name: Guido of Crema

Callistus III
Claimed the Papacy: 1168–1178
Given Name: Giovanni of Struma

Innocent III
Claimed the Papacy: 1179–1180
Given Name: Lando of Sezze

Nicholas (V)
Claimed the Papacy: 1328–1330
Given Name: Pietro Rainalducci

Clement VII
Claimed the Papacy: 1378–1394
Given Name: Robert of Geneva

Alexander V
Claimed the Papacy: 1409–1410
Given Name: Pietro Philargi

John XXIII
Claimed the Papacy: 1410–1415
Given Name: Baldassare Cossa

Clement VIII
Claimed the Papacy: 1423–1429
Given Name: Gil Sanchez Munoz

Benedict (XIV)
Claimed the Papacy: 1425
Given Name: Bernard Garier

Felix V
Claimed the Papacy: 1439–1449
Given Name: Amadeus of Savoy

Further Reading

Books and Articles

Bander, Peter. *The Prophecies of Malachy*. Rockford, Ill.: Tan Books and Publishers, 1973.

Brundage, James. *The Crusades: A Documentary History*. Milwaukee: Marquette University Press, 1962.

The Catholic League, "Frequently Asked Questions About Pius XII and the Holocaust." Article on www.catholicleague.com, 2001.

Chapin, John, ed. *A Treasury of Catholic Reading*. New York: Farrar, Straus and Company, 1957.

Chernow, Barbara and George Vallasi, eds. *The Columbia Encyclopedia*, 5th ed. New York: Columbia University Press, 1993.

Collins, Mary, OSB, et. al, eds., *The New Catholic Encyclopedia*. New York: The Publishers' Guild, 1997.

Cross, F.L, and E.A. Livingston, eds. *The Oxford Dictionary of the Christian Church*. Oxford: Oxford University Press, 1997.

de Montor, Artaud. *The Lives and Times of the Popes*. New York: The Catholic Publication Society of New York, 1911.

Duffy, Eamon. *Saints and Sinners: A History of the Popes*. New Haven, Conn.: Yale University Press, 1997.

Eberhardt, N.C. *A Summary of Catholic History.* St. Louis: B. Herder Book Company, 1961.

Graham, Robert A., S.J. "How to Manufacture a Legend: The Controversy over the Alleged Silence of Pope Pius XII in World War II." Article on www.nbci.com, 2001.

Herbermann and Pace, eds. *The Catholic Encyclopedia.* New York: Appleton, 1907–1912.

Jones, Alexander, ed. *The Jerusalem Bible.* New York: Doubleday and Company, 1966.

Kertzer, David I. *The Popes Against the Jews: The Vatican's Role in the Rise of Modern Anti-Semitism.* New York: Alfred A Knopf, 2001.

McManners, John, ed. *The Oxford Illustrated History of Christianity.* Oxford: Oxford University Press, 1990.

Maxwell-Stuart, P.G. *Chronicle of the Popes.* London: Thames and Hudson, 1997.

Sandmel, Samuel, general ed. *The New English Bible.* New York: Oxford University Press, 1976.

Smestad, John R. Jr. *Europe: 1914–1915: Attempts at Peace.* New Orleans: Loyola University Department of History, 1994.

Toropov, Brandon and Luke Buckles, O.P. *The Complete Idiot's Guide to World Religions,* 2nd ed. Indianapolis: Alpha Books, 2001.

World Wide Web Sites

Biography.com, a site of A&E Television Networks
www.biography.com

The Bishops of Rome
www.friesian.com/popes.htm

Catechism of the Catholic Church, available at:
http://www.vatican.va/archive/catechism/ccc_toc.htm

The Catholic Community Forum
www.catholic-forum.com

The Catholic League
www.catholicleague.com

Magyar's Links to Catholic Resources on the Net
http://astro.ocis.temple.edu/~tarantul/spirit.html

Medieval Music and Arts Foundation
www.medieval.org

Papal Encyclicals Online
www.geocities.com/papalencyclicals/

The Papal Library
www.saint-mike.org/library/papal_library/

St. Michael's Depot
www.piar.hu/councils

The Thirty Years' War Homepage
www.pipeline.com/~cwa/TYWHome.htm

The Timeline of the Roman Catholic Church
www.geocities.com/Athens/Ithaca/6461/

Vatican: The Holy See
www.vatican.va

Index

Q-R